# WHAT'S THE TRUTH ABOUT HEAVEN AND HELL?

## DOUGLAS A. JACOBY

HARVEST HOUSE PUBLISHERS
EUGENE, OREGON

*Cover by Dugan Design Group, Bloomington, Minnesota*

The views in this book do not necessarily reflect those of the publisher.

**WHAT'S THE TRUTH ABOUT HEAVEN AND HELL?**
Copyright © 2013 by Douglas A. Jacoby
Published by Harvest House Publishers
Eugene, Oregon 97402
www.harvesthousepublishers.com

Library of Congress Cataloging-in-Publication Data
Jacoby, Douglas A.
What's the truth about heaven and hell? / Douglas Jacoby.
    p. cm.
ISBN 978-0-7369-5172-2 (pbk.)
ISBN 978-0-7369-5173-9 (eBook)
1. Heaven—Christianity. 2. Hell—Christianity. 3. Future life—Christianity. 4. Theology, Doctrinal—Popular works. I. Title.
BT846.3.J33 2013
236'.24—dc23
                                                                                    2012041088

# Acknowledgments

Many people have propelled me in the search for biblical truth. Our conversations, correspondence, coffees, and meals have called me higher: David Bercot, Mark Cahill, Craig Evans, Everett Ferguson, Edward Fudge, Gary Habermas, Randy Harris, Tom Jones, Gary Knutson, Craig Keener, Bob Kurka, Denis Lamoureux, Michael Licona, Jim McGuiggan, and Peter Williams—I owe you a continuing debt of love and respect.

Other lovers of Scripture have uplifted me more than they may realize through kind words of encouragement: Francis Chan, Francis Collins, Bill Craig, Dinesh D'Souza, Kenneth Kitchen, Peter Kreeft, Josh McDowell, Timothy McGrew, Charlie Moule, John Polkinghorne, Graham Stanton, John Stott, Ben Witherington, and Ravi Zacharias. I owe you too profound thanks.

To the entire Harvest House staff—especially Gene Skinner, Terry Glaspey, and Bob Hawkins Jr.—as well as my unofficial editor, Joe Sciortino, I am grateful for your support and confidence in me. May it not prove to be misplaced.

# Contents

Part 1

# Think Again

If we are serious about examining what the Scriptures really say about the afterlife, we must be willing to approach the subject with an open mind. This is easier said than done. First of all, everyone interprets, whether he or she is conscious of this or not. Second, we cannot help but bring preconceptions to the discussion of the afterlife. Last, not all Scripture is intended to be read literally. Knowing the difference is key to making sense of the passages touching on the afterlife.

# A Fresh Look

## *Opening Minds*

*The unexamined faith is hardly worth believing.*

### Bullet, Darkness, Light

I was 18, and I was a young Christian. Like many new believers, I was burning to share my faith with everything that moved. That included the blonde from New York, who like me was a freshman at Duke University.

I had no idea she had a gun. One evening we were discussing Christianity. In mid-conversation, and without the slightest warning, she pulled it out of her handbag and shot me. Before everything went dark, I felt the bullet tearing into my chest. I clearly recall the surprisingly intense heat of this minuscule chunk of metal.

I was fading…blackness…then utter calm. I asked out loud, "Am I in heaven?" As my eyes focused, I saw a light, and then a series of numbers—3-5-0. What was happening? And why did I expect to be in heaven? As I came to and to my great disappointment realized I was still alive, the luminous alarm clock informed me it would soon be four a.m. It was all a dream. My question, "Am I in heaven?" was decisively answered by my roommate, Joe. "Go back to sleep, Doug."

What a dream. Would it perhaps be like this one day? What is on the other side?

I didn't have many answers—I'd become a Christian only weeks earlier. So why did my dream take the shape it did? My assumptions about the afterlife had almost certainly come from my religious surroundings. But were they correct? In John 3:13, just three verses before the most famous Scripture in the Bible, Jesus told us, "No one has ever gone into heaven except the one who came from heaven—the Son of Man." What about you—what do you believe about heaven and hell? And if you're a believer in Christ, if a coworker asks you at lunch what you think about the topic, what scriptural basis would you have for your response?

**Everyone's Interested**

It is indisputable that every culture has believed in life after death. Whenever I read the holy writings of the world's religions, attend a funeral, see a sarcophagus or mummy, or walk through a graveyard, this truth is impressed on me. For millennia humans have speculated about judgment, the afterlife, and how to tip the balance in one's favor lest the final outcome prove negative. Even in countries where religion is discouraged or banned, this orientation toward the future cannot be squelched, and powerful underground movements keep faith alive. Of course the fact that faith is strong is no proof that it is right, but it does—and should—make the nonbeliever stop and think.

In my work I travel a lot, usually explaining the Christian faith and teaching the Bible. Last week I sat next to a fascinating woman on a flight from Mozambique to South Africa. She was well educated, fluent in many languages, and she was an atheist. We had much in common, including two countries (Sweden and Malaysia), and soon she was sharing with me her life philosophy. In short, she reasoned, "There's no need for anyone to live past age sixty."

"Should they be euthanized?" I asked innocently.

"Of course not. But we need to consider the next generation and not be selfish," she explained.

I should probably tell you that this dear woman looked to me to be in her late fifties. Time was short, according to her philosophy. I sensed an opening. "What's your take on what happens after we die?"

"We decompose and become part of future generations of life."

"Okay, so we become part of the next generation literally. But if the scientists are right, in a few billion years our world will be burnt up by the sun. If nothing's going to last, then what's the purpose of it all?" (She had no answer, although she insisted some things in her life were deeply meaningful.) "Then it's like existentialism? Life is ultimately absurd, so we create our own meaning?" She didn't know what to say, and not because she didn't understand the question.

We had a great talk. I was able to identify several things in her life (things she had opened up to me about) that point to something beyond, to purpose and meaning. "You have to admit, the evidence suggests transcendence—something beyond this life."

"And you believe in God?"

"I do," I responded. "This world makes a lot more sense if there is a God. I'm a Christian writer, and one of my books is actually on this subject—why belief in God makes more sense than the alternative. I have only one copy left, but it's yours if you think you'll read it. When we land in Johannesburg, I'll be happy to give it to you."

"Yes, I'd like that." When we landed, she eagerly introduced me to her work associate, who was on the same flight, and I handed over the book. Was a seed planted? Yes—but long before we met. The Lord had been preparing this soon-to-be 60-year-old for this encounter. We exchanged contact information, and I'm waiting for her response.

What would you have said to her? How would you share your faith in a similar situation? Don't ever write off atheists as uninterested in the afterlife. In fact, many persons who wouldn't be caught dead in a church (well, perhaps unless you count funerals) are taken with the paranormal. I find a great response among young and old when I teach about angels and demons, ghosts, and a number of other supernatural topics.

This is a great way to start a conversation with an unbeliever, by the way. Ask what he or she thinks about popular themes (vampires, for example) and then steer the conversation in a spiritual direction. Or ask directly, "What do you think happens on the other side?" You'd be amazed how many people, regardless of whether they have faith, have been waiting for someone to bring this up.

The afterlife is a subject that interests everyone, because it is about the one thing that happens to us all. Ultimately, nothing could be more relevant. There's a pressing reason many long for this discussion: God has set eternity in their hearts (Ecclesiastes 3:11). We are spiritual creatures.

Everyone's interested, but nearly everyone is confused. What's on the other side? Do we go to heaven the second we die? What about near-death experiences? Are we reincarnated? Is hell forever? How literally should we read the book of Revelation? Are there ghosts? What if you aren't a Christian—are there other valid paths? These and many other questions are being asked—and will be addressed in this volume.

This is a crucial conversation. If anything is on the other side of the grave, then heaven and hell aren't just small talk. We need answers, and so do your friends, family, and neighbors. Care enough about others to have this conversation!

## Questions, Questions

Is heaven on earth? Is there a waiting place before judgment day? Do those who haven't heard the gospel get a second chance? Let's see what the Bible says and make an honest effort to sort out the confusion. This means wading into some of the controversies and seeing that sometimes sincere students of Scripture land in different places. And in the process, we may receive some much-needed personal assurance about life after death.

This book may take you into new territory. Even if you're a veteran Bible reader, it is intended to prod you, to push you to think. Though the book touches on matters of eternal significance, there is latitude for flexibility of thought, for acceptance of differing views.

The Bible will be the authoritative text for our discussion in this book.[1] Do you think you know the Bible—that you've already heard all there is to know about heaven and hell? Think again. Bible scholars and teachers worldwide are taking a new look at both heaven and hell. We should too. In researching this volume, I have tried to analyze the most influential as well as the most recent works on heaven and hell. The conversation isn't over your head or inaccessibly erudite. You can listen in.

We all wear colored lenses; no one is (fully) objective. This means we need to keep our minds open and our hearts humble. For that reason, the three chapters that follow—one on eternity, the other two on interpretation—are probably the most important chapters in the book. You may think, "I only want to know where the author comes out on those who haven't heard the gospel"—or the second death, or… (fill in the blank). But should you really care what *my* position is? Isn't it far more crucial to learn how the Lord wants us to read his word? So please don't skip ahead if you want to be able to weigh the various views on the afterlife.

It's just possible, once we dig into the Scriptures, that we may change our minds on something important. Let's not be numbered among the timid souls who cannot, or will not, reexamine their faith. It's time for a fresh look.

## In Brief

- Everyone is interested in the afterlife—nonbelievers as well as believers.

- Even if we have read God's word, our notions about the afterlife may require refining or even replacing.

- We all have presuppositions regarding heaven and hell. Our knowledge was not attained in a vacuum. Becoming aware of these presuppositions is the best starting place for our inquiry.

# The Lens of Eternity

## *Defining Terms*

*God, the blessed and only Ruler, the King of kings and Lord of lords,*
*who alone is immortal and who lives in unapproachable light...*

1 TIMOTHY 6:15-16

I've worn glasses since I was ten, or at least I was supposed to. Those were the days before wearing specs became fashionable. We all require "lenses" in order to make sense of the world, to be able to cope. Of course lenses can do far more than correct nearsightedness or astigmatism. They can take us into microscopic worlds or deep space. Not that anyone, when it comes to viewing eternity, has 20/20 vision. What are your "lenses"? To successfully navigate the various afterlife views, we first need to be aware of lenses that have refracted our view of the world to come.

### Defining Terms

Plentiful ideas compete about heaven, hell, and the afterlife—and not just the rival belief systems of Hinduism, Islam, and other worldviews. Even Christians only roughly agree on what happens after we die. Everyone has an opinion, and apparently many of these opinions are rooted more deeply in tradition and personal preference than in

Scripture. Like Pharaoh's chief baker, we are attracted to interpretations that bode well for us (Genesis 40:16). To some extent, our lenses distort our perception of reality.

To be sure that we are correctly hearing the multiple voices in the discussion, we need to define terms. In religion as in politics, without agreeing on what it is we are disagreeing about, we are doomed to talk past one another. Key terms for this chapter include *eternity, infinity,* and *immortality.* Sharpening our thinking about eternity and immortality will bear fruit in chapter 8 as we examine nonstandard views about the end of the wicked. All three terms are lofty, loaded, and to some degree more elusive than we may realize.

### Eternity

Woody Allen quips, "Eternity is really long, especially toward the end." In his unique and winsome way, he makes us laugh at ourselves. Who, after all, can even *begin* to appreciate eternity, let alone the part "toward the end"? We mortals must admit we face a basic limitation, a sort of vision impairment.

The biblical words often translated "eternal" are the Old Testament Hebrew *'olam* and the New Testament Greek *aion*. But what is eternity? One nineteenth-century Princeton scholar insisted that *aion* always denotes time (quantity), never quality or nature.[1] Yet few are so bold as to claim that the Greek adjective *aionios* always suggests "infinity in time"—such thinking has been rejected by most modern exegetes.[2] But isn't this how many readers understand the Bible? Other scholars, including those who believe that hell is eternal torment, are more tempered in their judgment. Bruce Milne is an example. "The word commonly rendered 'eternal' in our New Testament translations is in fact literally 'of the age (to come).' Thus it refers in the first instance to a particular quality of life, rather than to its durational quantity."[3]

The basic sense of *aion* (from which we get the English word eon) is "time, age." The listed definitions in the standard lexicon for New Testament Greek are "very long time, eternity; a segment of time, age; the world."[4] There is no inherent notion of everlastingness.

For example, the following list is based (only) on the Greek root *aion*, common in the Greek New Testament and the Greek version of the Old Testament.[5] There are a number of Scriptures where words such as "forever," "eternal," and "everlasting" entail no sense of infinite duration.

- Genesis 6:4—The Nephilim were heroes "of old."
- Genesis 9:12—The rainbow was to be a sign for "all generations to come."
- Exodus 21:6—Servants could choose to serve their masters "for life."
- Leviticus 25:34—The Levites' pastureland was their "permanent possession."
- 1 Chronicles 16:15; Psalm 105:8—"Forever" is equivalent to a thousand generations.
- 1 Samuel 1:22—Young Samuel was to serve at the house of the Lord "always," even though his death is recorded in 1 Samuel 15:35.
- Ezra 4:15,19—Jerusalem had a "long history" of resisting political domination, but Israel had existed as a nation less than a millennium.
- Psalm 24:7—The gates to Jerusalem were "ancient," as was the boundary stone of Proverbs 22:28.
- Jonah 2:6—The prophet was confined in (the fish) "forever."

This makes sense. In Exodus 31:17 the Sabbath was to remain a sign for the Jewish people "forever," yet the early church felt no obligation to keep it (Colossians 2:16; see Galatians 4:8-11). Similarly, circumcision was "for the generations to come" (Genesis 17:12), yet as Acts 15 and the letter to the Galatians make clear, the requirement was no longer considered binding under the new covenant. Think carefully about the meaning of "eternal" in these three passages in Hebrews:

- Hebrews 5:9—"Eternal salvation" refers to the effect of the cross. We are saved once; only the consequence that endures into the age to come.
- Hebrews 6:2—"Eternal judgment" refers to the

consequences of our rebellion against God; no one is repeatedly hauled before the judgment seat of God for pronouncements of guilt.

- Hebrews 9:12—"Eternal redemption" is nonrepeatable. Jesus doesn't redeem us over and over; the effect of his redemption lasts into the age to come.

For a final example, in Matthew 25:41,46, "eternal" punishment is illuminated by Matthew 21:19.

> Jesus even provides us with a graphic illustration of his use of the Greek root word *aion*, when he cursed the unfruitful fig tree on his way into Jerusalem: "Let no fruit grow on thee henceforth forward forever," Jesus commanded. "And presently the fig tree withered away" (Matthew 21:19 KJV). The desired effect was not something that happened over and over again throughout eons of time, but once for all time. Apply the imagery of *immediate withering* to "eternal fire" and you get the picture.[6]

This line of reasoning is important to follow if we are to understand, in a later chapter, why some take exception to the traditional concept of hell as infinite torment.

The New Testament announces that eternal life is now, not just something in the distant future (John 17:2-3). The age to come has already arrived; the kingdom has come (Luke 11:20; 17:20-21). As theologian Dallas Willard puts it, "Eternity is now in process."[7] Yet few Bible readers are even aware of these important distinctions. In short, we may *think* we grasp eternity, but how likely is this? Humility is needed.

### Infinity

If eternity is elusive, it certainly isn't any easier getting a handle on the concept of infinity. All the same, it's a term frequently bandied about in many a religious or scientific discussion—just as armchair physicists drop impressive names like Einstein and Hawking without actually understanding these scientists at all.

Speaking of human ignorance, I sometimes hear Christians say, "I guess I'll just have to ask Paul what he meant when I see him in heaven," or "I look forward to learning the theory of relativity when I meet the Lord." But how can we be sure that "know fully" and "see face to face" (1 Corinthians 13:12) denote omniscience? Isn't this passage referring to knowing God through Christ—a context that is relational rather than informational? And what makes us think we'd understand Einstein in the next life? (How did you do when you studied calculus and physics here on earth?)

"But if I had all eternity to learn…," you may be thinking. But what makes you think you'd get it even if the Lord took 100 years to patiently explain it? Some things we don't know now, and some things we may never know. After all, in the next world we still won't be omniscient—that's the province of God alone.

So shall we give up? Not at all. The point is to be humble—not inert. And so back to infinity. In the real world, infinity is more a concept than a reality. For example, if time extended to the infinite past, how could we ever have arrived at the present? An infinite gap would remain between the past and today? Perhaps that's why Augustine (AD 354–430) argued that time is not eternal; God created the universe *with* time, not *in* time. This agrees with modern cosmology. The big bang theory holds—and the evidence is strong—that matter and energy, space and time all came into being at a point in the distant past.

If that isn't mind-bending enough, there's more. For us, will eternity be infinite? Well, not in both directions; after all, our existence had a beginning. Our eternal life with God will last forever, so it is infinite in one direction, or halfway infinite—yet any fraction of infinity is still infinity. Eternity has to do with the age to come; infinity has to do with extent or duration. Neither concept is easy to grasp, and in some sense neither is fully intelligible to us, but that doesn't mean the words are interchangeable. We will do well to keep the distinction in mind.

## Immortality

Preachers sometimes proclaim there are only three eternal things: God in heaven, the word of God, and the soul of man.[8] Surely God's word is eternal (Psalm 119:89; Matthew 24:35). And there is no doubt that God is immortal (1 Timothy 1:17; 6:16). What about us?

The Barna people tell us that most Americans believe we have an immortal soul.[9] Sometimes this is assumed because God breathed his spirit into man (Genesis 2:7), investing us with his own immortality. But how can we sure? By every appearance, after sin entered the world, the Lord refused the first couple immortality (Genesis 3:22-24). Why would such an important teaching not be revealed until the New Testament—and especially if this vital truth had eternal implications for the hundreds of millions living before the time of Christ?[10] The New Testament teaches that eternal life is a gift for those who are saved by faith.[11] After all, God is uniquely immortal: "God, the blessed and only Ruler, the King of kings and Lord of lords, who alone is immortal and who lives in unapproachable light" (1 Timothy 6:15-16). Whether God is outside time, inside it, or both, he is certainly not subject to the same limitations we struggle under. That we may *become* immortal does not mean that we are *innately* immortal.

The idea of the immortal soul was baptized, in some quarters at least, as early as the second century. The Platonic notion entered Christianity by way of the second-century apologists, such as Athenagoras and Tertullian. Says the latter, "I may use, therefore, the opinion of Plato when he declares, 'Every soul is immortal.'"[12] In time, much of Judaism would follow suit.[13]

Says theologian Stanley Grenz, "The idea of the soul's immortality has been highly influential throughout Christian history…Despite its influence, the doctrine is problematic. It suggests that immortality is somehow intrinsic to the soul, rather than being God's gift."[14] During the great housecleaning known as the Protestant Reformation, Martin Luther, the Anabaptists, and Tyndale roundly rejected the immortality of the soul.[15] But Luther did not push his view; the Anabaptists were too radical for most, and by the end of the Reformation, Calvin and his opposing viewpoint had won the day. The traditional (Catholic) concept reigned virtually unchallenged until the nineteenth century.

Conditional immortality, the notion that the soul's immortality depends on God, gained traction in late 1800s through groups like the Seventh-day Adventists.[16] This belief is sometimes called *conditionalism*. It is widely recognized that human immortality stems from Plato (423–347 BC). But this is in conflict with what God has revealed in the Old and New Testaments.[17] Many biblical scholars now agree that the human soul is mortal, and several popular writers have taken the hint.[18] It is especially noteworthy that scholars of the conditional-ist persuasion hail from the entire spectrum of Christianity: Baptists George Beasley-Murray, Dale Moody, Clark Pinnock, and E. Earle Ellis; Anglicans Richard Bauckham, John Wenham, John R.W. Stott, and Michael Green; F.F. Bruce (Brethren); Edward Fudge (Churches of Christ); Philip E. Hughes and John McRay (Reform); and John Stack-house Jr. (J.I. Packer's successor at Regent College, Vancouver). These are just a few of the better-known names among this growing number.

If the soul is going to live forever, God will have to grant it immor-tality. Then the question is, will he give immortality to the lost? That is, will he keep them existing forever for the purpose of punishment, or will their punishment ever come to an end? (That will be our focus in chapter 8.)

Does science shed any light on the matter? According to Rodney J. Scott and Raymond E. Phinney Jr., experts in neurobiology, "There is little question that traditional exegetes have viewed the Old Testament picture of human nature through the lenses of Christian Platonism… a material body and an immaterial soul or spirit was simply taken for granted."[19] Malcolm Jeeves, a Christian neuroscientist, goes even fur-ther. He doubts the existence of an immaterial soul.[20] Of course he does not deny the soul, only its existence independent of the body—a far cry from Plato.

## The Timelessness of the Womb

> It is not unlike the unborn baby in the womb, who already has life, but hasn't yet been born. And who could possibly explain to that developing little person about life outside the womb? Or about the nature of time? The irony is that, in the womb, we've already experienced a timelessness in which we were perfectly content. An "eternity," as far as we knew, in which our every need was met without our ever asking![21]

We ought not to imagine that we perceive too clearly the essence of immortality, infinity, and eternity. Appreciating the contributions of scholars who have laid the groundwork for us laymen, we realize that there is often more than one way to look at things.

Doubtless there are other significant terms in the Bible related to the afterlife, such as *soul* and *spirit*. We will touch on several in the course of our investigation.

## A Second Lens

We began the chapter with the analogy of corrective lenses. My eyes are not the same. Although one is stronger than the other, neither sees clearly. Sometimes a lens will fall out of its frame, or a contact lens might slide out of position. At times like these it's almost easier to have no lenses than only one. Similarly, our interpretive presuppositions form a second, powerful lens, clarifying or distorting the truth, as the case may be. This will be our study in chapters 3 and 4.

Being aware of our biases goes well beyond rethinking eternity, infinity, and immortality—a task that weighs heavily on our puny minds. Everyone interprets—despite the claims of some who claim direct access to the meaning of Scripture without the difficult work of applying their minds to the text. Next, therefore, we will examine our method of interpretation.

## In Brief

- The logical starting place in the afterlife discussion is to define terms. In religion as in politics, without agreeing on what it is we are disagreeing about, we will talk past one another.

- As optical lenses refract light and enable us to make sense of our world, so our previous understanding of eternity affects our ability to discern clearly the will of God.

- *Eternal* is not a synonym of *infinite*.

- Only God is intrinsically immortal. The philosophical doctrine of immortality of the human soul is difficult to defend biblically, and many scholars reject it.

- In short, the concept of eternity is beyond our capacity to apprehend.

# 3

# Lenses of Interpretation, Part 1

## *Should We Take the Bible Literally?*

*It is never too late to give up our prejudices.*

THOREAU

In the last chapter we saw that when reading the Bible, we all bring something to the text. We aren't purely objective; our picture of reality is refracted or even fragmented by our personal "lenses." Three concepts fraught with presupposition are eternity, infinity, and immortality, and unpacking them is essential if we are to thoughtfully consider the passages usually regarded as informing us about heaven, hell, and the afterlife. While it may be tempting to skip to the book of Revelation or the parables of Christ, it is better to take our time—especially if we are really willing to reconsider the weighty matters of eternity. In fact, there is a great deal of language that affects our view of heaven, hell, eternity, and the afterlife that comes from the Old Testament, and a close look shows that much of this language is figurative or must be understood differently than a simple literal reading would propose.

## Self-Interpreting?

To say that "no prophecy of Scripture came about by the prophet's own interpretation" (2 Peter 1:20) is to say that the Scripture authors did not inject their own opinions in any way so as to distort the meaning. Or as the NASB translates this verse, "No prophecy of Scripture is a matter of one's own interpretation." The imperative for us is not that we should (or can) understand without interpreting. It is that we should understand the Scripture as the Spirit-led author intended it to be understood rather than as we wish it to be.

The idea of letting the Bible interpret itself can be better stated another way. We should understand the writings of Scripture in their most plain, straightforward manner unless another passage elsewhere in the Scripture makes it clear we must look for a more complex or subtle meaning. Actually, the Bible never claims that every part is easy to understand (in fact, quite the opposite—2 Peter 3:14-16). It urges us to meditate diligently on God's word (Joshua 1:8; Psalm 119) that the Lord may give us insight (2 Timothy 2:7,15).[1]

Therefore, *interpretation* is not a dirty word. It does take work to integrate our knowledge of all the Scriptures and to discern what the author meant for us to understand. That is the appropriate application of interpretation to the Scriptures. To neglect to do this is not to be spiritual. It is just to be lazy.

### Theology, Anyone?

Whatever goes for our tendency to deprecate interpretation goes double for a dismissive stance toward theology. I. Howard Marshall perceptively notes, "Although some people claim to be able to dispense with biblical criticism and to settle issues by the plain simple evidence of what the Bible says, they still have to use biblical criticism to find out just what the Bible does say."[2] He is right. Unless we are expert in the original tongues, we depend on armies of scholars who have translated the text for us. And what about those whose lives have been dedicated to painstakingly copying it or clarifying it through illuminating geography, history, culture, and so forth? Without theologians and other scholars, we would be completely disoriented in our trek through the pages of ancient cultures.

### Method or Madness?

Theology shouldn't elicit yawns, but gratitude and excitement. But what is the typical Bible reader's approach to interpretation?

- Theology is viewed with suspicion (sometimes for good reason, but too often it's a case of throwing out the baby with the bathwater).

- We assume we already know what the passage means.

- Or we assume our tradition (church culture) has it right.

- Or we assume it doesn't matter, or perhaps we dismiss the text as irrelevant to our modern age. ("It's cultural.")

- And if we bump into a possible discrepancy, we are asked to be patient, for God will make all things clear in time.

Moreover, most of us have only a sketchy knowledge of the Old Testament. Why would we think we could read just the last quarter of the Bible (the New Testament) without bothering to see how it connects to the first three quarters—and with nothing to guide us beyond common sense and local church tradition? Doesn't sound like much of a method, does it? Surely we can do better. To ensure our eyes are open and we see God's word clearly (Psalm 119:18), we must go back to the prophets.

## The Mother Lode

Compared to most prophets and biblical authors, Isaiah's language is highly descriptive and visionary, as opposed to the more straightforward writing of Nehemiah, the epistle penned by James, or the prophecies of Jeremiah. Its symbolic aspect makes it more interesting and yet also more complex. By virtue of its length—66 chapters—we are offered mountains of poetic and metaphorical material.

I reread Isaiah, with an eye on its symbolism, so that we can appreciate the scope of what Isaiah is doing. Several of these images are below; others—for the motivated reader—may be found in appendix A. For now, we will zoom in on three passages that will open a window into Isaiah's thought and speech. Each passage relates to the destruction of an earthly kingdom. The prophecies were fulfilled long before the time of Christ.

The principles in Isaiah, as in all the books of the Bible, are timeless, though of course he was dealing with particular historical situations—Israel before and after the exile. Much was written in the eighth century BC.[3] Isaiah is chock-full of poetry. In contemporary translations, you can usually distinguish prose and poetry at a glance, as verse is indented on alternate lines. Persons unfamiliar with poetry may misread the metaphors.

For our purposes, Isaiah also has the advantage of being a rich resource for New Testament passages relating to justice, reward and punishment, vindication of the saints, and tribulation for their opponents. The book of Revelation draws on many prophetic books, including Ezekiel, Daniel, and Zechariah, but Isaiah is the most quoted prophet in the New Testament.[4]

### Chapters 13–14: A Prophecy Against Babylon

> See, the day of the LORD is coming
>    —a cruel day, with wrath and fierce anger—
> to make the land desolate
>    and destroy the sinners within it.
> The stars of heaven and their constellations
>    will not show their light.
> The rising sun will be darkened
>    and the moon will not give its light.
> I will punish the world for its evil,
>    the wicked for their sins.
> I will put an end to the arrogance of the haughty
>    and will humble the pride of the ruthless.
> I will make people scarcer than pure gold,
>    more rare than the gold of Ophir.
> Therefore I will make the heavens tremble;
>    and the earth will shake from its place
> at the wrath of the LORD Almighty,
>    in the day of his burning anger (13:9-13).

If this were all Isaiah had written, one might be forgiven for believing he prophesied the end of the world. And yet context is king. Or maybe we should say that the king must be understood in context—he's the king of Babylon (13:1,19). Divine punishment in the Bible is often executed through the agency of a foreign army—in this case the Medes (13:17). Babylon "fell" without a shot being fired. The

Medo-Persian alliance simply took over. Nor was the city abandoned immediately.

> How you have fallen from heaven,
> > morning star, son of the dawn!
>
> You have been cast down to the earth,
> > you who once laid low the nations!
>
> You said in your heart,
> > "I will ascend to the heavens;
>
> I will raise my throne
> > above the stars of God;
>
> I will sit enthroned on the mount of assembly,
> > on the utmost heights of Mount Zaphon.
>
> I will ascend above the tops of the clouds;
> > I will make myself like the Most High."
>
> But you are brought down to the realm of the dead,
> > to the depths of the pit (14:12-15).

The Babylonian leader is compared to a falling star. The commonly heard assertion that the verse is about Satan is speculative, despite a possible echo of the tradition of the fall of Satan. This tradition was reinforced by the Latin version, where verse 12 renders "morning star" as "Lucifer" (light-bearer). The passage explicitly speaks of the king of Babylon (14:4). It is Babylon that will suffer destruction.

## Chapter 34: Judgment Against Edom

> For the LORD has a day of vengeance,
> > a year of retribution, to uphold Zion's cause.
>
> Edom's streams will be turned into pitch,
> > her dust into burning sulfur;
> > her land will become blazing pitch!
>
> It will not be quenched night or day;
> > its smoke will rise forever.
>
> From generation to generation it will lie desolate;
> > no one will ever pass through it again.
>
> The desert owl and screech owl will possess it;
> > the great owl and the raven will nest there.
>
> God will stretch out over Edom

> the measuring line of chaos
> and the plumb line of desolation.
> Her nobles will have nothing there to be called a kingdom,
> all her princes will vanish away.
> Thorns will overrun her citadels,
> nettles and brambles her strongholds.
> She will become a haunt for jackals,
> a home for owls (34:8-13).

The enemy is named—Edom (34:5-6). Notice how her destruction is described, and ask yourself whether this should be understood literally. (The answer is a firm no.) Her streams will turn to pitch, and her land to sulfur (34:9). Nothing could live in such an environment.

The smoke of her destruction was to rise forever, just like the smoke of burning Rome (Revelation 19:3). Jude 7 tells us that the burning of Sodom and Gomorrah, frequently referred to in Scripture, is an example of eternal fire. Is Sodom still smoking? Is Edom still ablaze? Does Rome still burn? No, but the lesson remains forever. As we saw in the last chapter, when we read words like *eternal*, we must determine whether biblical writers meant eternal in the sense of a continuous action or state, or eternal in the sense of a consequence or result.

The smoke of her burning "will not be quenched night or day" (Isaiah 34:10), another phrase suggesting there is no respite. This too turns out to be a figure of speech. Paul worked and prayed night and day (1 Thessalonians 2:9; 3:10), though not literally. Even if the apostle had some sleepless nights (2 Corinthians 6:5; 11:27), he still had to rest. The same phrase appears in Revelation 4:8; 7:15; 12:10; 20:10.

Despite the nonstop blaze, Edom is claimed by wild animals (Isaiah 34:11). The city is to become unsafe, wild, reverting from a state of order to one of disorder. Plants and animals will live there. No need to imagine a genetically modified jackal (verse 13); once the images are seen as figurative, the impossibility disappears.

Last, the passage speaks of Edom's loss of political sovereignty (34:12), which is the real point of the doom oracle. God himself brought an end to the kingdom of Edom, shattering her illusion of self-sufficiency.[5] Yet it continued to be inhabited. Even in Jesus's time we find Idumea (the new name for Edom). Was she destroyed? Yes.

Literally, as a wooden reading of Isaiah 34 might indicate? No. Then is the Scripture true? Of course. Where is the problem? There is none, unless the reader fails to appreciate the metaphorical language.

## Chapters 65–66: A New Heavens and Earth

> See, I will create
>     new heavens and a new earth.
> The former things will not be remembered,
>     nor will they come to mind.
> But be glad and rejoice forever
>     in what I will create,
> for I will create Jerusalem to be a delight
>     and its people a joy.
> I will rejoice over Jerusalem
>     and take delight in my people;
> the sound of weeping and of crying
>     will be heard in it no more (Isaiah 65:17-19).

Isaiah looks ahead to a day when Israel, now in exile in Persia, will return to her land. He foresees a political and spiritual golden age. In essence the prophet is saying, "It's a whole new world" (figuratively, not literally). The Jews did return by edict of the Persian king (538 BC), and they experienced a sort of revival under Haggai, Zechariah, Ezra, and Nehemiah (sixth and fifth centuries BC), but the golden age remained a lofty ideal. Ultimate fulfillment was to take place only through the kingdom of the Messiah, centuries later.

> "They will proclaim my glory among the nations. And they will bring all your people, from all the nations, to my holy mountain in Jerusalem as an offering to the LORD—on horses, in chariots and wagons, and on mules and camels," says the LORD. "They will bring them, as the Israelites bring their grain offerings, to the temple of the LORD in ceremonially clean vessels. And I will select some of them also to be priests and Levites," says the LORD.
>
> "As the new heavens and the new earth that I make will endure before me," declares the LORD, "so will your name and descendants endure. From one New Moon to another

and from one Sabbath to another, all mankind will come
and bow down before me," says the LORD. "And they will
go out and look on the dead bodies of those who rebelled
against me; the worms that eat them will not die, the fire
that burns them will not be quenched, and they will be
loathsome to all mankind" (Isaiah 66:19-24).

Notice the very Jewish context of the passage. This is not the end
of the world. The temple is standing (it has been rebuilt). Levites are
serving there. The enemies of Israel have been incinerated, their smoldering corpses visible to all.

Notice too that the insentient corpses are consumed by worms *after*
they are judged (see also 34:3). These enemies of God are no longer
conscious. The dominant emotion elicited is not one of pity, but of
disgust.

Thus we see that throughout the oracles of Isaiah, local events
(touching Israel and the surrounding nations) may be pictured in
poetic, even cosmic terms.[6] Does this sound like a picture of heaven
and hell? Of course not; there is a specific historical context and a specific fulfillment. To literalize is to misunderstand and to destroy the
meaning.

In light of Isaiah's language, we should hesitate to accept a literalistic approach toward metaphors in the Bible, especially in the poetic
sections. Isaiah's imagery is recycled in the New Testament. Here are a
handful of Isaiah's poignant images reused in Revelation.

- *Astronomical descriptions.* Falling stars, split heavens, and
  so on have a definite meaning, normally in connection
  with judgment, but not a literal meaning. Ancient worlds
  were ending. Although there may be prophetic parallels
  with our own day, this hardly justifies us in literalizing the
  poetic words of the ancient writers.

- *Consuming fire.* Fire is a stock image in the prophets, sometimes depicting cleansing or, more often, punishment.

- *Worms.* The enemies of God have no future. The worms do
  not torment living souls; they only speed up the decomposition of corpses.

- *Smoke.* This is a sign of burning and therefore of judgment. Smoke may ascend forever (like the smoke of burning Rome in Revelation 19:3), yet this is metaphorical.

## Is the Bible to Be Taken Literally?

So when someone asks, "Are we supposed to take the Bible literally or figuratively?" answer yes. We are to take it all seriously. Take it literally when dealing with straightforward language, figuratively at other times. We all understand the principle. Is it really raining cats and dogs when heavy precipitation falls to the earth? These are figures of speech. In the same vein, are we to literally believe rivers clap their hands, stones cry out, or stars plummet to the earth (Psalm 98:8; Luke 19:40; Revelation 6:13)? We need to distinguish the medium from the message. Sometimes the medium is colorful and poetic, other times prosaic. Once we discern the type of literature we are reading—and usually this is not too difficult—we can take the passage at face value. That is the best way to fully appreciate the inspired word of God.

If this makes you uncomfortable, recall that Jesus himself frequently taught through figures of speech, hyperbole (deliberate overstatement for effect), word plays, and even fiction (stories). Let's consider a few illustrations from the Sermon on the Mount (Matthew 5–7).

Figures of speech include salt, light, not allowing one's left hand to know what one's right hand is doing, throwing pearls to swine, and entering through the narrow gate (Matthew 5:13-14; 6:3; 7:6; 7:13). Here are some of Jesus's use of hyperbole:

- The surgical removal of eyes and hands (5:29-30). After all, would one enter heaven with missing limbs, given the doctrine of the resurrection of the body?

- Praying in one's inner room (6:6). Jesus never did so as far as we can tell, which suggests he is concerned with the attitude, not the place of prayer.

- The permanence of the law (5:18). Jesus upholds the law, though he clearly feels comfortable suspending or adapting parts of it, as in chapter 12:1-8, where he is Lord of the Sabbath.

- Marrying a divorced woman (5:32). If literal, this makes the book of Hosea problematic because God commands Hosea to marry, divorce, and remarry Gomer (Hosea 1:2; 2:2; 3:1).

- Exceeding the righteousness of the Pharisees (5:20).

- The Pharisees announcing their benevolence with trumpets (6:2).

There are many other instances where the Lord uses hyperbole or other literary forms that require careful interpretation. In Luke 14:26 he tells us to hate our parents. In John 6:35 he says he is the bread of life. In Mark 4:12 he says he speaks in parables so some people won't understand. It would be wrong to take him literally if that means we should despise our family, or imagine that Jesus is actual bread, or that he didn't want the crowds to respond to his words.

Those without literary sensitivity make mistakes. Failing to grasp that Luke 22:44 contains a simile—Jesus's sweat was *like* drops of blood—they conclude that Jesus was literally sweating blood. This is not impossible, but it is not what the text says. Or they may read Paul's words in Colossians 1:23 about the gospel being preached to every creature under heaven and think that the Native Americans, the Chinese, and Australian aborigines were all evangelized by the time Paul penned Colossians. Paul's sense becomes clear when we appreciate similar passages in the Old Testament, such as Psalm 98:3 and Jeremiah 25:26. In fact, we find Paul offering advice about interactions with outsiders in Colossians 4:2-6. If there were still persons who had not heard the gospel, the world was still unevangelized.

Of course, much of the Bible employs literal language. Our approach to interpreting the texts on the afterlife ought to reflect this fact. In the next chapter we will continue to discuss poetry and then take a look at a famous parable. Afterward we will explore the nature of apocalypse. Then we should be ready to tackle the meaty portion of the book—the central chapters on heaven and hell.

## In Brief

- There is no such thing as neutral interpretation, only careful and careless interpretation.

- Literal language should be taken literally, metaphorical language metaphorically. We must study and pray for the wisdom to know the difference.

- Going back to the prophets prepares us to understand the book of Revelation. Observing Jesus's own teaching method can also help us to avoid excessive literalism.

- The richness, depth, and actual meaning of many parts of the Bible can be discovered only when we read passages in context and with literary awareness. This is exciting stuff!

# Lenses of Interpretation, Part 2

## Poetry, Parable, Apocalypse

*Some students drink at the fountain of
knowledge. Others just gargle.
Conceit is what makes a little squirt think
he's a fountain of knowledge.*

In this chapter we'll focus on three types of biblical writing: poetry, parable, and apocalyptic. We need to appreciate them before we study the passages about the afterlife. Each part of our study will yield rich dividends to those who will invest the time required to think critically about Scripture. Not Scripture as we might prefer it to be—easy, straightforward, prosaic, and written for our own culture—but as it is: an uneven mix of poetry and prose, fiction and nonfiction, and familiar and not-so-familiar terms, people, place, empires, and concepts. We must use different approaches to interpretation for each of these types of writing.

## Poetry

A third of the Bible is poetry. Everyone recognizes that poetry is different from prose. In poetry, words paint pictures. Grammar is more flexible. Archaic terms pop up. Strict logic may or may not be honored.

That's why we err when we literalize, imagining things never intended by the writer. Let's consider a few passages from the book of Psalms, the longest poetic section in Scripture.

"The LORD is my shepherd" (Psalm 23:1). Are we literally sheep? Is he literally a shepherd? Not at all. We understand this most famous of psalms, but just to be awkward...

- We're supposed to lie down in green pastures. What about my hay fever?
- Our cup will overflow. What if we don't have a cup? And what beverage exactly is he putting into my cup?
- Where is this house that I am going to live in forever?

"In sin my mother conceived me" (Psalm 51:5). Is this a strong proof text for original sin?

- If this is literally true, do the wicked also literally speak lies from birth (Psalm 58:3)?
- If the passage in Psalm 58:3 is figurative, why should we take 51:5 differently?
- If the wicked are born in sin and deceivers from the beginning of their lives, are the righteous full of faith even in the womb? Psalm 22:9-10 and 71:6 seem to say so. Or is the point more an emotional one? A profound feeling of sinfulness (uncleanness) is being projected back to the earliest possible moment, as is faith. "I've trusted in you since birth" means my life is characterized by faith, not that I was born a Christian.

"Every animal of the forest is mine, and the cattle on a thousand hills" (Psalm 50:10).

- If God owns the cattle on a thousand hills, who owns the others?
- Maybe the earth has only a thousand "true hills." Or was this the exact number of hills in the part of Israel where the psalmist lived?

- Isn't it more reasonable that "a thousand" is symbolic, representing all the hills in the world and thus establishing God's title to all the cattle that graze there? (The point is that he doesn't need our [animal] sacrifices because he has his own livestock.)

To literalize these passages is to miss their meaning. Moreover, we are right to be cautious about deriving doctrine from poetry. With poetry we first *feel* what the writer intends to convey, and then we ponder the implications. With prose we *assess* what the writer is saying, and feelings are secondary.

## Parables

Strictly speaking, parables are comparisons (from the Greek *parabolé*, meaning "comparison, illustration, placing beside"). We are most familiar with the story parables. Jesus was a master storyteller, but he was not the first to utilize this literary genre. Two Old Testament examples are the parable of the vineyard (Isaiah 5) and the parable of the rich man and the ewe lamb (2 Samuel 12:1-4).

Parables are fiction; the details need not be realistic. Indebtedness was common in Palestine, but certainly no servant ever owed his master ten thousand bags of gold (Matthew 18:21-35)! The unjust judge (Luke 18:1-8) and the master of the shrewd manager (Luke 16:1-9) are hardly worthy role models of God, but that doesn't negate the points of the parables. Rather, we are to learn from the urgency of the persistent widow and the recently unemployed manager. Doubtless many were robbed on the road to Jericho, so there was no need for Jesus to bring his listeners a news flash (Luke 10:25-37). The robbery could well have happened, or Jesus could have made it up. It doesn't matter one way or the other.

Parables are better than journalistic accounts—truer, in a way. Two of the magazines to which I subscribe are *Scientific American* and *The Economist*. I like to keep current with what's happening in science and world events. I hope I am reading truth and not nonsense. When I put down my magazine, I may be shocked at the state of the world or thrilled that a new planet was discovered, yet rarely does anything

make me a better husband, father, or friend. But in the case of parables, there are lessons for the heart, truths that can shape our destiny.
Do you agree? Good fiction trumps nonfiction.

Several parables are frequently mined by Bible believers for doctrine about the afterlife. The most popular might be the parable of
the rich man and Lazarus (Luke 16:19-31). (You may already be balk-
ing. "It's not a parable; it really happened." Perhaps it did, but we will
address that issue soon enough.)

Scholars have discovered parables with a similar message in earlier
Egyptian and Jewish texts.[1] A doctoral dissertation at the University of
Amsterdam identified seven versions of the parable circulating in the
first century.[2] The fortunes of a rich man and a poor man are reversed
in the afterlife. As often happens in the Bible, a preexisting story is
adapted to present a theological truth. And here's where it gets interesting. What does Jesus do? Jeremias pointed out that, as in Matthew
20:1-16 and 22:1-14, Jesus grabs his listeners' attention with a familiar
story and then adds a twist, or an epilogue.[3] One of the most respected
evangelical Bible scholars, N.T. Wright, explains.

> The story carries clear echoes of well-known folk tales to
> which Jesus is giving a fresh and startling twist. The empha-
> sis falls at the same point that was made twice—i.e., with
> great stress—in the prodigal son: "resurrection," i.e. "return
> from exile," is happening all around, and the Pharisees can-
> not see it. The parable is not, as often supposed, a descrip-
> tion of the afterlife, warning people to be sure of their
> ultimate destination.[4]

Though the story contains echoes of the afterlife, this is not the
point. The story appears in a chapter almost entirely focused on money
matters. Apart from three verses, all of Luke 16 concentrates on proper
and improper attitudes towards wealth: The parable of the shrewd
Manager (verses 1-9), stewardship of earthly riches (verses 10-13), the
Pharisees' love of money (verses 14-15), a few brief additional teachings
(verses 16-18), and then our parable.

Why does the rich man fare so badly in the afterlife? He had ignored
Lazarus, the beggar at his gate. He'd hardened his heart to his fellow
man, failing to show love. In a culture that considered wealth a mark

of divine blessing, Jesus makes a radical point. It's what we *do* with our wealth that indicates whether or not we have God's blessing. That's a point that challenges all of us living in the affluent West. As the parable concludes, for someone whose heart is hardened by mammon, even the resurrection of Christ will have no impact.

Now to the matter of whether the event itself actually happened. As mentioned, the story was already familiar; Jesus's contribution lay in how he shaped the story. Like the other parables, the situation is general. In fact it begins in the same way as the previous parable: "There was a rich man…"

"Yes, but no one else in a parable is *named*." So what? His name is symbolic, meaning "God has helped"—an apt name for one whose fortunes have been favorably reversed.[5] "But these are physical persons and experiences, so it must be a true story." As N.T. Wright points out, "It is hard to imagine how else the characters could be portrayed except as physical."[6] Of course it's a true story, but true in what way? Parables serve as vehicles to bring us divine truth. It's the message of the parable that is true.

How about the details? In the parable, they are in tension with the biblical teaching on judgment (see chapter 12), as it appears these men received their eternal reward before the judgment day. The rich man is in Hades, not Gehenna.[7] For such reasons, New Testament scholars, anticipated by Luther, Bullinger, Lightfoot, and a host of earlier commentators, unanimously interpret this story as a parable, though some popular writers think differently. The literal interpretation of the parable was common in the Middle Ages, but it has been largely abandoned in more recent theological articles.[8]

What about "Abraham's bosom" (Luke 16:22 KJV—"Abraham's side" in the NIV)? Does the phrase tell us anything about the Jews' expectation of the afterlife? In the intertestamental period (from about 400 BC to the time of Christ) there was a growing expectation of meeting Abraham and the prophets in paradise.[9] During the Middle Ages, churchmen envisioned a warm embrace by the prophet (hence his bosom). Though a few scholars contest it, the majority of contemporary commentators see here an image of table fellowship. People reclined to eat, lying around a table, resting on their left elbow, and eating with their right hand. This is surely the way we are to picture the Last Supper, with "the disciple whom Jesus loved" (John 13:23) leaning into Jesus's side. It is a picture of intimacy, connection, unrushed fellowship. This is not to say that we should think of heaven as a literal banquet, for while it may be that, it will certainly be far more. Besides, in the parable, Lazarus is not in heaven. For the Christians of the first few centuries, the term "Abraham's bosom" was simply another way of conceiving of paradise.[10] And as we will see in chapter 10, paradise is not heaven, but rather the joyous waiting place of the departed righteous. Thus the parable relates the common view of the intermediate state of the dead. It is not intended to correct it or to supply fresh afterlife doctrine.

One further comment is in order. Earlier versions of verse 23 in the NIV followed the KJV, errantly rendering Hades as hell. This is somewhat understandable, considering the fire in which the rich man is suffering, yet the Greek is clear. The KJV renders four terms, *Sheol*, *Hades*, *Gehenna*, and the rare *Tartarus* (2 Peter 2:9), by the same English word, *hell*. Hades (equivalent to Sheol in the Old Testament) is the waiting place of the dead, not hell.

Strikingly, no early Christian writer understood the Hades of Luke 16 to be hell. Still, scores of writers equate the two. Based on Luke 16:22, some conclude that angels will escort us to heaven when we die.[11] Even though the story tempts us, we must not extract doctrine from minor details in a parable. Perhaps angels do escort us, perhaps they don't. Probably it was part of the folklore of Jesus's day, and he has little interest in correcting minor issues in people's theology.[12] To illustrate the error of turning parabolic details into doctrine, how would you assess a claim that God will always send a Samaritan if we're in trouble (Luke 10:33), or that we are always sure to find our lost possessions (Luke 15:9)? These are just details in stories. What about the talking trees in Jotham's parable—are trees conscious (Judges 9:7-15)? What if we find buried treasure in a field—are we to deceive the owner as to its presence (Matthew 13:44)?

Luke 16 is certainly suggestive of punishments and rewards in the afterlife, but the purpose of the parable is not to describe them. Robert Morey, a strong defender of the traditional view of hell (eternal torment—one of several positions we will inspect in chapter 8), agrees that Luke 16 does not provide details of the world to come.[13] No wonder a widely used evangelical theology textbook holds that it is probably better not to look to Luke 16 for details of life after death at all.[14]

By now you may be feeling leery of *any* interpretation. "I'll never be certain what poetry and parables mean!" But that's not quite right. We *can* know what they mean, but not when we misinterpret them, which is likely to happen if we treat them like prose or historical narrative.[15]

## Apocalypse

We need to cover one more type of literature in the Bible before we wrap up this chapter, and it's a jawbreaker: apocalyptic literature. The word *apocalypse* has three meanings. In the popular sense, it is the cataclysmic end of the world. Second, The Apocalypse is the alternate name for Revelation, the last book of the Bible. Both words mean unveiling, or revealing.[16] Third, apocalypse is a literary genre used in both testaments. This genre is poorly understood by casual Bible readers, and it will be well worth our while to become familiar with it.

This ancient genre appears in various sections of the Old Testament and became extremely popular between 200 BC and AD 200. Often employed by the prophetic writers, apocalypse especially spoke to the hearts of the people in times of turmoil, oppression, and hopelessness. The curtains are pulled back to reveal what is truly going on in the heavenly realms. In times of stress, God's people increasingly looked ahead to a time when God would penetrate our world, ushering in a glorious future. Evil would be requited, good rewarded, all things fulfilled. Christians believe this is precisely what began when Jesus Christ entered our world.

In apocalypse, local problems (including persecution, warfare, and oppression) are seen in cosmic terms. The following description may help.

> Apocalyptic speech is lurid in its colours and very often violent in its tone. It strikes the imagination and grabs hold of the mind. Who, having read it, can forget the seven-headed sea beast or the scarlet prostitute on its back? Whose mind does not boggle over the falling of the stars and the rolling up of the heavens? Apocalyptic speech is vivid and easily

remembered. It appeals to our imagination. It is the language of conflict and victory. It is the language used when God smites the oppressor and vindicates his people. It is the language of crisis if not of persecution.[17]

Here is a sampling of apocalyptic passages in the Bible: Isaiah 24–27; 33–35; Ezekiel 2:8–3:27; 38–39; Daniel 2; 7; 8; Joel 3:9-17; Zechariah 12–14; Matthew 24; Mark 13; Luke 21:5-36; and Revelation. There are scores of examples of extrabiblical apocalyptic literature, both Jewish (1 Enoch, 4 Ezra, Apocalypse of Abraham) and Christian (Apocalypse of Peter, Shepherd of Hermas, Revelation of Bartholomew).[18]

The two most familiar apocalyptic passages are Matthew 24 (with parallels in Mark 13 and Luke 21) and the book of Revelation. In Matthew 24 Jesus foretold the destruction of Jerusalem. In doing so he chose the language of apocalypse. Although scholars differ, most concur that the prophecy alludes to the Roman destruction of 70 AD. Many readers of Matthew 24 fail to see that there was a fulfillment within one generation of the oracle itself. As Jesus predicted, everything he described would take place *in that generation* (Matthew 24:34). If it had to be fulfilled literally, then his prophecy was a failure. But if he was utilizing apocalyptic, the problem vanishes. There is no reason to deny that the sun was darkened (verse 29) metaphorically, that the Lord came against Jerusalem (verse 30) through the Roman army, or that he gathered his elect from the four winds (verse 31) when believers heeded Jesus's prophecy and so fled the city.

Most modern readers don't understand the genre, so they frequently imagine apocalyptic prophecy as referring to political events in modern times. They have things backward because they have forgotten to *reverse the rules of interpretation.* In normal prose, we take everything literally unless forced to do otherwise. In apocalyptic, we take everything figuratively unless forced to do otherwise.[19] Here are some features of apocalyptic literature:

- An unveiling of previously unknown or secret knowledge, often by one who sees into the spiritual world by means of dreams or visions.

- Symbolic numbers (such as 7 churches, 1000 years, 144,000 saved in heaven). Other symbolic numbers are *gematria* (alphanumeric code spellings), including 666—the number of Nero Caesar (when the Greek names are spelled in Hebrew).

• Prophetic imagery about future events, pertaining not necessarily to the end of the world, but rather to the end of certain lives, eras, and nations.[20]

• A phantasmagorical cast of messenger angels, exotic animals with supernatural qualities and abilities, uniquely acting astronomic bodies, awesome phenomena and natural disasters, cosmological anomalies, and composite beings.

• Typically imaginative, stylized, and creative depictions of past, present, and future events in coded language. Cryptic imagery is rarely interpreted.

• A view of a struggle between cosmic powers of good and evil, typically in times of oppression, upheaval, and chaos, leading to a transformative future that is typically surreal, fantastic, and awe-inspiring.

If the details aren't *literally* true, is apocalyptic overdone? Not at all. It is effective. It is powerful. Revelation 12 is saturated with symbolism. The woman clothed with the sun is the church. Satan is the dragon. After the birth of a male child (Christ), the woman is protected in the desert—symbolizing God's faithfulness to his persecuted saints. These details are not literal; any reader must come to grips with what they represent. John is patently describing historical realities in the first century.

Hans Lilje, who finished his commentary on Revelation while imprisoned by Gestapo, wrote about God's undoing of Rome, the evil empire:

> The very moment when this purpose of God is fulfilled, the mighty power of the beast shrivels up like a collapsed balloon, as if it had never been. It has been unmasked, and its true character revealed: it was empty, futile presumption... Fire from heaven falls upon these hosts, and annihilates Satan and his armies. God's will has triumphed gloriously; the "lake of fire" means no more than this...
> Annihilation is itself annihilated. All that remains is the

majesty of life, which is God himself. He will be all in all
(1 Cor. 15:23,28). [21]

I like the way Eugene Peterson put it: "Apocalypse is arson—it
secretly sets a fire in the imagination that boils the fat out of an obese
culture-religion and renders a clear gospel love, a pure gospel hope, a
purged gospel faith."[22]

## Paradigm Shift

Admittedly, for many people, learning to read apocalypse requires
a paradigm shift. When an American rents a car in countries where
people drive on the left, everything—at first, anyway—feels backward.
But you get used it. Or think of making the shift from English mea-
surements to metric (pounds to kilos, yards to meters). When my wife,
who is British, moved with me to the United States, she had to stop
using the more logical metric system and revert (ironically) to the older
English measures.

And yet I believe most people in effect *do* understand how to read
apocalypse. Consider specimens of modern apocalypse: The Lord of
the Rings series, the Narnia books, or the world of Harry Potter. No
one asks where on the map they can find Frodo's shire or how the lion
Aslan is able to talk. Such questions belie the understanding of the
questioner. Tolkien and Lewis were more effective in communicating
their message through the use of fiction than if they had written his-
tories. This is not because they didn't know the truth but because they
knew the power of story.

Everyone knows that the story can only go one way: Things will
get worse before they get better, though in the final showdown evil will
be vanquished.

## How Do Bible Experts Interpret Revelation?

What do the experts say about this method of reading the Apocalypse—a method that contradicts popular teaching about the end of
the world found in bookstores and on the radio, television, and web?
That is, what do professional Bible scholars think about this, especially
those with a high view of the inspiration of the Bible? The great textual
expert Bruce Metzger says this:

[Revelation] contains a series of word pictures, as though a number of slides were being shown upon a great screen. As we watch we allow ourselves to be carried along by impressions created by these pictures. Many of the details of the pictures are intended to contribute to the total impression, and are not to be isolated and interpreted with wooden literalism.[23]

Most see a sequence of impressions, not a chronology as such.

Robert H. Mounce, a world-renowned Greek expert and the author of the volume on Revelation in the *New International Commentary on the New Testament*, insists that among the "essential questions" as we come to Revelation is the type of literature it is. "An informed sensitivity to the thought forms and vocabulary of apocalyptic is the *sine qua non* of satisfactory exegesis."[24]

Craig Keener, one of the most intelligent, evangelistically sensitive, and prolific New Testament scholars I have ever met, doubts that the "millennium" of Revelation 20:1-6 is meant to be literal, and he points out that this issue has been debated since early times.[25] In fact, earlier scholars, such as Augustine, Calvin, and Luther, took the millennium metaphorically.

Heavyweight New Testament scholar N.T. Wright observes that the new Jerusalem (Revelation 21:2) cannot be heaven because it comes down *out of* heaven.[26]

Cambridge scholar Richard Bauckham interprets the 144,000 in heaven (Revelation 7:4-8; 14:1,3) symbolically, as representing all the martyrs.[27] This seems more reasonable than the Jehovah's Witness position that most of the saved ("the great flock") will live on the renewed earth, and only a few of the saints will occupy heaven. (Bad news: Nearly all the 144,000 vacancies in heaven have now been filled.)

## Many Popular Writers Understand Apocalypse

By *popular* I do not mean to denigrate. The term simply designates works written not for specialists or scholars (those who have studied Greek, theology, church history, and so forth), but for the reading public.

• Wayne Martindale, a C.S. Lewis scholar, observes that the

dimensions of the city are symbolic and are in the same shape as the Holy of Holies, thus indicating God's presence among men.[28]

- Kenneth Boa and Robert Bowman take the dimensions of the new Jerusalem symbolically, as they do the 12,000-member tribes, the 144,000 in heaven, and the 144 cubits (Revelation 7:5-8; 14:1; 21:17).[29]

- They also call it "nonsense" that "the book of Revelation literally describes the new universe."[30] As we shall see in our next chapter, interpreting the apocalyptic of Revelation literally is problematic.

- F. LaGard Smith notes that, for all its hype, the millennium (Latin for the thousand years of Revelation 20:2-7) is never once mentioned by Jesus or Paul.[31] We have noted that Augustine, Calvin, and Luther refused to literalize the millennium.

- Smith notes that the difficulty of literal torment in the presence of the Lamb (Revelation 14:10), would contradict Matthew 7:23 ("*Away* from me, you evildoers!").[32]

- Commentator Jim McGuiggan explains that the millennium is probably not a period of time at all, but instead a picture of Christ's triumph through the cross over the kingdom of evil.[33] The 1000 years need not be any more literal than the 1000 years of Psalm 90:4 and 2 Peter 3:8, the 1000 hills of Psalm 50:10, the 1000 shields of Song of Songs 4:4, or the thousand generations of Deuteronomy 7:9 and 1 Chronicles 16:15.

All these writers demonstrate literary sensitivity. They understand the way apocalypse works and have managed to interpret it consistently.

## Other Popular Interpretations

Some popular writers approach Revelation as if it were a timetable. They seek to coordinate prophecies in the Apocalypse with events in history or modern times.[34] Yet, as Keener observes, "This book is in logical rather than chronological sequence."[35] There is no timetable.

In the same way, popular writers often misunderstand the apocalyptic language of the prophets, such as Joel 2:10: "Before them the earth shakes, the heavens tremble, the sun and moon are darkened, and the stars no longer shine." One writer states, "This did not occur when the Babylonians invaded Judah." He goes on to explain that it was fulfilled in the eruption of an Icelandic volcano in April 2010.[36] Yet apocalyptic language recasts local situations in cosmic language. It is simply not true that they refer to specific modern political or meteorological events.

Many see heaven in Revelation 21–22, and they may literalize the new Jerusalem.[37] As we saw in chapter 3 and will continue to explain in the next two chapters, this approach does not work.

Two writers offer what they call a "safe rule" for interpreting Revelation. "When uncertain, err on the side of caution and accept the literalness of inspired writing until it's clearly and convincingly proven otherwise."[38]

But this is *not* a safe rule—not because it is completely wrong, but because it is naive. We should take the Bible at face value, yet as we have seen, God's word employs a mixture of straightforward prose, figures of speech, poetry, and even apocalypse. Unless the reader has been trained to appreciate the (sometimes subtle) differences, he or she is likely to go astray.

Some popular writers' implausible conclusions reveal a failure to interact with the best of conservative scholarship. Of course the question is not whether the various descriptions in Revelation *could* be taken literally, or whether God is powerful enough to make them a literal reality. All the writers referenced in this chapter have a strong faith in the word of God and in his power to accomplish his will. The real question is, what does it mean? How would this have been understood by its original readers?

### How Confident Can We Be?

Do you want a firm place to stand—confidence in what the word of God says about the afterlife? Confidence comes when we have a consistent method. When we keep flipping from literal to figurative

without warrant, we are double-minded and unstable (James 1:8)—
like a national leader whose policies vacillate, a boyfriend who blows
hot and cold, or a driver who constantly changes lanes. People are
going to get hurt. Fortunately, we don't need a thick manual to "decode"
Revelation, nor is an appreciation of the nature of poetry or parable
beyond the reach of the average Bible reader.

When we are aware of our presuppositions, we become better readers. We are less likely to fall for shoddy reasoning or sensationalism.
We better appreciate the unity of Scripture. "The Old Testament is the
New Testament concealed; the New Testament is the Old Testament
revealed." We won't hold so tightly to tradition, because we know every
church, like every individual, makes mistakes, and we want to be corrected (Psalm 141:5).

On the basis of our study in chapters 2–4, we stand at the verge of
tackling the texts relating to the afterlife. We won't find all the answers—
no promise there! But at least we should make fewer mistakes.

## In Brief

- Poetry, parable, and apocalypse are common biblical
  genres that must be studied with care. Literalism tends to
  obscure the intended message, reading too much into the
  text and ignoring the unique ways God chose to express
  his inspired message.

- Many notions about the afterlife have been shaped by certain texts in the prophets, the story parables, and Revelation. Thus it pays to become familiar with the conventions
  of prophecy, parable, and apocalypse.

- Implicit in our study is another caveat: We must exercise
  caution when it comes to deriving doctrine from the most
  figurative book in the Bible (the Apocalypse).

## Questions for Self-Examination

- Do I have more to learn? Am I humble, teachable?
- Are my study habits healthy, or do I study haphazardly? Am I consistent, or do I miss days?
- Am I a careful student of the Bible? Do I have a clear method for distinguishing figurative passages from literal ones?

Part 2

# Destinations

In the previous chapters we acquired some tools for life-changing study of God's word. We learned to better distinguish literal passages from figurative ones. We saw that a mastery of the Old Testament is critical if we are to unravel the afterlife mysteries in the New Testament. Perhaps most importantly, we were led to humbly admit that our collective interpretive strategies leave much to be desired and that sometimes talk about interpretation is really a cover for poor Bible reading habits.

We now move on to our main subject. We will consider not only heaven and hell but also the possibility of a third destination. Heaven and hell are not as straightforward as we might think. For centuries Christian thinkers have reached differing conclusions, and they clearly were not ignorant, stupid, or devious. As men and women of faith, we strive to understand their reasoning in a spirit of respect. The fundamental task is to determine what is right, not who is right.

# The Good Place

## *Heaven*

*To those who by persistence in doing good seek glory,*
*honor and immortality, he will give eternal life.*

Romans 2:7

M y body was not acclimatized to the high altitude. We were high
in the Himalayas, hoping to glimpse Everest (not from the
top, mind you, just from the middle). The mountain is nearly always
obscured by fog and snow. Atmospheric oxygen was thin; walking too
quickly made us lightheaded. Eventually our persistence was rewarded
as the clouds blew off the mountain and the world's tallest peak came
into clear view. We celebrated. That night we slept with the curtain
pulled back. At 2:30 in the morning I awoke, stunned again—Everest glistened under a crescent moon. This is not unlike our glimpses of
eternity. They are worth the effort but dizzying.

### Other People

We were created for heaven, for a relationship with God. The Lord
Jesus Christ prayed these majestic words on the night of his arrest:
"Now this is eternal life: that they know you, the only true God, and
Jesus Christ, whom you have sent" (John 17:3). Eternal life is to know
God. In some sense, as mind-boggling as it is, Christians affirm and

have already experienced that Jesus Christ "is the true God and eternal life" (1 John 5:20).

Heaven will be completely satisfying. "As for me, I will be vindicated and will see your face; when I awake, I will be satisfied with seeing your likeness" (Psalm 17:15). Could it be that some don't desire heaven because they don't value a relationship with God? Whose likeness do we long to see—our own? Some not only have no desire for God but even find other people annoying, like the residents of the gray city in Lewis's *The Great Divorce*, who keep moving farther and farther apart. They can't stand one another. For them, as for one of Sartre's characters, "Hell is other people."[1] If we're completely content to be alone, away from people, then do we really desire fellowship with God?[2]

Whatever eternal life turns out to be, we can be sure that it's relational. Of course it is personal, but it's not something we do alone; there's a strong social element. It's not a private experience, but a public, shared event—or an eternal series of events. Boa and Bowman put it brilliantly:

> The extremes of a purely God-centered view of Heaven as endless contemplation of the Divine and a purely man-centered view of Heaven as unending theme park adventure with our earthly family and friends must both be rejected. In its place we must develop a Christ-centered view of eternal life in the New Heavens and New Earth, in which God dwells with the redeemed human race, in which a new extended divine "family" of God enjoys God and each other forever. [3]

The Lord taught us to pray, "Our Father." We come to God as his people. In eternity we continue to be his people. Jesus's powerful prayer continues for his disciples and for all those who will come to faith through their ministry. Heaven isn't for you and me; it's for *us*.

## Where Is Heaven?

We've taken quite some time to sharpen and calibrate our interpretive tools. Are we in a better position now to understand the nature of heaven? Nineteenth-century evangelist Dwight L. Moody described heaven as "upward and beyond the sky."[4] Such a statement sounds simple, even childish, but it can't be totally wrong. C.S. Lewis noted that any motion away from earth is "up." One clue to heaven's location is found in the nature of God. Theologians speak of his transcendence and immanence. He is transcendent—wholly beyond this world—as Solomon acknowledged when he dedicated the temple: "But will God really dwell on earth? The heavens, even the highest heaven, cannot contain you. How much less this temple I have built!" (1 Kings 8:27). God is also immanent—within our world—as Paul explained to the Athenians.

> The God who made the world and everything in it is the Lord of heaven and earth and does not live in temples built by human hands. And he is not served by human hands, as if he needed anything…God [made mankind] so that they would seek him and perhaps reach out for him and find him, though he is not far from any one of us. "For in him we live and move and have our being" (Acts 17:24-28).

Will space travelers ever reach heaven? Not likely. It does not greatly help to conceive of heaven as located in deep space or in the inner space of the human heart—though there may be a grain of truth in each possibility. Why could heaven not be another dimension?[5] Limited to our own dimensionality, we don't perceive any higher dimensions. This hardly means they aren't real. Lewis gives us more to think about:

> Heaven relates to earth tangentially so that one who is in heaven can be simultaneously present anywhere and everywhere on earth: the ascension therefore means that Jesus is available, accessible, without people having to travel to a particular spot on earth to find him…When the Bible speaks of heaven and earth it is not talking about two localities related to each other within the same space-time continuum, or about a nonphysical world contrasted with a physical one but about two different kinds of what we call space, two different kinds of what we call matter, and also quite possibly…two different kinds of what we call time.[6]

On a simpler level, Lewis conceives of heaven as a place, yet more as a relationship than a place—somewhat like the experience we have in our homes.[7]

God and heaven have been taught, hymned, and pondered universally as far back as human civilization can be measured. Do the world's religions offer any insight in their scriptures and stories?

## By Popular Demand

Heaven is certainly not the worldly paradise of wine, women, and song found in Islam, nor is it anything like the heaven of Hinduism or other faiths.[8] The Vikings had their Valhalla, the banquet hall of Odin, where the Valkyrie maidens waited on the warriors who fought by day and feasted by night. "Valhalla was not the only paradise that provided escort services for its male clientele: the Celts had a Land of the Women, medieval Germans had the ambiguous Venusberg, and of course the dark-eyed houris of the medieval Muslim paradise are famous."[9] The world's religions have not succeeded in finding the heaven of which Jesus and his followers spoke.

Despite the self-serving heavens some religions have constructed, all have a deep-felt need for a place of reward as well as a place of punishment. For example—and an ironic one at that—Buddhism, which started off as an atheistic worldview, eventually created many heavens and eight or more hells. That is, modern Buddhism resembles Islam, Christianity, and other religions in their evolution away from their starting principles. Popular Hinduism, too, has heavens and millions of hells. When a religion becomes too intellectual, losing a sense of sin, morality, absolutes, and judgment, the people reconstruct it. Heaven and hell come back by popular (emotional) demand. There is something in the spiritual heart of man that knows that he, as a sinner, deserves punishment—that justice must be served (Ecclesiastes 3:11; Romans 2:6-8). This isn't "salvation by works." It's fair and biblically correct.

## What Does the Old Testament Say?

It is often noted that the Old Testament reveals little about heaven and nothing about hell. But this isn't quite true. The word *hell* doesn't appear, but the enemies of God being destroyed by fire is a common image.[10] Let's take a look at Malachi 4.

"Surely the day is coming; it will burn like a furnace. All the arrogant and every evildoer will be stubble, and the day that is coming will set them on fire," says the Lord Almighty. "Not a root or a branch will be left to them. But for you who revere my name, the sun of righteousness will rise with healing in its rays. And you will go out and frolic like well-fed calves. Then you will trample on the wicked; they will be ashes under the soles of your feet on the day when I act," says the Lord Almighty.

The imagery here entails fire, judgment, and the complete destruction of the wicked. This is virtually the same as that at the end of Isaiah (66:15-16,24). Theologian and ethicist Stanley Grenz summarized this about heaven:

> The Old Testament community came to the conclusion that the forces of death and *Sheol* may not speak the last word. On the contrary, God had shown to his people the path to life by means of which they might avoid this fate (Ps. 16:8-11; Prov. 15:24). Consequently, the righteous psalmist could anticipate future bliss: "You guide me with your counsel, and afterward you will take me into glory" (Ps. 73:24)...Job spoke for the entire tradition when he affirmed: "I know that my Redeemer lives, and that in the end he will stand upon the earth. And after my skin has been destroyed, yet in my flesh I will see God; I myself will see him with my own eyes—I, and not another. How my heart yearns within me!" (Job 19:25-27).[11]

### Does the Apocalypse Tell Us Anything About Heaven?

Popular views on heaven and hell have been deeply influenced by Dante and Milton, no doubt, but also by the book of Revelation. For many, the new Jerusalem *is* heaven.[12]

> Then I saw "a new heaven and a new earth," for the first heaven and the first earth had passed away, and there was no longer any sea. I saw the Holy City, the new Jerusalem, coming down out of heaven from God, prepared as a bride beautifully dressed for her husband. And I heard a loud voice from the throne saying, "Look! God's dwelling place is now

among the people, and he will dwell with them. They will be his people, and God himself will be with them and be their God" (Revelation 21:1-3).

In fact nowhere in Revelation do people actually go to heaven. The new Jerusalem, the city of God described in the closing chapters, comes down *out of* heaven. Besides, the final vision has non-Christian nations still living on the earth (21:24). How can this be the end of the world?

What about the streets of gold (21:21)? In John's vision it's not only the streets that are gold, but the entire city (verse 18). Does this tell us anything about heaven? Directly, no; indirectly, perhaps. The vision is allusive. That is, without giving us any direct information, it tantalizes us, piques the imagination, prods us to envision what being in the presence of God might be like. If heaven were a literal city with golden streets, of course that would be beautiful. There is no need to literalize this detail in order to be faithful to the text, any more than we need to literalize other details of the Apocalypse. Let us consider a few.

Names written on people's foreheads indicates that they belong to God (7:3; 22:4; see Deuteronomy 11:18; Ezekiel 9:4). The star that fell to earth, part of an image of judgment against those who preferred death to repentance (Revelation 9:1-6), is not a literal star. If it were, the earth would have been annihilated. Nor will it do to claim it's really a meteor. Rigid literalism rules out flexible interpretation; the passage simply "means what it says." The vanquishing of the sea (21:1) connects with the biblical theme of the raging waters of the primeval chaos, which, like the enemies of God's people, threatens to drag them back into a spiritual wilderness (see Genesis 6:1-10; Isaiah 17:12). We cannot literalize the images of those faithful to the covenant to the point of death in Revelation 7 and 14; otherwise, only virgin Jewish males would reach heaven. (Sorry, no women, married persons, or Gentiles allowed.) The souls of the martyrs are depicted as being beneath the altar, which is before the heavenly throne (6:9; 8:5). They cry out for justice, in the same way the blood of Abel, slain for his righteousness, continues to cry out (Hebrews 11:4; 12:24). There is no necessity of taking any of these images literally.

Scores of images in the Apocalypse tell us something about God: his power, his sovereignty, his will. There are hundreds of references and allusions to the Old Testament. Revelation is only 404 verses, so the text is saturated with the Hebrew Scriptures. These images paint a picture—an encouraging one. But it will not do to overanalyze each brushstroke. We must stand farther back from the canvas.

One more example may prove helpful, if only to assure the reader of my orthodox Christian faith. Is Jesus literally a lion and a lamb (5:5)? Just to be sure you are following me, of course I believe he is *truly* the Lamb that was slain (Isaiah 53:7), as well as the Lion of the tribe of Judah (Genesis 49:10)—but not *literally* a lion or lamb, for the Bible tells us that the Son of God took on the robe of humanity. Human—not leonine or ovine.

Revelation speaks of the ultimate triumph of the kingdom of God over the kingdoms of the world. Yet there is no timetable of end-time events, not a word about the antichrist or a rapture, no description of World War III or the conversion of Israel. It does, however, make veiled allusions to the Roman Empire, and it incorporates hundreds of images and motifs from the Jewish Scriptures. Sensationalistic books and documentaries, displaying little awareness of the nature of apocalypse or the context of Revelation (the persecuted church), direct our attention to developments in the Middle East, Russia, or China, or they warn us of elaborate government conspiracies at home.[13] There is so much misinformation out there that, for most of us, the first step in making sense of this book is to forget everything we've ever heard about it! At the fundamental level, the book of Revelation directs us to faithful Christian living—even at the expense of our lives.

Some may take exception to this understanding of the Apocalypse, but let's ask some questions of those who think Revelation describes the end of the world and heaven rather than the church emerging through the Roman persecution.

- If Revelation 21–22 refers primarily to heaven, why does the new Jerusalem come down *out of* heaven? (21:2).

- Who are the people who dwell outside the city of God? Their kings are said to bring their splendor into the holy city (21:24).

- Why are the nations (Gentiles) still on the earth? (21:26).

If they weren't consumed in the lake of fire (20:15), why aren't they with God's people?

- Why do they require healing? (22:2). Weren't all things made new, and all sickness and sorrow removed?

- How can "dogs" (the impure and irreligious) exist outside the new Jerusalem (22:15)?

These questions must be answered not with assertions of opinion, tradition, and anecdote, but by a consistent and repeatable method. Just as we ask ourselves whether our own method is sound, so ought we to ask others how they come by their biblical knowledge, especially when it is held as dogma.

Revelation may not give us the details we seek. It does, however, point us in the right direction. It's a kind of sign. Nearly all readers of the Apocalypse sense the transcendence of the message. They are directed to a point beyond. It is quite impossible to read Revelation and not think of God's ultimate intervention, justice, and making all things new.[14] When we extend these metaphors beyond the time of John and the cessation of persecution to the end of time, we are not erring. But we must be cautious.

### What Heaven Is Not

Given the failure of human attempts to define heaven and the allusive nature of the biblical material, we might gain a higher degree of certainty as to the nature of heaven by pursuing a different course. Once the false ideas have been knocked down, only the most conclusive truths will remain standing. Even though the resulting structure may be a bit bare, we will have greater confidence in the results, and we will better be able to see God. So let's proceed by examining what heaven is *not*.

### It Is Not a Place of Lethargy

After life on earth, we will be weary, and we will appreciate refreshment. When God comforts his people—and there are many Scriptures to this effect, in both testaments—all our needs will be met. We will not be troubled by bad memories, fleshly temptations, nagging doubts, or aching muscles. This does not entail an existence of indolence. Even in Eden, God had work for man to do (Genesis 2:15). Heaven will not change that. We will still be "gardening"—though, as someone put it, without the weeds.[15] We were created to be busy, to be active, to function with a certain level of pressure and intensity. Recreation is never more rewarding than when we know we have been pouring ourselves out for what we believe is worthwhile.

Jesus more than hinted that this would be the case (Matthew 24:45-47; 25:21-23). First John 3:2-3 assures that when Christ comes, we will be like him, for we will see him as he is. This is motivating; the drive to be with Christ and like Christ keeps us holy. In this life we are becoming something—or someone.

Christians stand on Romans 8:28: "And we know that in all things God works for the good of those who love him, who have been called according to his purpose." But why stop there? Disciples of Christ want to be like their Lord. Nor do they lightly take verses out of context. So let's continue: "For those God foreknew he also predestined to be conformed to the image of his Son, that he might be the firstborn among many brothers and sisters" (Romans 8:29).

Our destiny is to become like Christ. This happens only through the fiery process of suffering (Romans 5:1-5; 8:17). We wish there were some other way, but this is God's plan. This is not a case for purgatory (more on that in chapter 9), but the reality of our earthly existence. It's a process of ongoing sanctification, of transformation in the direction of holiness. We are transformed only as we are conformed to the image of Christ (Romans 12:2; 2 Corinthians 3:18; Philippians 3:21; see also 1 Peter 1:14-16).

## It Is Not Becoming God

Doubtless heaven involves a closer relationship with God but not identity with him. Despite the wish of one writer, "Imagine the unspeakable benefits of a state where we will know all things perfectly," there's little reason to buy in to such thinking.[16] Omnipotent, omniscient, omnipresent—these are attributes of God alone.

And yet the Bible assures us we will partake of the divine nature (2 Peter 1:3-4)—something the Orthodox churches have historically emphasized far better than their Catholic or Protestant cousins. But we are already becoming *like* God. The Eastern concept that we will become one *with* God, and the New Age idea that we were god all along, are empty.

## It Is Not Boring

A friend wrote candidly of his dread of heaven. "Living in a place for eternity, singing or worshipping or whatever they do up there with no endings, transitions, or changes? I couldn't see how anyone would want to be in a place like that, especially one that was never, ever going to end. I felt trapped; it was either that or hell, and I wanted neither of them. There were days when the idea of complete annihilation appealed more to me."[17]

We find ourselves almost forced to come up with colorful analogies to convince ourselves that heaven will not be dull. We imagine a place where we can eat mountains of sumptuous foods without expanding the waistline. Or a place where we can fly, accomplish superhuman feats, or participate in incredible adventures. The more intellectually inclined may conceive of heaven as an infinite library, chock-full of scintillating reading. But these fantasies pale in comparison to heaven. Paradoxically—and in contrast to the opinion that we will have perfect knowledge—a full understanding of everything might well make heaven boring. Nothing new to learn, no mystery, no suspense—think about it.

Perhaps most of our questions about life, science, and even the Bible will be too trivial to pursue when we see the Lord as he really is (1 John 3:2), when we are transformed (Philippians 3:21). Lewis put it well:

> There is no need to be worried by facetious people who try to make the Christian hope of heaven ridiculous by saying that they do not want to spend eternity playing harps. The answer to such people is that if they cannot understand books written for grown-ups, they should not talk about them at all. All the scriptural imagery—harps, gold, and so on—is of course a symbolical attempt to express the inexpressible...People who take these symbols literally might

as well think that when Christ told us to be like doves, he meant that we were to lay eggs.[18]

According to Robert Mankoff, longtime cartoon editor for *The New Yorker*, heaven is second only to desert islands as a favorite setting for his cartoonists.[19] I doubt the cartoons would even be funny if the public could catch only a glimpse of heaven. Unfortunately, as long as faux believers live insipid lives instead of being on fire for God, the misperception that sinners have more fun than saints do will continue.

## It Is Not Flat

It is usually assumed that heaven is the same for everybody there—those who began working at the eleventh hour receive the same as those who bore the heat of the day, as in the parable of the workers in the vineyard (Matthew 20:1-15). This feels unfair to us as it did to the workers in the parable. But remember, this is a parable, and it highlights particularly God's scandalous grace. The workers who began later probably correspond to the Gentiles, whose reception into the early church, which was principally Jewish, was problematic. Were they going to be admitted without circumcision, Sabbath keeping, kosher eating, and Torah observance? What!—just repentance and a bloodless baptism ceremony? It was too easy, reducing the whole thing to justification by faith. The parable is not intended primarily to tell us about heaven. As always, we must proceed cautiously if we are attempting to derive doctrine.

In the flat view, everyone receives the same reward. That may be true enough in the parable, and if at the end of it all we are completely saved, we are saved (not 90 percent saved). One can certainly reason that the reward is heaven itself (Matthew 25:46). Some passages are harder to read this way: There are differences in reward (Matthew 6:4,6,18; 10:41-42). And others make much better sense if there are differing rewards (Matthew 6:2; 13:12; 25:29). A similar rationale applies to judgment (Luke 12:47-48), and we will return to this—a nonflat view of hell—later in the book.

The flat view confuses the reward with the experience of the reward. Might treasure in heaven signify differing experiences of heaven? Two persons can attend the same party. One enjoys it, happy he came. The other has had the time of her life. It's not that one was served iced tea and the other martinis. It is inherent within our own psyches to experience identical events in differing ways. My wife laughs, smiles, and chats much more easily than I do. Sometimes she has to ask me, "Douglas, are you enjoying yourself?" even when I am. Similarly, the more invested you are in your work, the more rewarding it is. If you work hard with your sports team to win, the victory is even sweeter than if you only gave 80 percent. There is thus a little extra reward for those who truly went the distance. You get out what you put in. This isn't salvation by works. But then, it isn't salvation without works either, as Jesus's brother James was quick to point out (James 2:24).

Another reason heaven will be truly fulfilling is that we will be doing what we love to do. Not because free will is quashed, nor is there any biblical indication that we will be forced to worship God. Whether we can still sin in heaven may be a moot point. Whatever temptation there might be will be so eclipsed by God's majesty and glory that we will no longer have the desire to sin. It will be that good.

## It Won't Be Lonely

Our human fears have been catalogued by psychologists. Fear of death, fear of public speaking, fear of rejection...High on the list is the fear of being alone. We were created for connection. Heaven is fellowship with God and with others. We will not be lonely.

So there we are. Heaven isn't idleness, tedium, or even a uniform experience for all. Nor is it lonely, for God and those who love him will be there. Heaven will be magnificent! It is the place where "glory, honor and immortality" (Romans 2:7) will be nonstop elements of our very existence.

## Are the Souls of the Saved in Heaven?

Are we catapulted to heaven the moment we die? Or is there an intermediate state between our earthly lives and the heavenly afterlife? There is a strong consensus among Christian writers that we do not have to wait for heaven. Dwight Moody and E.M. Bounds believe the departed saints are already in heaven, as does Max Lucado. John MacArthur believes Psalm 23:6 and 2 Corinthians 5:8 mean heaven is now. Oswald Sanders writes, "The moment we take our last breath on earth, we take our first breath in heaven." Similarly, Paul Enns writes, "Your last breath on earth will be your first breath in heaven." Ron Rhodes believes we go to heaven at the moment of death, as does Mark Cahill. Most writers, such as James Garlow and Keith Wall, teach that our deceased loved ones are already in heaven. Bill Wiese, whose story we will examine in chapter 16, is certain that the unsaved are cast into hell immediately at death. Randy Alcorn writes, "More than 250,000 people every day go either to Heaven or Hell."[20]

Moreover, tradition is strong. For centuries the church has taught that the departed saints are in heaven. The Roman Catholic Council of Florence (1438–1439) stated that the souls of the saints are assumed immediately into heaven. Protestants followed suit in the Second Helvetic Confession (1562), written for Swiss Reformed churches and adopted by Protestants throughout Europe.

So why are more and more Old and New Testament scholars rethinking this belief? There is a growing general recognition that the last day must come before we are assigned our eternal destinies. The New Testament never records the dead as being in heaven. Hebrews 12:22-24 is ambiguous at best.[21] Passages like Luke 15:7 and 1 Peter 3:22 name beings that are in heaven, and humans are not mentioned. Of course this is an argument from silence. Can we find any more compelling (direct) biblical evidence on this matter?

We can. The apostle Peter stated, "For David did not ascend to heaven" (Acts 2:34), even though David was a man after God's own heart (Acts 13:22). Jesus affirmed, "No one has ever gone into heaven except the one who came from heaven—the Son of Man" (John 3:13). Most commentators read John 14:1-3 in a similar light:

> Do not let your hearts be troubled. You believe in God; believe also in me. My Father's house has many rooms; if that were not so, would I have told you that I am going there to prepare a place for you? And if I go and prepare a place for you, I will come back and take you to be with me that you also may be where I am.

At first blush the Lord seems to promise that he'll take us to be with him only when he returns. We wait. (We'll examine what the early church taught about the intermediate state of the dead in chapter 10.) Protestant Martin Luther (1488–1546), defiant of popes, councils, and creeds, was adamant that the dead are not in heaven yet, as was Tyndale (1492–1536), the English reformer strangled and burned at the stake for translating the Bible into English.[22] However, there is an alternative understanding of this passage, which we will engage in the next chapter.

If the dead aren't in heaven, where are they? And what about near-death experiences—aren't they verification that some at least have already made it? We will take time to answer these important questions in chapters 10 and 16. More intriguing is this query: Does heaven mean that we will escape the earth or live on it? This last question is so widely discussed that we will need to devote our next chapter to it.

### Your Heaven Is Too Small

Someone said, "If our God is small enough for us to understand, he isn't big enough for us to worship." The same goes for heaven. Whenever we try to describe it, we get into trouble. We mistake the metaphor, the analogy, for the real thing. We forget the puniness of our thinking.

> Your heaven is too small. Mine is too small. If all of us together tried to outdo one another with wilder, bolder and more outrageous thoughts of heaven—we would still fall short. In fact, a whole mountain of wonderful thoughts, gathered together and lifted up, would not suffice. This exercise would leave us exhausted and happy, to be sure; but we would look up from that summit of superlatives only to realize that we had not yet begun to ascend the real peak, still towering hundreds of miles into the sky before us.
>
> Ten times more? One hundred trillion times more? How about *infinitely* more? Heaven is infinitely more than our best, our most wonderful and most outrageously creative thoughts. What, after all, do Biblical expressions like these tell us: "unsearchable," "immeasurable," "indescribable" and "inexpressible"? In heaven, we will dwell in the kingdom of an infinite God. We will enter into and become part of God's very own life—his abundant, eternal, creative, life-giving life. Mortality and every other limitation of this creation will be swallowed up by the life of the Eternal One.

So why try to imagine it at all? Because we are encouraged to do so again and again, and even commanded to. You see, thoughts of heaven elevate us. They purify us (1 John 3:3), releasing us from the grip of this world (Colossians 3:1-4). They give us hope and endurance. They fill us with "inexpressible and glorious joy" (1 Peter 1:8). And besides, it's just plain fun.[23]

## In Brief

- Heaven is not a place of tedium, lethargy, or loneliness. Heaven involves activity, not passivity.

- Heaven is more about relationship than anything else.

- The book of Revelation supplies lovely imagery that points us beyond this world to our Judge and Redeemer, but it does not *directly* teach about heaven.

- Perhaps people's heavenly experiences will vary, depending on such factors as personality and how invested they were as disciples of Christ during their earthly lives.

- The consensus of Jesus, the apostles, and the church of the early centuries is that all the dead are still waiting for the judgment day. No humans are in heaven yet.

# Heaven on Earth

## *Up There or Down Here?*

*The kingdom of this world is become the
kingdom of our Lord and of his Christ.*

HANDEL'S MESSIAH, BASED ON REVELATION 11:15

The heavenly realm can be described only indirectly and is best understood in terms of character and relationship, not geography and physics. That is, until we get there, we may never know where heaven is or what sort of science—if any at all—correctly describes transactions in the celestial realm. Yet we *do* know what sorts of persons we need to become as we are transformed into the likeness of God's Son. Heaven is about him, not us.

When I was a new believer, the only persons I knew who taught that we would live in an earthly paradise were the Jehovah's Witnesses. Their official literature (the *Watchtower*), with its 1950s-style drawings of smiling white American suburbanites, made it hard to take the notion seriously. Nevertheless, where heaven is—"up there" or "down here"— is energetically debated in the theological world. Maybe the Witnesses were onto something?

Warning: The analysis in this chapter is fairly technical. Please skip immediately to chapter 7 if you feel a headache coming on. But for those who persevere, enlightenment is just around the corner.

## The Traditional View: From Earth to Heaven

The concept most of us grew up with was that when Christ returns, he will take us away from the earth to be with him in heaven. The new heaven and new earth are merely symbolic. We couldn't stay here even if we wanted to because it's all going to burn. Let's take a look at five of the Scriptures most relevant to the conversation. As we consider alternate views, you can make your choice as to which is best supported.

> My Father's house has many rooms; if that were not so, would I have told you that I am going there to prepare a place for you? And if I go and prepare a place for you, I will come back and take you to be with me that you also may be where I am (John 14:2-3).

> According to the Lord's word, we tell you that we who are still alive, who are left until the coming of the Lord, will certainly not precede those who have fallen asleep. For the Lord himself will come down from heaven, with a loud command, with the voice of the archangel and with the trumpet call of God, and the dead in Christ will rise first. After that, we who are still alive and are left will be caught up together with them in the clouds to meet the Lord in the air. And so we will be with the Lord forever (1 Thessalonians 4:15-17).

> But the day of the Lord will come like a thief. The heavens will disappear with a roar; the elements will be destroyed by fire, and the earth and everything done in it will be laid bare. Since everything will be destroyed in this way, what kind of people ought you to be? You ought to live holy and godly lives as you look forward to the day of God and speed its coming. That day will bring about the destruction of the heavens by fire, and the elements will melt in the heat. But in keeping with his promise we are looking forward to a new heaven and a new earth, where righteousness dwells (2 Peter 3:10-13).

> See, I will create
> new heavens and a new earth.
> The former things will not be remembered,

nor will they come to mind.
But be glad and rejoice forever
   in what I will create,
for I will create Jerusalem to be a delight
   and its people a joy.
I will rejoice over Jerusalem
   and take delight in my people;
the sound of weeping and of crying
   will be heard in it no more (Isaiah 65:17-19).

Then I saw "a new heaven and a new earth," for the first heaven and the first earth had passed away, and there was no longer any sea. I saw the Holy City, the new Jerusalem, coming down out of heaven from God, prepared as a bride beautifully dressed for her husband. And I heard a loud voice from the throne saying, "Look! God's dwelling place is now among the people, and he will dwell with them. They will be his people, and God himself will be with them and be their God" (Revelation 21:1-3).

Admittedly, when we read each of these texts on its own (out of context) and without the benefit of any interpretive tools (which we covered in chapters 2–4), the traditional view is strong. At Jesus's return he will take us away from the planet, which will then be destroyed.

## A Second Possibility: From Heaven to Earth

Is there another way to look at these passages? Perhaps heaven comes to earth. The earth itself, like our bodies, is resurrected—brought from death to life in a glorious transformation. In fact, heaven and earth are united in a cosmic wedding.[1] This view is growing in acceptance.

### John 14:1-3

N.T. Wright, with an eye on John 1:14 and 2:21, explains that "the Father's house" in John 14:2 refers not to a future heaven but to the present. The "house" is no physical structure (such as the temple) any more than the body of Christ is made with bricks and mortar. McGuiggan agrees, though he believes John 14 refers to our future life on earth.[2] John 14 in this case has nothing to do with a rapture, but the restoration of the dwelling of God with man.[3] Such an interpretation fits the context and flow of John 14 better than the traditional view. Jesus promises his presence; he will come (through the Holy Spirit) to those who obey him (14:23). This would be a sudden change of subject if the early verses were talking about a rapture.

Accordingly, Bartholomew and Goheen criticize the standard translations of John 14:2-3 as not fitting the context.

> David Lawrence (*Heaven: It's Not the End of the World! The Biblical Promise of a New Earth* [London: Scripture Union, 1995], 32) has offered a paraphrase of this text that much better fits Jesus's words to his disciples: "In my Father's presence [i.e., house] there is room for all. As I go to the Father via the cross I prepare the means for you to enter his presence wherever you may find yourselves. Having opened the way for you to enjoy the same intimacy with the Father that you have seen me enjoy, I will return to you in the form of the Spirit, so that even while you live on earth you will share with me in the heavenly places." The metaphor of preparing a place in the Father's house is not of heaven but living in the presence of God with Jesus. It is here the disciples are to dwell (cf. John 15:1-17).[4]

Jesus comes to us through the indwelling Holy Spirit. In that case, 14:2 dovetails perfectly with 14:16,18,23,26. The new view is attractive, and I would like Wright to be right. Yet I stumble at 14:3, where Jesus says he will take us to be with him. Let's look at the other key Scriptures to see if such an understanding can be sustained.

### 1 Thessalonians 4:13-18

Here the question is *where* we will be forever with the Lord—heaven or earth.[5] Grenz is one of many theologians who notice that God never intended to rescue us from the earth or from our physical bodies. Through Christ he rescues us from evil and emptiness. Then why would we rise in the air to meet the Lord? Wright explains that the verb *meet* in 4:17 suggests welcoming a returning king. Just as citizens of a city might walk outside the walls to usher in a returning or visiting emperor, after which they would accompany him back inside, so we will meet the Lord to usher him to his rightful place as ruler of the new earth.[6] This interpretation is coherent, though those who have been nurtured in the twin doctrines of the rapture and the tribulation will not be easily convinced.[7] If there is a rapture, the proof is slim. First Thessalonians 4:17 is the clearest passage. First Corinthians 15:52 has us raised from the grave, but no higher.

### 2 Peter 3:10-13

Peter does not foretell the total destruction of the earth. His analogy is the deluge, which only "destroyed" the world in an incomplete way (3:3-7). It is not the annihilation of the old earth, but a surface cleansing.[8] What makes this hard to swallow are Peter's words that the elements will be destroyed by fire and even melt in the intense heat—more reminiscent of a nuclear Armageddon than a surface cleansing or a metaphorical new start (3:10,12). But it is clear that the purpose of the deluge and of Peter's fiery cleansing is the destruction of "the wickedness of the human race" (Genesis 6:5,11-13) and "the ungodly" (2 Peter 3:7), which also entailed an apocalyptic cleansing of the earth.

We saw in our short study of Isaiah (chapter 3; see also appendix A) that the apocalyptic annihilations of Babylon and Edom were figurative (Isaiah 13; 34), not literal. Second Peter 3 also appears to be employing apocalyptic language, so there is no need to assume a literal conflagration. Will the elements (Greek *stoicheia*) really melt in the heat, destroying all matter?[9] The Arndt-Gingrich lexicon lists these entries for *stoicheia:*

1. elements (of learning), fundamental principles
2. elemental substances
3. heavenly bodies

As for Galatians 4:3 and Colossians 2:8,20 ("elemental spiritual forces"), the lexicon notes that the meaning of *ta stoicheia* is "much disputed."[10] If sense (3) is in mind, then there may be a connotation of divine judgment on the false gods of paganism. In the ancient world, the heavenly bodies were often regarded as persons and were sought out for guidance by means of astrology. Thus, whether the fire is metaphorical or intended to denote a surface cleansing, the new view—that heaven will come to earth—has an answer. Second Peter 3 appears to be less conclusive than at first blush.

There may also be a theological reason God would never completely destroy the world.

> If God would have to annihilate the present cosmos, Satan would have won a great victory. For then Satan would have succeeded in so corrupting the present cosmos and the present earth that God could do nothing with it but to blot it totally out of existence. But Satan did not win such a victory. On the contrary, Satan has been decisively defeated.[11]

This is a mirror image of the argument for the ultimate annihilation of Satan and his kingdom. Lest there be a victory on the diabolic side, God would not allow the dominion of darkness to exist in eternity side-by-side with his kingdom of light. Only in this way, at the end of all things, would God be all in all (1 Corinthians 15:28). However, it is not completely clear how God's sovereignty would be compromised if he created an entirely new world, as opposed to simply transforming the current one.

But our God is a God of order. It is somehow comforting to think that in the first two chapters of the Bible, God lived with sinless Adam and Eve in a pristine garden suitable for both God and them, and that in the last two chapters of the Bible, God returns sinless humanity to another pristine garden to live with him.

### Isaiah 65:17-19 and Revelation 21:1-3

Evangelical New Testament scholar Ben Witherington III is hardly alone when he affirms, "The final state is represented as transpiring not when believers go up to heaven but when God and heaven come down permanently." Other scholars heartily concur. Grenz notes that the prophets of both testaments anticipated a new earth blanketed by a new heaven.

> Rather than resurrected believers being snatched away to live forever with God in some heavenly world beyond the cosmos, the seer of Revelation envisioned exactly the opposite. God will take up residence in the new creation (Rev.

21:3). The dwelling of the citizens of God's eternal community, therefore, will be the renewed earth.[12]

Bartholomew and Goheen agree.

> John's vision in Revelation, indeed, in the whole New Testament, does not depict salvation as an escape from earth into a spiritualized heaven where human souls dwell forever. Instead, John is shown (and shows us in turn) that salvation is the restoration of God's creation on a new earth. In this restored world, the redeemed of God will live in resurrected bodies within a renewed creation, from which sin and its effects have been expunged. This is the kingdom that Christ's followers have already begun to enjoy in foretaste.[13]

N.T. Wright and a host of other respected academics construe Revelation 21 this way. Many popular writers are on board too.[14]

Doubtless the easiest way to understand "new earth" is to take it literally, although we have demonstrated that it was not presented that way in Isaiah. On the principle of allowing Scripture to interpret Scripture, the new earth does not appear to be literal. A scientific point is in order. If the new earth is here, would it survive? In a short few billion years (short in the light of eternity) our planet will be consumed by its sun. At least that is what nature tells us (according to astrophysicists)—and nature itself is a means of God's revelation (Psalm 19:1-2; Romans 1:19-20). We can always theorize that God will intervene with a miracle, but when a theory requires backup theories, we ought to reconsider it.

The visions of Isaiah and Revelation do not necessarily refer to the end of the world. They foretell the end of earthly kingdoms and the vindication of God's people.[15] Isn't it possible that these prophetic visions prefigure a more solid reality? Could they, on a deeper level, be glimpses of what is to come—something more real and substantial than what is pictured by the prophetic language? That remains, in my mind, a possibility.

Furthermore, in commenting on Romans 8:18-24 (which we will discuss in chapter 11), Witherington observes, "Paul's vision of the future, though involving a transformed condition called resurrection, definitely entails life on earth...He looks forward to a new earth and new earthlings, not merely a new heaven." Wright makes the same observation: There is no point in having a resurrected body if there's no resurrected environment. Just as there is continuity (and discontinuity) between our present bodies and our resurrection bodies, so there is between the present earth and the new, resurrected earth. This attractive thesis, endorsed by many evangelical writers, finds confirmation in Acts 3:21, where Peter tells his audience that the ascended Jesus must remain in heaven "until the time comes for God to restore everything, as he promised long ago through his holy prophets."[16]

This restoration (Greek *apokatastasis*) is the same unusual word used by first-century Jewish writer Philo of the "new earth" following Noah's flood. The word was also used by first-century Jewish writer Josephus of the rebirth of the Jewish nation following exile—a more figurative sense.[17] Doubtless both sides of the debate can claim this as evidence.

## Marriage

If heaven comes to earth, the liaison is more than temporary. It is a marriage (Revelation 19:7; 21:2). As noted in the *International Standard Bible Encyclopedia,* after Revelation 21:1, there is no more separation of heaven and earth.[18] As in Handel's *Messiah,* the kingdom of this world has become the kingdom of our Lord and of his Christ.

## Alternatives?

Is it either/or? Do we have to decide whether the earth will be literally renovated or completely obliterated? It's difficult to conceive of a third possibility. If the new earth is not made out of the old earth, then that means the old one has disintegrated.

- As we have seen, more and more Bible expositors take Revelation quite literally (or try to).

- Some have weighed the evidence yet still hold that the next world is *away* from this world. Once the apocalyptic language of Revelation has been interpreted, this position is easier to retain.[19]

- Others believe that Christians are to work to bring in the millennium through political activism.[20] This muscular Christianity resembled nineteenth-century millennialism, which claimed conditions will gradually improve.[21] If Revelation envisions a marriage of heaven and earth, this is the shotgun-wedding version.

• Or perhaps we're creating a false choice or asking the wrong questions. To return to Lewis,

> When the Bible speaks of heaven and earth it is not talking about two localities related to each other within the same space-time continuum, or about a nonphysical world contrasted with a physical one, but about two different kinds of what we call space, two different kinds of what we call matter, and also quite possibly... two different kinds of what we call time.[22]

In some sense God will renew nature, though we are fuzzy on the details. This is the most natural reading of Romans 8, and it resonates best with the biblical teaching on the general resurrection in 1 Corinthians 15. Actually, not everyone is fuzzy. Randy Alcorn is probably the most influential popular writer on this topic. His bestseller *Heaven* caused a sensation in the evangelical world.[23] Most recent books on heaven cite him, even if they (like me) only partially agree. In the book jacket, Alcorn is billed as "a leading authority on heaven." What does he have to say?

## Salient Points in Alcorn's Theology of Heaven

I admire the man—and for that matter any author who gives away all his royalties. But being a fine person doesn't guarantee correct interpretation. I embrace Alcorn as a fellow believer, but I am convinced his interpretive method is inconsistent. This harsh claim is justified, however, in four problem areas.

### Inconsistent Literalization

About Revelation 5:6, Alcorn writes (as noted previously), "When Jesus is described as a lamb with seven eyes, it contradicts known facts to take that literally. But would it contradict known facts to believe that on the New Earth there will be a great city with streets of gold and gates made of pearls (Revelation 21:21), and with trees and a river (22:1-2)?"[24] But this approach fails to correctly read the genre of apocalypse, and it encourages speculation. The streets *are* gold, and the Lamb *does* have seven eyes—just not literally. Common sense is simply not enough if we are going to correctly interpret apocalyptic literature. Interpreting it as feels reasonable is one reason why we have so much confusion about the afterlife. Alcorn seems to be saying, "Why *not* take all the descriptions of heaven and the new earth literally?" But can this be done consistently? We can't just ignore the Scriptures that militate against our view.

1. He takes the image of the souls of martyrs under the altar (6:9) literally, concluding there are already people in heaven. But why should this picture be any more literally true than the earthquake and falling stars we read about only a few verses later? The earthquake actually appears to cause the other phenomena, which works only with the ancient cosmology. No earthquake could actually knock a star out of its place.

2. Alcorn believes Isaiah and Revelation both reveal details of the new earth. In Isaiah, the new earth has a new temple (Isaiah 44:28; 56:5; 60:7; 64:11; 66:6,20), but in Revelation, it doesn't (21:22). The details don't match, yet the author sweeps the problem aside.[25]

3. He claims there will be "nations" in heaven (21:24). What about 22:15—the dogs? Like the nations, they are outside the holy city. The context makes clear that John is referring to people. If one is to take Revelation at face value, there are unsaved persons outside the holy city on the new earth. This poses a serious threat to Alcorn's position and shows the impossibility of sustaining a literalistic approach.

4. The books mentioned in Revelation 20:12 are literal books.[26] Why is this necessary? What about 20:10 and 20:14? Was the false prophet (idolatrous worship of the emperor) literally thrown into the lake of fire? How does that work? What does it mean that death and Hades were cast into hell? Was Hades, which had been the abode of the righteous, being punished?

### Speculation

Alcorn literalizes highly symbolic passages in Isaiah and Revelation even though they have specific historical contexts. His interpretation leads to some interesting conclusions. He ends up with meat substitutes and catch-and-release fishing on the new earth. Our eyes might function as telescopes and microscopes. Jesus Christ may appear in multiple bodies simultaneously in order to have simultaneous fellowship with many people in different parts of heaven.[27] Extinct animals will probably return to life. (*Jurassic Park,* move over!) Certainly we will see our pets in heaven, and don't be surprised if some of the animals are talking too.[28]

## Disregard for Context

Alcorn ignores the religious (Jewish) and historical context of Isaiah, whose promises were fulfilled in the return from exile. Will animal sacrifices continue in heaven (Isaiah 60:7)? Alcorn admits the problem but doesn't deal with it. The entire book of Revelation applies most directly to the persecuted church during the time of the Roman Empire. We may extrapolate some of its principles, but we cannot lift passages from their context and then reinterpret them according to our enlightened common sense.

## Sentimentality

First Corinthians 3:12-15 is construed to mean that anything our hands have ever made will be redeemed, whereas Paul is clearly speaking about church building. Psalm 90:17 supposedly suggests that whatever our hands have made will be recovered in heaven. Nothing good will ever be truly lost, whether our children's kindergarten finger paintings or the works of the great masters. Everything worthwhile will reappear! The idea has great sentimental appeal, and there are plenty of things I wish I could receive back (documents, toys, pets)—but this passage has nothing to do with Alcorn's point. He has not substantiated his claim.

Alcorn is right that at the resurrection we will have transformed bodies (1 Corinthians 15), but much of what he has written about heaven in his book—its location, activities, and its nature—is unpersuasive. The handling of biblical texts is inconsistent, and major problems are glossed over. We have seen four areas in which *Heaven* leaves much to be desired. An expanded version of this critique, with seven problem areas, will be found in appendix B.

## How Do Others Evaluate Alcorn's Work?

Reactions to *Heaven* range widely, from high praise to deep concern.

- *Insane.* F. LaGard Smith responds, "This book is theological lunacy born of an overliteralization of text (mostly from Isaiah and Revelation), and a gross misunderstanding of the spiritual nature of the kingdom of God, which is not associated with place, only salvation and sanctification."[29]

- *Inane.* Dinesh D'Souza, an intellectual and expert on the evidence for the afterlife, doesn't follow Alcorn, although he sees no harm in imagining such a heaven.[30]

- *Brilliant.* Rick Warren, hailed by some as the most influential Christian author and speaker in the twenty-first century, exclaims, "This is the best book on Heaven I've read." He is joined by Joni Eareckson Tada, Hank Hanegraaff, and Gene Getz.[31]

The question is not whether the book is well written or interesting. The real questions are whether it's right and whether it guides its readers into paths of understanding. We could not apply Alcorn's method to the rest of the Scriptures. Alcorn tells us to take Scripture literally unless our interpretation "contradicts known facts." What facts would be contradicted if we chopped off hands (if it were a matter of our eternal destiny), prayed only in closets, or kissed each other (men kissing men, women kissing women, as was the biblical custom)? None, but these examples (Matthew 5:30; 6:6; Romans 16:16) suffice to show the inadequacy of this hermeneutic. Besides, the rules for reading apocalypse are different from the rules for reading narrative, gospels, letters, or psalms. The Bible is a library as much as it is a book, and each genre must be identified and carefully read. Alcorn is a theology graduate and an adjunct professor, but I cannot accept his interpretive scheme.

## Which View Is Correct?

We have considered two views. One posits that heaven will be away from earth, and the other asserts that heaven will be on earth. (Just to be clear, let me emphasize that not all commentators holding to the second position embrace Alcorn's literalism.) Which is correct?

It's always safest to stick with tradition. But tradition itself has a tendency to evolve, and we can easily but mistakenly equate the teaching of our local church or respected Christian authors with the original apostolic teaching. To take the new earth literally is doubtless bolder and more interesting, and yet given that the phrase did not require literal fulfillment for the ancient Jews, it is difficult to see why it would require a literal fulfillment today.

Even if we are to look forward to a new planet (not just a new world—everyone agrees that will come), still no one has ever taken Revelation literally. Not the Jehovah's Witnesses, not Alcorn, nobody. Every interpreter ends up being selective, depending on his or her agenda. The most obvious of several insuperable difficulties is the presence of unsaved persons in heaven.

But these things we know for certain:

- Heaven will be awesome whether it's down here or up there. Surely it will be even better than the various stabs authors have made at describing it.

- The earth is already a beautiful planet, although it is marred by human sinfulness (including warfare, greed, and ecological irresponsibility). Yet we must not make the mistake of drifting into nature worship. James Cameron's 2009 film *Avatar* comes to mind, where the pristine people of Pandora worship Eywa, the mother goddess, redolent of Gaia, the Greek earth goddess. We have a Father in heaven. We do not, and never will, have a mother in earth.

- There is a parallel between the resurrection body and the new earth. With N.T. Wright, we can appreciate the logic that a resurrected body requires, in whatever sense we understand it, a resurrected environment.

- We're already part of a new universe. "If anyone is in Christ, the new creation has come: The old has gone, the new is here!" (2 Corinthians 5:17). For believers in Jesus Christ, the old has already passed away.[32] When Christ came to earth, a new day dawned.[33] We are living in the new creation now.[34]

I asked my wife about the new earth—is it a metaphor or a literal reality? I shared about the controversy we've been discussing in this chapter. As a European, she hears the debate with different ears. For many American evangelicals, life on earth isn't that bad. It's comfortable. Ask a Syrian, Congolese, or North Korean—for them, leaving this world entirely behind sounds pretty good. Then she added that for many on our planet, if they saw how we lived, they'd jump at the chance to have what we have. She thought the idea of remaining here forever was a little suspicious, smacking of American materialism. We should be suspicious of our interpretations when they conveniently complement our socioeconomic lifestyle—and all the more when they differ from the radical discipleship to which the Lord has called us.

Then I asked Vicki for her take on eternity. She immediately compared our ignorance to that of a fetus. The baby's entire world (for all it knows) consists of the womb. No words could adequately explain what lies in store. Earth is our reference point, our womb. Are we not guilty of presumption? Paul enjoyed a visit to the third heaven yet could not tell us anything about it.[35] This doesn't mean we shouldn't try to understand. Faith seeking understanding makes our spiritual journey an adventure. We must balance intellectual pursuit and trust in the Lord. Our attitude ought to be the spirit of Psalm 131:1-2:

> My heart is not proud, LORD,
>     my eyes are not haughty;
> I do not concern myself with great matters
>     or things too wonderful for me.
> But I have calmed and quieted myself,
>     I am like a weaned child with its mother;
>     like a weaned child I am content.

## In Brief

- There are two basic understandings of the location of the afterlife. One says we will be brought to heaven, the other that heaven will be brought to us. Either way sounds great to me! In addition, there are hybrid views.

- Both views are prone to unnecessary literalization of the relevant texts, in part because wrapping our heads around eternal realities is so difficult. We must all guard against wild speculation.

- The phrase "new heaven and new earth" means a new creation. The term was first fulfilled metaphorically in the sixth century BC when the Jews returned from exile. The onus is on those who insist it is to be taken literally in reference to the end of the world. If we allow the Old Testament to guide us, there is no need for literalism.

- The truth about heaven may well turn out to be a reality reflecting parts of both views, each of which has fastened on to one facet of a larger whole. The ultimate heavenly reality may be more solid, more physical (as in Lewis's *The Great Divorce*) than the prophets in their temporal oracles ever imagined.

- The point that a resurrected body requires a resurrected environment is reasonable, yet what shape that new environment will take—the nature and location of heaven— will probably remain an open matter.

# The Other Place

## *Hell*

*[Hell] was not made for men. It is in no sense parallel
to heaven: it is "the darkness outside," the outer
rim where being fades away into nonentity.*

C.S. Lewis

The preacher was expounding Luke 16—yes, the rich man and Lazarus—and making a sermon illustration out of an unsaved relative
of ours who had died only days before. (No, not the most sensitive message we've heard.) The preacher had reached out to the dying man, but
the gospel message fell on deaf ears. Dramatizing the pain of the flames,
in which doubtless our family member was now squirming in agony,
he explained that the rich man had already been there 2000 years—but
he was only just getting started, not even making a dent in the infinite
punishment incurred by all the lost. The audience was mesmerized—
or were they traumatized? Was it right for the speaker to play on the
audience's sentiments and fears to compel a response to the gospel?

John Piper comments, "I know of no one who has overstated the
terror of Hell...We are meant to tremble and feel dread. We are meant
to recoil from the reality. Not by denying it, but by fleeing from it into

the arms of Jesus, who died to save us from it."[1] Scaring people into the kingdom of God has a long history. In the medieval cathedrals, such as that at Chartres, the scene of the last judgment was sculpted over doors so that people would see and fear. Even in Victorian England, after most thinking Christians had rejected their belief in hell altogether, the vicars continued to preach it, if for no other reason than for its salutary effect—the lower classes needed to be reined in. Was this the strategy of Jesus or the apostles?

## Jesus and His Apostles

It is true that no one in Scripture mentions hell more than Jesus, at least explicitly. (Recall that the word was not in use during Old Testament times, but the prophets frequently spoke of the fire of judgment.) "Jesus himself stands out as hell's chief defender—no medieval preacher ever spoke as fearsomely about the horrors of hell as Jesus did."[2] Is this accurate? The Gospels record Jesus using the word *Gehenna* (hell) on four occasions. The context of his comments includes repentance from sin, fear of man, causing others to stumble, and the unhealthy spiritual influence of the clergy of the day.[3] Warning the crowds to flee from the fire was an important part of John the Baptist's message, but then he seems to have had a more fiery preaching style than the one who came after him.[4] Compare the preaching of Charles Haddon Spurgeon:

> Suffice it for me to close by saying, that the hell of hells will be to thee, poor sinner, the thought that it is to be *forever.* Thou wilt look up there on the throne of God, and it shall be written "For ever!" When the damned jingle the burning irons of their torments, they shall say, "For ever!" When they howl, echo cries "For ever!"[5]

Did the apostles attempt to frighten people into becoming Christians? In the book of Acts, which covers about 30 years of church history, the word *hell* never even shows up. Judgment is mentioned three times, but never in connection with the flames of perdition.[6] This is not to deny that judgment was a fundamental of the faith. It was, and it remains so. But we are talking about hell. Even in the most intense of the apostolic encounters, they did not raise the specter of hell to frighten their opponents (5:1-11; 13:6-12). Notice Peter's emphasis on the first day of the church—Pentecost, AD 30:

> With many other words he warned them; and he pleaded with them, "Save yourselves from this corrupt generation." Those who accepted his message were baptized, and about three thousand were added to their number that day (Acts 2:40-41).

The truly frightening reality from which Peter urges his audience to save themselves is their corrupt generation. We all know the corrupting influence of materialism, narcissism, and spiritual apathy. Why didn't Peter plead, "Save yourselves from hell"? Surely that would not have been an unbiblical warning, but to truly help his listeners—to wake them from spiritual torpor—it was more effective to focus on the peril at hand than a distant threat on the far horizon.[7] Besides, there are other motivations for repentance.

### Revisioning

The Bible foresees two ultimate outcomes: heaven and hell. The Roman Catholics have added a third, though it is more of an intermediate stop than a final outcome: purgatory. Just as heaven is being revisioned by Christian thinkers, so are hell and purgatory. The nature, duration, and purpose of hell have all been meticulously examined in the past 30 years, and we will drop in on the conversation in this chapter and the next.

### Do We Send Ourselves to Hell?

It has become fashionable to deny that God sends anyone to hell.[8] It is our choice. C.S. Lewis's famous statement in *The Great Divorce,* one of the most helpful books ever penned on the topic, is often cited: "There are only two kinds of people in the end: those who say to God, 'Thy will be done,' and those to whom God says, in the end, '*Thy* will be done.' All that are in Hell, choose it. Without that self-choice there could be no Hell."[9] This makes sense, but we must be careful that we aren't scandalized by the biblical doctrine of judgment. (More on that in chapter 12.) It is God's choice too. The Bible certainly holds us accountable for our freewill decisions. Hell is portrayed as a place of privation, punishment, and perishing.

> The Lord Jesus will be revealed from heaven with His mighty angels in flaming fire, dealing out retribution to those who do not know God and to those who do not obey the gospel of our Lord Jesus. These will pay the penalty of eternal destruction, away from the presence of the Lord and from the glory of His power (2 Thessalonians 1:7-9 NASB).

Sin separates us from God (Isaiah 59:1-2; Romans 6:23; Colossians 1:21), and we miss out on eternal glory. We are cut off from his grace, from everything that is good. The "flaming fire" is more than being uninvited to the party; it is punitive. We will be destroyed. This is in keeping with Jesus's own emphasis:

> Do not be afraid of those who kill the body but cannot kill the soul. Rather, be afraid of the One who can destroy both soul and body in hell (Matthew 10:28).

> And if your eye causes you to stumble, pluck it out. It is better for you to enter the kingdom of God with one eye than to have two eyes and be thrown into hell, where "the worms that eat them do not die, and the fire is not quenched" (Mark 9:47-48).

In the first Scripture, Jesus teaches us that God has the power to destroy us—which is what hell is. In the second, he quotes the final verse of Isaiah, where God's enemies have already been destroyed. Their corpses are being consumed by fire and worm. Please keep in mind this detail: Insentient corpses are being destroyed. The natural result is that nothing is left. This will be important as we consider one of the alternative understandings on the duration of hell. At any rate, it is only half true that we send ourselves to hell. It is not merely a self-pronounced sentence; it is God's just verdict.

## Nomenclature

*Sheol.* The abode of the dead, the underworld—the standard word in the Old Testament (used 67 times) as the equivalent to Hades in the New Testament. It is never associated with hellfire.[10]

*Hades.* The abode of the dead, the underworld; equivalent to Sheol. The standard word in the New Testament (used six times) as the equivalent to Sheol in the Old Testament. In the Greek translation of the Old Testament, *Sheol* was always rendered *Hades.* Hades has two compartments: an upper, bright, happy section for the righteous, and a lower, dark place of dread for the wicked.

*Paradise.* The part of Hades reserved for the righteous (Luke 23:43; possibly 2 Corinthians 12:4). Although it can be a synonym for heaven, it is not used this way in the New Testament. In the Ante-Nicene Fathers, the term appears in Tertullian (3.52), Cyprian (5.474-475), and Methodius (6.377).[11]

*Bosom of Abraham.* This is a Jewish synonym for paradise.[12] At a supper, with the diners reclining around the table, you would be almost in the arms of the person on your left. Consequently, *Abraham's bosom* probably indicates intimate fellowship, more than warm embrace or support.

*Tartarus.* In Greek mythology, this was the place of punishment for the Titans, Cyclops, and certain humans. In Jewish literature, it was where wicked angels were consigned.[13] It appears only once in the Bible (2 Peter 2:4). Some people consider it the part of Hades reserved for the wicked.

*Intermediate state.* The state of human existence in Sheol (Hades) between death and the resurrection.

*Purgatory.* The Catholic term for the place of purgation of the saved, in which holy desire for God will be perfected. It has no biblical support, though some claim that Paul refers to it in 1 Corinthians 3:12-15.

*Resurrection.* The physical revival and transformation of a dead body. Jesus was the firstfruits of the resurrection (1 Corinthians 15:20). The resurrection of all humanity at the last day is sometimes called the *general resurrection.*

*Heaven.* The abode of God, probably also called the third heaven.[14] (More on this in chapter 17.)

*Hell.* The usual translation of Gehenna.[15] The word appears in the New Testament but not the Septuagint.

*Gehenna.* Hell, a place of fire and destruction. It is adapted from the Valley of Hinnom, a place of human sacrifice, disposal of corpses, and perhaps a garbage dump.[16] Gehenna is a Jewish word, and in the New Testament it appears only in the Gospels and James.

*Lake of fire.* In the book of Revelation, hell is depicted as a lake (20:14-15). Psalm 140:10 may be behind the image. In some Jewish writings, the lake was believed to exist within Hades.[17]

*Second death.* The destruction of death and Hades is the second death in the book of Revelation (2:11; 20:6,14; 21:8), correlating with the death of body and soul referred to by Jesus (Matthew 10:28). Some rabbis understood the second death to refer to non-resurrection (that is, de facto annihilation). Others took it to mean eternal life or an eternal death.

*Annihilation.* The destruction of the wicked, normally conceived as happening after they have been punished for their sins in hell.

*Eternal torment.* The mainstream Christian interpretation of hell since at least the mid-second century. Also called *infinite torment.*

*Universalism.* The belief that in time all humans will receive God's grace.

## Is Hell Currently Vacant?

In the parable of the sheep and the goats (Matthew 25:31-46), the goats, for their lack of care for others, are ordered into the eternal fire. In the judgment scene of Revelation 20:11-15, the wicked experience the second death in the lake of fire. If these scenes are both future, then just as no one has ascended to heaven except Jesus (John 3:13), so no one has gone to hell. Not before the judgment day. We will consider the sequence of events in greater detail in later chapters. The upshot is that the final judgment hasn't taken place. Hell, however we envision it, is as yet empty.

## Is Hell a Literal Fire?

Many Bible readers, with Franklin Graham, foresee a literal "eternity filled with grief and pain, an unquenchable fire." Charles Stanley writes, "Hades is a place of torment and agony...As much as I dislike the idea, I do believe that the lake of fire (Hell) is a real, literal place." Chuck Smith, senior pastor at Calvary Chapel, Costa Mesa, goes even further in the literal direction: "The abyss is literally a shaft. Somewhere upon the surface of the Earth there is a shaft. The entrance to this shaft leads down into the heart of the Earth where Hades exists. Hades is often translated 'Hell' in the Bible. Hell does exist. It is in the center of the Earth."[18] Stanley and Smith both equate hell with Hades.

Many strong Bible believers deny a literal hell, including Billy Graham. Boa and Bowman don't think hell is physical pain, but rather a spiritual form of suffering.[19] (But then, which is worse, emotional torment or physical torment?) Princeton's William Shedd was one of many who interpreted "fire and brimstone" (Revelation 14:10 KJV) as sin and conscience.[20] The suggestion is plausible but lacks proof. Many evangelical theologians reject a literal hell, but that isn't to say they don't believe in hell.[21] If we allow golden streets and pearly gates to serve as a sign, something pointing to the beauty and magnificence of heaven, why couldn't we allow the lake of fire to serve as a sign of hell? Many go wrong in the discussion of symbolism. If heaven is not a celestial city with literal streets of gold, it is surely something better. And if hell isn't a lake of fire (literally), it is surely something worse. The sign is, in a sense, less substantial than that to which it points.

Perhaps it will help in the discussion to remember that *literal* isn't another word for *real*. The fire may or may not be literal, but its effects are very real. The divine fire is surely painful. "It is a dreadful thing to fall into the hands of the living God," "for our 'God is a consuming fire'" (Hebrews 10:31; 12:29). Thus the better question is not whether hell is a literal fire, but whether hell is real. The Bible answers in the affirmative.

### Gnashing of Teeth

Those who are judged are said to be cast to a place where there is weeping and gnashing of teeth.[22] In the popular mind, gnashing is an uncontrollable reaction, born of the agony of the flames. However, this is incorrect. Gnashing is an indication of anger (Job 16:9; Psalms 35:16; 37:12; 112:10; Lamentations 2:16; Acts 7:54). In the case of hell, it represents a stubborn refusal to back down and admit God is in the right. The recalcitrant hate God. "What burns in hell are the soul's putrid, hate-filled remains."[23]

The gnashing is a significant detail and often misunderstood. Most Bible readers see gnashing, along with weeping, as a sign of regret. Luther supposed that the teeth were chattering on account of the cold.[24] (In traditional Christian thought, hell has been conceived of as both hot and cold.) As we will see in the next chapter, this detail refutes the universalist opinion that the lost will undergo a change of heart over their sentence. Those condemned to hell are not softening; they are hardening.

### Celebrate, Apologize, or Rationalize?

Hell should humble us. It should disturb us. Bible believers respond in a variety of ways to the doctrine of hell. Brian Jones writes, "Apocalyptic urgency is not about saving your friend from hell. It's about saving your friend *from God*... Until you understand how violent and inhumane God really is...you'll never feel the urgency to help your non-Christian friends escape His detestable clutches."[25] But this makes God out to be some monster or somehow unjustified in his judging. In about AD 1100, Peter Lombard wrote, "Therefore the elect shall go forth...to see the torments of the impious, seeing which they will not be grieved, but will be satiated with joy at the sight of the unutterable calamity of the impious."[26] To me, this sounds even worse.[27] In modern times, a strong advocate of the infinite torment of the lost writes this:

> If [a Christian] loves God, he must love hell too. If God decrees it, it must be good and for God's glory, and the evangelical knows that he will sing God's praises eternally as the smoke ascends from the burning pit. AMEN!…When Christ asks, "Do you love me?," he is also asking, "Do you love hell?"…Even *now* while the evangelical is singing the praises of his Lord and Savior, Jesus Christ, he knows that multitudes are suffering the torments of the damned…The true Christian, aware of this, is happily, exuberantly, gladly praising the Judge of the Last Day, Jesus Christ, who has sentenced to such merited damnation millions of souls."[28]

We are right to distance ourselves from such sentiments. They are sub-Christian.[29]

So how should hell affect us? It should sober us and motivate us. "We must all appear before the judgment seat of Christ, so that each of us may receive what is due us for the things done while in the body, whether good or bad. Since, then, we know what it is to fear the Lord, we try to persuade others" (2 Corinthians 5:10-11). It may not be the main message in our evangelism, but it is a valid reason to open our mouths. There is no room for triumphalism here. We are all sinners, and we have a debt to reach out to our fellow man in love and humility and with gentleness and respect (1 Peter 3:15). No one needs to go to hell. The tragedy of a life lost—missing one's eternal purpose and being separated from the goodness of God, punished, and destroyed—is deplorable. Christ-followers will do all they can to prevent their friends and family as well as strangers from meeting such a fate. Jesus bore our sins, tasting hell so that we would not need to.

Some think hell should be celebrated. Others shun the very word. For some, it is a staple of preaching, while other evangelists practically refuse to bring up the topic. Some deny it exists or psychologize it away. Others say it exists but comes to an end (a position we will examine in the next chapter). Others consider hell a deterrent regardless of whether it is real. Fifty-nine percent of Americans believe in hell, but few think they will be going there—just as most people believe they are better than the average driver.[30] Yet the only thing that counts is what the Bible says.

## In Brief

- Hell is a sobering reality whether it is understood literally or otherwise.

- In a sense, we do send ourselves to hell, yet hell essentially is a place of punishment, privation, and destruction.

- Hell gives no cause for rejoicing. Triumphalism is not a Christian attitude.

- The early church taught about the judgment day, but they did not dramatize hell or use terrifying imagery to frighten their listeners into becoming Christians.

- If we really believe in hell, we will not only prepare ourselves for the day of judgment but also make it our mission to help as many as we can during the short course of our lives.

# No Exit

## *Does It Ever End?*

*The punishments of sin in the world to come, are everlasting
separation from the comfortable presence of God, and most grievous
torments in soul and body, without intermission, in hell fire forever.*

WESTMINSTER LARGER CATECHISM

*[There are] endless opportunities in an endless amount of time
for people to say yes to God. As long as it takes, in other words.*

ROB BELL

*The destructive process will include distress, fury,
tribulation, and God's wrath. No one should think that
the wicked simply go quietly asleep. This is not an easy
demise. The second death is not a peaceful death.*

EDWARD FUDGE

I recently attended a dialogue on the duration of hell. Three schol-ars, representing infinite torment, universalism, and conditionalism, shared the floor.[1] I was most intrigued by the spirit of mutual respect. At times, it was more than respect—verging on collegiality, even cama-raderie. If only that spirit would always typify the debate on hell. In some books the battle lines have long been drawn, no side willing to cede an inch. As I have seen with my own eyes, it does not need to be this way.

I embraced the traditional view when I became a Christian at Duke University. I was unaware that there were any other serious contenders. The seminary at which I got my next degree, Harvard Divinity School, is universalist. (Universalists believe that no one will be lost.) The Bible was discredited as the word of God; we needed only to march to the beat of the drummer within. To me, universalism did not seem a serious contender. A couple of years later I stumbled across the writings of the annihilationists (or conditionalists, as they believe humans will become immortal only on the condition that God grants them this gift). I knew that advocates of the first and third views had many Scriptures to back them up, but I was taken aback to learn that some universalists also have well thought-through positions.

In this chapter we will lay out these three principal views on hell. All three were present in ancient Judaism, from which Christianity emerged, as they were in early Christianity. We will also look briefly at medieval thought on hell. After developing the positions and covering the history, we will see that each has its modern proponents.

- the traditional view: infinite torment

- the universalist view: eventual salvation for all

- the conditional view: punishment followed by annihilation

## The Traditional View

The traditional view, also called infinite torment, has the weight of church history on its side. Infinite torment is the official position of most churches and has reigned unchallenged since at least the fifth century. *Eternal* in Matthew 25:46 is understood to mean "infinite." The consuming fire of Mark 9:48 is interpreted as infinite punishment. (Actually, the passage is ambiguous.[2])

Given the ambiguity of *eternal*, the traditional view relies on three passages to give color to eternal punishment. They are the parable of the rich man and Lazarus (Luke 16:19-31) and two passages in the apocalypse (Revelation 14:10-12 and 20:10,15). The theological basis is that the lost have sinned against an infinite being and thus deserve infinite (endless) punishment. As a result, there will be forever two kingdoms—the kingdom of God and the kingdom of evil.[3] "Evil is an eternal element in the universe, no less positively real than the good itself."[4]

## The Universalist View

Universalists reason that since it is God's will that all be saved (2 Peter 3:9; 1 Timothy 2:4), and he is all-powerful, all will be saved. They also reason from God's essence as love (1 John 4:7,16). It would be unloving, and thus against his nature, to allow anyone to suffer forever.[5] His overarching purpose, to bring everyone into the heavenly kingdom, will not be frustrated. God will be all in all (1 Corinthians 15:28) only when evil has been universally destroyed. (This is also a point made by the conditionalists.) Further, passages such as Revelation 21 seem to depict unbelievers alive and well in the next world.

Universalists reason that if God can forgive sinners in this age, there is no reason why he couldn't forgive them in the age to come. Some regard the fire of judgment either as restorative or as both retributive and restorative.[6] Note that we are not critiquing secular or liberal universalism, neither of which is based on the gospel.[7] Our concern is rather with the position of Bible believers who lean in the universalist direction. "There has been a more or less continuous tradition of universalism within (and on the penumbra of) Christianity." Since 1998 a new species of universalism has emerged—evangelical. Advocates accept the reality of sin, the uniqueness of Jesus, the atonement, judgment, and hell.[8] They are not numerous, but they are publishing a lot of books.

## The Conditionalist View

This view entails two doctrines: the immortality of the soul, which some people see as an intrusion from Platonism, and the efficacy of the fire of judgment to annihilate those who are condemned.

The consuming fire does not preserve, but destroys, just as weeds are burnt up in a furnace (Isaiah 34:10-11; Ezekiel 20:47-48; Amos 5:6; Matthew 3:12; 13:41-42,50). Sodom serves as an example of eternal fire (2 Peter 2:6; Jude 7). The fire does not consume forever; it destroys forever. Annihilation is the eventual result, though it would be wrong to suppose that conditionalists reject hell. "This is no gentle and passive death, but a fearful extinction wrought by potentially excruciating destruction in the fiery pit of the age to come."[9] I recall a scene from the film *Terminator II*. The terminator ends his robotic existence in a lake of molten metal. Slowly he slips beneath the surface; his destruction is not instantaneous, but it culminates in complete destruction. At last he is unconscious, extinguished forever.

Support for this view is found in the Old Testament (Psalms 2:7-9; 110:5-6; Isaiah 66:24; Malachi 4:1-3) and in the New Testament (Matthew 10:28; 2 Thessalonians 1:7-9). This is the position of the Seventh-day Adventists. In addition, the Church of the East (not to be confused with the Eastern Orthodox) holds to this position and may have done so since before it branched off of the Western Catholic Church in the early 400s.[10]

| The Penal Justice of God | |
|---|---|
| **View** | **Analogy** |
| Infinite torment | Infinite corporal punishment |
| Universalism | Corporal punishment (if any at all) and then release |
| Conditionalism | Corporal punishment and then capital punishment |

### First-Century Jews

I'll never forget a lecture by New Testament professor James Charlesworth, who once visited King's College London when I was a postgraduate student there. He demolished the notion that Jews in the time of Jesus all believed the same things.[11] There was diversity then, just as now. "What did the Jews believe about ___?" is the wrong question. On many subjects there were multiple understandings. This was eye-opening for me; imagining that everyone thought alike had been so much easier. I still hear people say that all Jews in New Testament times believed in eternal torment, but this is not accurate. There was a diversity of positions among the rabbis.

No Old Testament passages clearly support infinite torment (Isaiah 66:24 seems to teach the opposite), but the notion is found in many later works.[12] The immortality of the soul and infinite punishment were part of Greek religion and philosophy, but the Jews had a long history of resisting such influences.[13] Conditional immortality (annihilation) also finds wide support.[14] In the Dead Sea Scrolls, the wicked are completely consumed. The first passage (chronologically) to unambiguously promote eternal torment is Judith 16:17, which is part of the Old Testament Apocrypha, accepted in Catholic and Orthodox churches as canonical.

> The nations who rise up against my people are doomed.
> The Lord Almighty will punish them on Judgment Day.
> He will send fire and worms to devour their bodies,
> and they will weep in pain forever (Judith 16:17).[15]

Notice that in Judith, Isaiah's corpses being devoured by fire and worms have become sentient—not a subtle change. There were two Jewish views on Gehenna: It consumed sinners, or it tormented them forever. In the Babylonian Talmud, the worst sinners were sentenced to Gehenna for 12 months, after which "their bodies are destroyed, their souls are burned, and the wind strews the ashes under the feet of the pious." There is no Gehenna in the future world.[16]

As for universalism, in the oldest rabbinic reference to Gehenna (Talmudic tractate Sanhedrin 13:3), the disciples of Shammai interpreted it as purgatorial, not merely punitive—though only in the case of those whose transgressions and merits balance one another.

Annihilation is taught in every book of the Apocrypha except Judith (as we saw above). In the Dead Sea Scrolls, the wicked are always completely destroyed. The Targums (Aramaic paraphrases of Scripture with commentary) explain the term "second death."[17] This expression, found in six Targums, refers either to nonresurrection (annihilation) or resurrection followed by eternal life or an eternal death.[18]

The most careful scholars admit that first-century Judaism was far from monolithic.[19] Popular writers like Francis Chan candidly admit that first-century Jews regarded hell as a place of punishment, though they differed over its duration.[20]

## Early Christian Positions on Hell

There are no unambiguous Scriptures supporting infinite torment in the New Testament, unless Revelation 14:10-12 and 20:10,15 are meant to be taken literally. (If they are, this is strong support for infinite torment.) However, a few generations after the New Testament period, some Christians were cooking up horrific tortures for the damned (as in the Apocalypse of Peter, the Acts of Thomas, and the Apocalypse of Paul). Some second-century apologists, including Athenagoras and Tertullian, accepted the Greek doctrine of the soul, typically in defending the Christian doctrine of the resurrection of the body.[21] Irenaeus held both annihilationist and traditionalist views simultaneously.

Universalism was always a minority view. Its most illustrious advocates were Clement of Alexandria (AD 150–215) and Origen (AD 185–254).[22] Both taught that *apokatastasis* (restoration) purified sinners so that they would ultimately be made holy. Gregory of Nyssa (335–395) continued Origen's thought, keeping the universalist strain alive.[23]

Conditional immortality (annihilationism) was taught by the apostolic fathers, the Epistle of Barnabas, the Didache, and Justin Martyr (late first to mid-second centuries). Irenaeus, as mentioned, seems to have held to annihilationism *and* infinite torment, while Arnobius (who died about AD 330) rejected the traditional view outright.

Summarizing the early church period, annihilationism was prevalent until the mid-second century. It seems to have been the de facto position of the apostolic fathers, churchmen living within two or three generations of the apostles.[24] They used words like *perish, destroy, consume,* and *kill,* without explicitly concluding that such terms were being used in a special sense entailing immortality. Yet over the *entire* period (between about AD 30 and 325), infinite torment was unquestionably dominant. David Bercot, an expert on the church fathers, estimates that as many as 85 percent of writers in the early church stood for the traditional view, followed by conditionalists and (in last place) the universalists.[25]

I find three things noteworthy about the early period. First is the incredible diversity of opinion. Even such a stalwart defender of infinite torment as John Walvoord admitted that there was diversity of opinion from the beginning of the Christian era.[26] Second, despite the diversity, no one was excommunicated for his or her difference of opinion about the nature of hell. Last, all writers took Luke 16:19-31 to describe Hades (verse 23), the location of those in the intermediate state, not hell. (In chapter 10 we will amplify this claim.)

## The Medieval Church

The medieval period stretches from the time the Roman Empire favored Christianity (from around AD 311) to the Renaissance (around 1400). Persecution came to an end. There is little doubt the most influential churchman was Augustine (354–430). Whereas in the first three centuries there were different opinions on hell, Augustine pushed hard for uniformity.[27] Augustine's position on infinite torment determined the direction of the church thereafter.[28] Although he was a staunch traditionalist, no dissenter on the topic of hell was ostracized. However, in the century after his death, things changed. At the Council of Constantinople (AD 553), Origen was anathematized.[29] The one who thought all might be purified by the fire was, ironically, sentenced to be consigned to the fire—he and anyone who might dare to follow him.

Three other important figures deserve mention, all from the High Middle Ages. One is Anselm (eleventh century), who argued that infinite punishment was required because of God's offended judgment. Just as an offense against a nobleman was more serious than an offense against a commoner, an offense against God required the greatest punishment—an infinite one. Biblically speaking, Anselm's model is wrong. The degree of the offense is not rated by feudal thinking; with God there is no such favoritism (Exodus 23:3; Leviticus 19:15; 24:19-22; Deuteronomy 1:16). The notion of infinite sin is also found in Thomas Aquinas (thirteenth century). Aquinas reasoned that at death the soul begins to suffer in hell, joined later by the body after the general resurrection. The third person of influence was Dante Alighieri (thirteenth–fourteenth centuries). His graphic descriptions of the pains of purgatory and hell in *The Divine Comedy* still haunt the modern mind.

## Modern Christian Thinkers

### Infinite Torment

In our era, and with arguably greater religious freedom than at any time since before Augustine, all three of the ancient views are proliferating. Needless to say, infinite torment is the strongest position, at least if it came to a head count.[30] Adherents follow Anselm's reasoning that any sin demands infinite punishment because it is directed against an infinite being.[31] One advocate states, "God has given the wicked *resurrection* bodies so that they *cannot* die."[32] Isaiah 66:24 is interpreted in terms of eternal torment.[33] Another eloquent proponent claims Paul "teaches most directly about hell in 2 Thessalonians."[34] Second Thessalonians 1:7-9 refers to the Lord's coming, fire, vengeance, destruction, and banishment.

Several writers assert that backing away from a view of hell that includes eternal torment is a cowardly capitulation to peer pressure and political correctness.[35] We are called not to decide which parts of the Bible we find palatable, but to take an uncompromising stand on the word of God. Interestingly, a number of traditionalists de-emphasize hell by suggesting that the number of souls actually consigned there is small.[36]

For many Protestants, eternal torment is a major point of doctrine. Moreover, the Westminster Confession of 1646 says that the wicked proceed immediately to hell, the souls of the righteous to the highest heavens.[37] (There is no intermediate state.)

### Universal Salvation

Friedrich Schleiermacher (1768–1834) was the first influential theologian since the Patristic period to consider universalism. Hell, he reasoned, should be reformative—a process. Many have followed in his train.[38] Hell is a remedy, "a pedagogic cleansing process."[39] To put it less pedantically, "God will put on the screws tighter and tighter until we come to ourselves and are willing to consider the good he has prepared for us."[40]

There are variants of universalism, like the idea that although everyone can expect a postmortem chance to respond to the truth, those who persist in rejecting God will be destroyed.[41] Sharon Baker holds that in the fire (which is God's very presence), we have a choice to repent and be purified or to be consumed. This combines universalism with annihilationism.[42] "While we were still *enemies* of God, as opponents, still steeped in our sin, still unrepentant, deserving nothing but evil in return for our rebellion (retributive justice), God reached out to reconcile us through Jesus (restorative justice)." Why may he not do so after death? "How does eternal damnation, burning forever in unquenchable fire, redeem and restore?"[43] God's goal of restoration (*apokatastasis*, as we discussed in chapter 6) is broader than human salvation; he purposes to restore the entire cosmos.

Universalism has been recently considered by Rob Bell (endorsed by Eugene Peterson), founder of Mars Hill Bible Church. Even if we die unprepared, we may be purified by "flames in heaven" so that "we can actually handle heaven." God is able to provide "endless opportunities in an endless amount of time for people to say yes to God. As long as it takes, in other words." Bell stops short of committing himself, but it seems fair to call him a quasi universalist. "Renewal and return cause God's greatness to shine through the universe; never-ending punishment doesn't."[44] The book has been heavily criticized by Mark Galli, senior managing editor of *Christianity Today*,[45] and addressed, among others, by Christian speaker and writer Francis Chan.[46] Brian McLaren, prominent leader in the emergent church movement, says "we need to have this conversation."[47] With so many big names in the conversation, perhaps we should respond to universalism with more than a yawn. Its position feels compelling to many, especially among the younger generation. Right or wrong, its stance on hell is perceived as more reasonable (less barbaric) than the traditional view, and its proponents more gentle and winsome—qualities all who love the Lord certainly appreciate.

### Annihilation

The best-known advocate of conditionalism, the third of the major views on hell, is undoubtedly Edward Fudge. His magnum opus, *The Fire That Consumes*, has been in print for more than 30 years.[48] Three theological heavyweights, much respected across the spectrum of evangelicalism, have written the forewords for its three editions: F.F. Bruce, John Wenham, and Richard Bauckham.[49] That he was able to enlist the support of scholars of such stature says a lot about the respectability and influence of conditionalism. Fudge is well aware that tradition is against his thesis. But why couldn't the majority be wrong? "Most of the Christian Church was confused about the core doctrine of justification by grace through faith from about the time of Augustine until the Protestant Reformation—a period of more than a thousand years."[50] Baptist minister and professor of theology at Baylor University Roger E. Olson shares a helpful perspective:

> Annihilation does not strike at the heart of the gospel or even deny any major Christian belief; it is simply a reinterpretation of hell. More importantly, its harsh condemnation by a few fundamentalists should not deter Christians from accepting one another equally as believers in the gospel of Jesus Christ in spite of differences of opinion about the nature of hell. Contrary to what some fundamentalist critics have charged, annihilationism is not tantamount to universalism or *apokatastasis*. It is simply a minority view of the nature of hell, not a denial of hell.[51]

Fudge says "The destructive process will include *distress* (Rom. 2:9), *fury* (Rom. 2:8), *tribulation* (Rom. 2:9) and God's *wrath* (Rom. 2:8; 1 Thess. 1:10, 5:9). No one should think that the wicked simply go quietly asleep. This is not an easy demise. The second death is not a peaceful death."[52] Another notes: "While John baptized in water, a symbol of the eschatological judgment and purification, the one to come... would purify the righteous and burn up the unrighteous."[53]

In Galatians 1:8-9, where false teachers are cursed, Paul has in mind their utter destruction. Greek *anathema* translates the Hebrew *ḥerem* (Deuteronomy 7:26; Joshua 6:17-18; 7:12). *Anathema* and *ḥerem* refer to destruction. Thus the onus is on those who assign a metaphorical meaning to words like *kill, destroy, consume.*[54]

A belief in conditionalism is not based on emotion, although one's view of God—his justice, love, and essential goodness—is no doubt a factor in the types of ultimate scenarios one can tolerate. John Stott famously told the evangelical world, "I find the concept [of eternal conscious torment] intolerable, and do not understand how people can live with it without cauterizing their feelings or cracking under the strain."[55] In response, biblical scholar F.F. Bruce wrote to him, "Annihilation is certainly an acceptable interpretation of the relevant New Testament passages…For myself, I remain agnostic. Eternal conscious torment is incompatible with the revealed character of God."[56] Professor Richard Bauckham of the University of Cambridge is just one of many living scholars standing for the conditionalist view.[57]

Conditionalism recognizes that in some sense the lost become less than human, like the grumbler who becomes a "grumble" in Lewis's *The Great Divorce*. N.T. Wright, who steers a middle course between the traditional view and conditionalism, believes that humans cease to bear the divine image by their own effective choice, yet "still exist in an ex-human state, no longer reflecting their maker in any meaningful sense…" However, he holds this view lightly, admitting speculation: "I am well aware that I have now wandered into territory that no one can claim to have mapped."[58]

Francis Chan leans towards the infinite torment view but concedes there is abundant evidence for annihilation. His comments on 2 Thessalonians 1:9 are apropos: "This verse is not crystal clear, and anyone who thinks it is needs a good dose of interpretive humility."[59]

### Assessment: Infinite Torment

The traditional view has the strong weight of tradition on its side, but that does not exempt its advocates from the need to prove their position. Too often supporters read the conclusion into the texts instead of properly deriving them. One expositor claims that the apostle Paul "teaches most directly about hell in 2 Thessalonians [1:7-10]," where Christ comes at the last day to bring retributive justice, with exclusion from the presence and majesty of the Lord and eternal destruction. Yet this passage can just as easily be read to support the conditionalist view. Another, commenting on Isaiah 66:24, tells us "The worms do not die and the fire is not quenched because these dead people are not dead! They are burning 'dead' in torment…One does not have to be a traditionalist to see that 'carcasses' which do not die are ever-living 'carcasses.'" But he hasn't proved his point, only asserted it. A third writer comments on Jesus's use of Isaiah 66:24: "The corpses of those enduring everlasting torment will serve as a vivid reminder to the grievous nature and terrible consequences of rebellion against God. In referring to this verse, Jesus spoke of the Valley of Hinnom (i.e., Gehenna) where a continually burning trash heap pictured the never-ending pain of the lost (Mark 9:47-48)." In fact, Jesus never mentions "never-ending pain," which is read into the text. These are common examples of begging the question.[60]

Expositors of infinite torment commonly fail to interpret the genre of apocalypse. For example, the nonstop burning of Revelation 14:9-12 should be read in the light of Isaiah 34:8-17.[61] We have already discussed the limitations of Revelation 14 and 20 (and the rest of the Apocalypse) for deriving doctrine about the afterlife. There is no need to literalize the richly symbolic apocalyptic metaphors.

Advocates of the traditional view, discussing human sin, speak of "the infinity of the evil." This concept seems to be an import from theology or philosophy rather than an explicit teaching in the relevant texts themselves. Sinners are "always infinitely guilty of what one has done; the sentence never overtakes the crime."[62] Several advocates reason that in hell, sinners continue to hate God, accruing to themselves more guilt and punishment continually.[63] Some have backed away from Anselm's argument, which relies on a sense of feudal justice, but others try to salvage it. "Culpability is determined largely by the identity of the victim," writes one author, who abandons Anselm's sequence of slave, commoner, nobleman, and God, and in its place talks about ants, flies, frogs, squirrels, puppies, humans, and the "infinite and holy God."[64] Of course one who kills a human should be punished, and no one would be charged with murder in the case of swatting a fly. But no one kills God (in the sense of bringing his life to an end), and "offended justice" hardly relates to squirrels and puppies, so the argument fails. Further, regardless of the degree of pain felt by the impenitent, still their "total" misery is infinite. Every sinner thus receives the same punishment—violating the principle of Luke 12:47-48 and calling into question God's fairness.

"Infinite hell protects society from lawlessness. Fear of hellfire is a powerful deterrent against sin"—or at least that is commonly said. Even if there is no hell, it is still better for society if we preach it. But is that true? Has anyone demonstrated a positive correlation between belief in hell and virtue? This argument was asserted by the educated upper class, who often merely pretended to believe in hell for the greater social good. But if a belief in hell did lead to virtue, criminals who believed in hell should have been more virtuous than their social superiors who did not.

We do not determine doctrine based on how we feel about God's righteous standards (Romans 9:20), but one aspect of the traditional position elicits a strong emotional response and deserves an answer. "How could heaven be heaven if just off the back porch of heaven is a fiery pit of screaming souls?"[65] The first conditionalists I spoke with (some 30 years ago) asked, "What kind of a father rewards the good children upstairs, while down in the basement he is torturing the naughty ones forever?" If we predicate such a sternness of God and it turns out not to be true, would we not be impugning his character? It makes sense that God punishes sin (see chapter 14), but to torment someone *infinitely*?

On the other hand, we must agree with Miroslav Volf that, "With some notable exceptions, especially in recent centuries, most Christians have thought that the self-giving character of God's love is not incompatible with the reality of eternal [infinite] punishment of those who refused to be redeemed by God's love. That punishment has itself been seen as a mode of God's love...a difficult thought that underscores the fundamental importance for Christians of the conviction that God is love."[66] Perhaps most believers' natural repulsion at the thought of hell is more culturally conditioned than we may realize.

In a related thought, Yarbrough (who holds the traditional view) writes, "With Stott, I affirm that eternal conscious torment strains our sense of justice. It weighs heavily on our emotions. But so does the daily news. Can anyone take it in?...Can anyone make sense of things to...the bereaved of suicide bombers in Israel? To hapless victims of a Western serial killer? To any of their moms and dads?...I cannot make sense of any of it, and I am suspicious of anyone who says they can— anyone, that is, except Christ."[67] In other words, regardless of whether hell lasts forever, we still have to process horrific pain and suffering in our world. There are coping mechanisms that allow adherents of infinite torment to still affirm the love of God.

The weight of tradition is firmly on the traditionalist side. Its long pedigree, from the second half of the second century to the twentieth, is impressive indeed. Millions of godly persons believe it. The position may be right, but it is hardly a slam dunk.

The title of a recent book in favor of infinite punishment is *Is Hell Real or Does Everyone Go to Heaven?* But this presents a false choice. Most conditionalists believe in hell, just not in its infinity. And quite a few universalists accept hellfire as God's means of purifying and saving everyone. Let us now assess the two main rivals to infinite punishment.

### Assessment: Universalism

Universalism, like Calvinism, underscores the success of God's sovereign plan. He will save whom he will—which in the case of universalism is all the world.

The view also highlights God's wisdom and love. He is not willing that anyone be lost, and he takes no pleasure in the death of the wicked (Ezekiel 18:32). And yet the rest of Ezekiel 18 makes clear that judgment and death are realities. They will not be bypassed by God's goodness, only by repentance and faith.

There are several verses that seem to support universalism, though it is quickly seen that they have been wrested from their contexts. The universalist slant on 1 Timothy 2:4 is belied by 1 Timothy 4:16. Second Peter 3:9 is contradicted by 2 Peter 2:20-22.

Besides, many passages seem incapable of sustaining a universalist interpretation, such as Matthew 12:32; Romans 9:3-4; 10:1. Robert Mackintosh, a prominent universalist of the last century, admits that universalism cannot challenge the traditional doctrine on exegetical grounds.[68]

As we saw in chapter 7, the "gnashing of teeth" apparently rules out postmortem conversion. The damned are depicted as angry, not remorseful. In fact, nearly all commentators miss the biblical meaning of gnashing. If the lost are defiant, they can hardly turn to God. If the devil and his angels have for ages past chosen to resist God, despite the overwhelming evidence that they are on the losing side (James 2:19; Revelation 12:12), then there is no strong reason for believing that even with eons of time to consider one's fate, any would actually change sides.

Universalists ignore the "point of no return" often found in Scripture (Proverbs 29:1; Hebrews 6:4-6; 10:26-31; 2 Peter 2:20-22). Even if we grant the hope for postmortem salvation, not everybody will make it. The Bible speaks of a line people can cross, after which there is no repentance or even a desire for repentance.

The universalist claim that *apokatastasis* ("restoration," referred to in Acts 3:21) applies to all the lost does not work. The Greek word is found in Jeremiah 16:15 in connection with the restoration of the land of Israel (also in Josephus *Antiquities* 11.63), in medical texts, legal texts (referring to hostages and to property), and political writings (referring to order). The word never, however, refers to the restoration of persons—only of things.[69]

As Kreeft and Tacelli have pointed out, universalism takes away free will.[70] God always gets his way. Unless free will is only a sham, this is a serious problem.

J.I. Packer's critique is insightful: "Its sunny optimism may be reassuring and comfortable, but it wholly misses the tragic quality of human sin, human unbelief, and human death set forth in the Bible... It needs to be actively opposed so that the world may know the truth about the judgment, the love, and the salvation of our God."[71]

Two sorts of universalism run through both testaments. First, God desires that Gentiles (outsiders to the Jewish covenant) be included among the people of God (Psalm 67:2-5; 117:1; Isaiah 49:6; Zechariah 8:20-23). Second, God desires the welfare of all mankind, though he does not coerce them to respond to his offer of salvation. God's care extends beyond the elect. In this respect, universalism outperforms Calvinism.

We commend the universalists for their vision that ultimately God will be all in all and that sin and the dominion of darkness will be done away with. But not many serious Bible students will be won over given the thinness of the scriptural case.

### Assessment: Conditional Immortality

The conditionalist works well with the biblical doctrine of the soul. The soul is not innately immortal; eternal life is a gift only to those in a right relationship with God. Traditionalists might counter that the resurrection body is imperishable (1 Corinthians 15:42). However, Paul is dealing with the resurrection of the righteous, who "bear the image of the heavenly man" (1 Corinthians 15:49). Nothing is said about the lost becoming immortal. Universalists and traditionalists may appreciate the mortality of the soul, but the best fit is with the conditionalist interpretation.

The most common objection to the conditionalist view is that *eternal* means "eternal." If *eternal* is a synonym for *infinite*, the objection is sustained. But in chapter 2 we explored the meanings of eternity and infinity and concluded that the common understanding of *eternal* is too narrow.

Revelation 14:9-12 seems to support infinite torment. As an apocalyptic passage, however, it will not bear a literal interpretation.[72] Further, conditionalists respond that the entire traditional view hinges on two highly figurative chapters in a single book of the Bible (Revelation 14 and 20).

Those on the traditionalist side affirm that *unquenchable fire* means that not only the fire but also those cast into it must always burn. But Homer uses the same phrase when the Trojans burned the Grecian ships, as does Eusebius when speaking of the martyrs who have been reduced to ashes.[73] In neither case does the phrase involve conflagration in perpetuity. Pompeii comes to mind, and especially the images of those unfortunate souls incinerated in the volcanic eruption of AD 79. They had no hope of survival in such ferocious heat. Whatever goes through unquenchable fire will be burned up. This implies destruction.

The apocalyptic passages become the lens through which eternal punishment is understood as infinite torture. In Matthew 25:46, eternal punishment is parallel to eternal life, so the lost must be in torment as long as the saved are in heaven. If they were merely snuffed out, how would this be an "eternal" punishment? Wouldn't they be getting off easy? Herman Witsius (1636–1708), a shaper of seventeenth-century Reformed orthodoxy (and a traditionalist), asked, "May it not, in its measure, be reckoned an infinite punishment, should God please to doom man, who was by nature a candidate for immortality, to total annihilation, from whence he should never be suffered to return to life?" Witsius admitted that sinners deserve punishment infinite in measure, but not infinite in intensity. Annihilation would deprive sinners of the enjoyment of infinite good (God) forever. He admitted that whether the sinner would exist forever or be annihilated, "I own that I am ignorant."[74] So respected was Witsius, J.I. Packer suggested that Witsius's writings have "landmark status as summing up a whole era" of Reformed theology. Therefore we should take note of his openness to a broader definition of *eternal* than many Bible-believers hold today.[75]

Actually, Jonathan Edwards made the same point as Witsius, as did Augustine before him: "Where a very serious crime is punished by death and the execution of the sentence takes only a minute, no laws consider that minute as the measure of the punishment, but rather the fact that the criminal is forever removed from the community of the living."[76]

The conditionalist view takes sin seriously (a strength of the infinite torment view) but also embraces the complete obliteration of evil in the universe (a strength of universalism). No more incongruous "concentration camp" in the middle of heaven. The Lord will not be angry forever (Psalm 103:9; Isaiah 57:16).

Like universalism, conditionalism deserves a better hearing than it has received. Unlike universalism, conditionalism has ample scriptural support.

### Five Scholars Offer Perspective

As we have seen, diversity of opinion about hell has characterized Christianity since the second century. My goal is not to vindicate one particular view, but to present them all so that they may be evaluated in the light of Scripture. Five highly respected scholars will now bring our discussion to a close with apt words of counsel.

Ben Witherington III holds a hybrid view. This is from one of his blogs:

> Based on all my work on the theology and ethics of the NT…if I were a betting man (which I am not), I would bet that probably the annihilationist view is closer to the truth [than the traditional view], based on the revealed character of God in Christ as both just and loving. But I don't know that I can be sure about this when the evidence is so imagaic and so metaphorical…I have to be honest and say either

> conclusion is possible, and equally orthodox…Equally
> orthodox Christians can agree to disagree and should not
> question each other's orthodoxy because of it.[77]

John Wenham holds the conditional view. He admits, "The temptation to twist what might be quite plain statements of Scripture is intense. It is the ideal situation for unconscious rationalizing."[78] (Nevertheless, he believed he was led by careful Bible study to the conditionalist position.) This degree of introspection in a Christian thinker is rare. Wenham was aware of his "lenses," and he reminds us that none of us are as objective as we might like to think.

J.I. Packer holds the infinite torment view. He shows the spirit of respect that is essential for meaningful dialogue on this sensitive subject. "It is distasteful to argue in print against honored fellow evangelicals, some of whom are good friends and others of whom…are now with Christ, so I stop right here."[79]

C.S. Lewis adheres to the traditional view and believes in purgatory.

> That the lost soul is eternally fixed in its diabolical attitude
> we cannot doubt: but whether this eternal fixity implies
> endless duration—or duration at all—we cannot say…
> [Hell] was not made for men. It is in no sense parallel to
> heaven: it is "the darkness outside," the outer rim where
> being fades away into nonentity.[80]

Early church historian David Bercot supports an independent view. He is loath to believe in eternal torment, but in the final analysis, he is agnostic. "What happens?" says Bercot? "I don't know and you don't either."[81]

## In Brief

- The three basic positions on hell are infinite torment, eventual annihilation, and universalism.

- All three were present in the early church. One's position was not made a test of fellowship until the sixth century.

- Infinite torment has the support of some 1600 years of tradition.

- Annihilation has biblical support and has become much more prominent in the last few decades.[82]
- Universalism is the most difficult of the three positions to support biblically.

## Questions for Self-Examination

- Am I looking forward to heaven?
- Are my concepts of heaven and hell static or dynamic? Have I made up my mind long ago, or do I still expect to learn more from the Scriptures?
- How does my understanding of hell affect my concept of God?
- Do I still have a sense of wonder at these eternal mysteries?
- How often do I talk to others about the next world? Do I generally keep the gospel message to myself, or do I allow the Lord to use me as a conduit for his grace?

Part 3

# Postmortem

We have already walked around heaven and hell, scrutinizing them from various angles. Our concern now is on what happens immediately after death. In this section we address three further themes: purgatory, Hades, and the resurrection.

# A Third Place?

## *The Logic of Purgatory*

*Less than a drop of blood remains in me that does not*
*tremble; I recognize the signals of the ancient flame.*

DANTE ALIGHIERI

### What Is Purgatory?

Roman Catholics believe in purgatory, a postmortem place of cleansing from sin (purgation). The *Catechism of the Catholic Church* reads, "All who die in God's grace and friendship, but are still imperfectly purified, are indeed assured of their eternal salvation; but after death they undergo purification so as to achieve the holiness necessary to enter the joy of heaven."[1] It is also believed that the living can assist souls in purgatory through prayers and the Eucharist. Purgatory is a place primarily of purgation, not punishment. Although some think of it as a postmortem opportunity to be saved, purgatory is *not* a second shot at salvation. It exists for those already saved in order to be made fully holy.

Of course, purgatory is not reincarnation. Surprisingly, many people assume they are the same thing. (We will address reincarnation in chapter 17.)

Dante Alighieri (1265–1321), who wrote more about purgatory than any other medieval writer, portrayed it as a state of suffering but also of joyous anticipation. Does that surprise you as it surprised me?

Though painful, this "antechamber of heaven" enables us to reach a state of holiness so that we may enter the presence of God. In Dante's *Divine Comedy*, purgatory is a mountain with seven terraces, one for each of the seven deadly sins: pride, greed, lust, envy, gluttony, anger, and sloth.

> Each person willingly undergoes the discipline to correct the sin of each terrace until the sin is turned from a perversion of love to true love. Each pilgrim on the way to Heaven emerges from Mount Purgatory fully purged of sin and loving everything perfectly. Then, truly, each can be "comfortable and unguarded."[2]

We emerge from the mountain of purgatory purged of sin and now able to love God perfectly.

That idea of purgatory certainly wasn't the one I had heard about (and made fun of). For Dante, purgatory is a place of suffering *and* anticipation, even joy. Similarly, the Eastern Orthodox purgatory is a place not so much of punishment as of growth in holiness.

### The Evolution of the Concept of Purgatory

How did such a notion develop? The early church was kept more or less purified by societal pressure (Christianity was countercultural) and the fires of persecution. Official Roman persecution was greatest in the second and third centuries. By the second decade of the fourth century, persecution came to an end, and the church began to slip into worldliness. As church membership became the norm in the Roman Empire, the majority were no longer living holy lives. Members lived and died with little evidence of God's power in their lives. What about their sin? The necessary purging must take place in the afterlife, it was thought.

The roots of purgatory can be found in such third-century writers as Tertullian and Origen.[3] The doctrine gradually evolved during the third and fourth centuries, and by the fifth century, it was generally accepted throughout Christendom. Various penalties for specific sins were supposed. At first purgatory was seen as a state. In the following centuries, it was understood as a physical place. Purgatory received official confirmation in the Second Council of Lyon (1274), the Council of Florence (1439), and the Counter-Reformation Council of Trent

(1563). As we have seen, it remains an important plank in Roman Catholic faith.

Jesuit theologian Karl Rahner tried to combine the Roman Catholic purgatory with the Eastern Orthodox teaching on the intermediate state of the dead. And Joseph Ratzinger, now Pope Benedict XVI, points out that the Lord himself *is* the fire of judgment that effects our transformation. These two major Catholic thinkers have moved away from a traditional stance on purgatory, so further developments may be on the way.[4]

### Is There Any Biblical Justification?

How does purgatory square with biblical teaching? Catholics say that after Adam rebelled, he was in God's grace, but he still had to pay for his sin by the sweat of his brow (Genesis 3:16-19). Moses was forgiven but excluded from the Promised Land (Numbers 20:12). David's life was spared, yet still he paid severe penalties for the incident with Uriah and Bathsheba (2 Samuel 12:10-12). However, all of these consequences of sin transpired in this life, not the next, so the parallels are unconvincing.

### 2 Maccabees and 1 Corinthians

One passage in the Old Testament Apocrypha seems to justify prayers for the dead and imply that they may be suffering in purgatory—2 Maccabees 12:39-46.

> Judas and his companions went to gather up the bodies of the fallen and bury them with their kindred in their ancestral tombs. But under the tunic of each of the dead they found amulets sacred to the idols of Jamnia, which the law forbids the Jews to wear. So it was clear to all that this was why these men had fallen…Turning to supplication, they prayed that the sinful deed might be fully blotted out…He then took up a collection among all his soldiers, amounting to two thousand silver drachmas, which he sent to Jerusalem to provide for an expiatory sacrifice. In doing this he acted in a very excellent and noble way, inasmuch as he had the resurrection in mind; for if he were not expecting the fallen to rise again, it would have been superfluous and

foolish to pray for the dead. But if he did this with a view to the splendid reward that awaits those who had gone to rest in godliness, it was a holy and pious thought. Thus he made atonement for the dead that they might be absolved from their sin.

The soldiers had committed idolatry. According to Catholic theology, this is a mortal sin and can be forgiven only through confession and penance, not through third-party prayer. They should have gone straight to hell. Thus this proof text backfires. Some claim Matthew 12:32 as implying purgatory, but the verse is inconclusive. By far the most commonly cited passage is 1 Corinthians 3:12-15.

> If anyone builds on this foundation using gold, silver, costly stones, wood, hay or straw, their work will be shown for what it is, because the Day will bring it to light. It will be revealed with fire, and the fire will test the quality of each person's work. If what has been built survives, the builder will receive a reward. If it is burned up, the builder will suffer loss but yet will be saved—even though only as one escaping through the flames.

Yet the larger context (verses 5-15) has to do with church planting and ministry. *The Catholic Encyclopedia* admits, "This passage presents considerable difficulty," and several authors I've read who support purgatory admit that there is little if any biblical justification.[5] The grounds for purgatory are thus more philosophical than biblical. First Corinthians 3 contains nothing about the afterlife and certainly no hint of a purgatory. What is burning is not the not-yet-holy sinner, but substandard construction of a local church fellowship.

### Purgatory and the Protestants

The doctrine of purgatory has always been accepted by some Protestants, including Luther.

> The existence of a purgatory I have never denied. I still hold that it exists, as I have written and admitted many times, though I have found no way of proving it incontrovertibly from Scripture or reason…I myself have come to the conclusion that there is a purgatory, but I cannot force anybody else to come to the same result.[6]

C.S. Lewis accepted purgatory, and many high Anglicans still accept the Roman doctrine. In his superb book *The Great Divorce,* where he develops the logic of judgment, purgatory is envisioned as the outer fringe of heaven.[7] Anglican priest and physicist John Polkinghorne is another supporter of purgatory.[8] Philosopher Jerry Walls is open to the idea.[9] George MacDonald, J.B. Phillips, and William Barclay—all widely read and beloved by Bible believers—lean in this direction too.

If you are a Protestant, I know at least one other Protestant who believes in the idea of purgation from sin after death—*you!* You may not subscribe to the doctrine of purgatory, but all Protestants accept the basic idea that after death the saved become like Christ (1 John 3:2). Before we are admitted to heaven, we undergo some transformation. We will sin no more, for without holiness no one will see the Lord (Hebrews 12:14). Most of us are somewhere in between rejecting God outright and being perfect in love of God and neighbor, so we all need a boost.[10] After all, as (Catholic) theologian Terence Nichols notes, "If we say that one does *not* need to be sanctified to come fully into God's presence, then heaven won't be heaven; it will be full of unloving people."[11] And why couldn't there be further personal spiritual growth after we die? For example, many evangelicals believe that babies mature after death so that their eternal "age" will not be fixed at six months.

So it seems the real dispute is over how long this process of transformation takes place, whether over a period of years in purgatory or in a split second at the point of death or the last resurrection.

## Problems with Purgatory

Despite the logic of purgatory, there are several profound difficulties in accepting it.

- N.T. Wright reminds us that if anything, the Bible teaches purgatory is *now,* not after we die, for it is in this life that we face fiery trials (1 Peter 4:12).[12]

- LaGard Smith notes, "It is not until the day of judgment (post-purgatory) that the motives of men's hearts will come to light and be judged. If souls had already been fully cleansed in purgatory, there would be no evil motives remaining to be exposed."[13]

- Paul Enns notes that the promise to the thief on the cross (Luke 23:43) is an implicit denial of the doctrine of purgatory.[14]

- Zachary Hayes, a major proponent of purgatory, concedes that the fire of 1 Corinthians 3—purgatory's principal proof text—is the judgment itself, not purgatory.[15] As the *New Catholic Encyclopedia* frankly admits, "In the final analysis, the doctrine of purgatory is based on tradition, not Sacred Scripture."[16]

If the church had not lost its fire (Revelation 3:14-20), perhaps the fires of purgatory would never have been ignited. Let us learn from history—we can do better. It is up to us as disciples of Christ to ensure that our brothers and sisters are holy in *this* life (Colossians 1:28–2:1; Hebrews 3:12-14).

## In Brief

- Purgatory has some logical support but no scriptural support, as most Roman Catholics freely admit.

- All believers accept some postmortem process of purification. Protestants generally believe this transformation is instantaneous at the moment of death.

- Jesus's death was enough to completely forgive our sins. We do not need to pay for them in the afterlife.

- The Bible teaches that motives will be revealed only at the judgment day (1 Corinthians 4:5; Hebrews 4:13). That is the time, not before, when we will be fully sanctified.

# The Intermediate State

## *Hades*

*Let no one imagine that souls are immediately judged after
death. For all are detained in one and a common place of
confinement—until the arrival of the time [of] the great Judge.*

LACTANTIUS

*One of the criminals who hung there hurled insults at
him: "Aren't you the Messiah? Save yourself and us!"
But the other criminal rebuked him. "Don't you fear
God," he said, "since you are under the same sentence?
We are punished justly, for we are getting what our deeds
deserve. But this man has done nothing wrong."
Then he said, "Jesus, remember me when
you come into your kingdom."
Jesus answered him, "Truly I tell you, today
you will be with me in paradise."*

LUKE 23:39-43

## The Thief on the Cross

Jesus promised the thief that he would be with him in paradise that
very day. How could he be with Jesus in paradise when Jesus had
not yet ascended to the Father (John 20:17)? Is "today" perhaps a psychological instant? Was the penitent thief to be with Jesus in the next

moment of consciousness (even if thousands of years later)? Or is "today" not chronological at all—as a day is normally understood?

If we took Jesus literally, which is the simplest way of understanding his promise to the thief, then that very day, as mortals reckon time, the thief was to be with Christ in paradise. Jesus didn't ascend to heaven until more than 40 days later, so if by *paradise* Jesus meant heaven, we would excuse the thief for being confused when he finally reached heaven after a wait of 40 days (or 2000 years!). Yet that is the way many teachers take the passage.[1]

Others assume Jesus must be talking about the end of time. Those who advocate soul sleep deny that the thief would have been conscious. But how encouraging would it have been had Jesus said, "In a few thousand years you will be with me in paradise, and it'll seem like it happened today. Between now and then you'll be unconscious"? It sounds as if paradise was *not* heaven and that it *was* a condition of which the thief would be aware.

Of course the meaning of a word can change according to its context. When we look at the dictionary definition of *paradise*, we realize that the early Christians usually used the term in the third sense listed in the Oxford English Dictionary.

> Paradise: 1. the garden of Eden. 2. heaven, the abode of God and his angels and the final abode of the righteous. 3. an intermediate place or state where the departed souls of the righteous await resurrection and the last judgment.

The righteous wait. In 2 Peter 2:9 we read of the wicked being held before the day of judgment. No one is actually ushered into heaven or hell until the judgment day, which has not yet occurred. This means there is an interim state.

Paradise is the waiting room to heaven. Paradise is also a place of reward. The belief that souls proceed immediately at death to heaven, hell, or purgatory is a Western Christian notion. In Eastern Christian thinking, Christians await the day of resurrection and judgment in paradise (the bosom of Abraham). As we will see as we examine the patristic evidence (the writings of the church fathers), this is the more original doctrine. But first, to set the stage, we need to pause and talk about cosmology.

## The Underworld

We think of the cosmos as consisting of heaven and earth, but the ancients included an underworld (Ephesians 4:9-10 [probably]; Philippians 2:9-11; Revelation 5:3). The underworld was no more *literally* under the world than heaven is literally above the earth. It's a theological direction, not a geographical one. But it's a helpful way of visualizing Sheol (Hades).

The Egyptians believed that after death your soul proceeded to the underworld, where the jackal-headed Anubis weighed your heart against the feather of truth. If your heart was too heavy or too light, it was devoured by the crocodile-headed Attim. In other words, you were annihilated—this was the second death.[2] But if you were righteous, you went to paradise. Such scenarios contrast with the religions of Canaan and Mesopotamia, where all the dead were conscious in the netherworld.[3] Even though Sheol was a gray and gloomy place, no one wanted to be turned away from its dismal gates because the alternative was to be a wandering spirit. Israelite religion was more like the Mesopotamian variety, although it did not have ghosts (more on this in chapter 17). Everyone, the wicked and the righteous, departed to the same underworld.

The inhabitants of Sheol are *shades*, also called *rephaim* (Job 26:5; Psalm 88:11; Proverbs 2:18).[4] G.E. Ladd, Baptist minister and theology professor at Fuller seminary, describes the shade as "some kind of pale replica of man himself."[5] Terence Nichols writes, "What survives is therefore not a *part* of a living man but a shadowy image of the *whole* man."[6] Like the shades in the underworld of the ancient Greek poet Homer, the inhabitants of Sheol are not immaterial, and they still look like themselves.

In the intertestamental period, Hebrew ceased being the mother tongue of the majority. The Jews translated their Scriptures into Greek, and Sheol became Hades.

Christianity grew out of Judaism and retained its tripartite cosmology: heaven, earth, and Hades. Although there was considerable diversity of thought in the New Testament period, all agreed that the dead waited in Hades until the Last Day.[7]

### The Church Fathers

Now the stage is set for our examination of patristic texts. They all date from the second century to AD 325, the year of the Council of Nicaea. (References in the text of this chapter are to volume and page number in the standard edition of *The Ante-Nicene Fathers*.[8])

- "The souls of the godly remain in a better place, while those of the unjust and wicked are in a worse place, waiting for the time of judgment" (Justin Martyr, 1:197).

- "We speak of Paradise, the place of divine bliss appointed to receive the spirits of the saints. There, the saints are cut off from the knowledge of this world by that fiery zone, as by a sort of enclosure" (Tertullian, 3:52).

- "No disciple is above his master...Our master, therefore, did not at once depart, taking flight [to heaven]. Rather, he awaited the time of his resurrection, as determined by the Father...Likewise, we also should await the time of our resurrection determined by God" (Irenaeus, 1:560-61).

- "We regard paradise as our country...Why do we not hasten and run so that we may behold our country? Why do we not hurry to greet our fathers [the patriarchs]? For a great number of our dear ones are awaiting us there" (Cyprian, 5:474-75).

- "Let no one imagine that souls are immediately judged after death. For all are detained in one and a common place of confinement—until the arrival of the time [of] the great Judge" (Lactantius, 7:217).

Justin Martyr, the Samaritan philosopher who converted to the faith, reflects the unanimous Christian view that all the dead waited in the underworld—which is divided into two sections, one for the righteous and one for the wicked.[9] The righteous are already enjoying their reward, or at least they are anticipating it. The lost are already filled with dread, and Peter implies that some degree of punishment begins in Hades (2 Peter 2:9 NASB). Tertullian, the North African lawyer who became a Christian, locates paradise in Hades, as do the other patristic writers. Odd as that may sound to our ears, paradise was in the underworld.[10] Irenaeus, the church leader in Gaul (France), and Lactantius (another North African) stated that the dead do not proceed to heaven until the time of the resurrection. Cyprian offers us a cheerful reminder that paradise is not dismal. It may be a waiting area, but still it is a grand reunion.

The parable of the rich man and Lazarus may not be literal, though it is suggestive of the rewards and punishments of the afterlife. At least one third-century commentator understood it as a literal description of a pre-judgment situation.

> The rich man was in torment and the poor man was comforted in the bosom of Abraham. The one was to be punished in Hades, and the other was to be comforted in Abraham's bosom. Yet they are both spoken of as before the coming of the Savior and before the end of the world. Therefore, their condition is before the resurrection (Methodius, 6:377, quoting Photius).

Did any of the ancient Christians teach that the dead are taken directly to heaven? None taught this. However, there was a heretical movement, the Gnostics, that rejected the resurrection. Anything the wicked god of the Old Testament created—the earth, the body, sex... anything material—was evil. Notice Justin's strong condemnation of the Gnostics:

> You may have fallen in with some [Gnostics] who are called Christians. However, they do not admit this [intermediate state], and they venture to blaspheme the God of Abraham...They say there is no resurrection of the dead. Rather, they say that when they die, their souls are taken to heaven. Do not imagine that they are Christians! (Justin Martyr, 1:239).

## What Happened?

If it's so clear that there is an intermediate state, why do so few Protestants teach it? Early Protestantism did acknowledge the intermediate state. Luther (1483–1546), Calvin (1509–1564), and Zwingli (1484–1531), the fathers of the Reformation, all believed in an interim state between death and final judgment. Yet in time the Reformers yielded to a popular understanding of death—without the waiting period. Many Protestants today assume that if you believe in an intermediate state, you must be affirming purgatory. As we have seen from the early Christian writers, this isn't necessarily so. Thus this sequence of beliefs emerges: intermediate state (early church) to purgatory (medieval church) to immediate heaven or hell (later Reformation). Many of us reading this paragraph are heirs of the Reformation.

### Difficulties

Often when I give this historical overview, people are positively stimulated. Others are disturbed—not necessarily because it is a challenge to their church tradition, but because they cannot study the Scriptures without reading their view into them—that believers immediately go to heaven when they die. Some claim that David expected to rejoin his dead son in heaven (2 Samuel 12:22-23). But David merely said they would be together—he does not indicate *where*, though presumably this is Sheol, the abode of the dead.[11] Similarly, when Stephen sees Jesus in heaven and prays that the Lord will receive his spirit (Acts 7:56,59), many people infer that heaven was his *immediate* destination, but the text does not say so.

Didn't Paul say that to be away from the body was to be at home with the Lord—that as soon as we die we are with him (2 Corinthians 5:8; Philippians 1:21-23)? Yes, Paul is looking forward to being with God, but we are not told whether that is to be in heaven or in paradise. The Lord will be with us even in Hades (Psalm 139:8), so being in paradise (Hades) doesn't mean we aren't with God (even though many ancient Jews dreaded that possibility). Moreover, our sojourn in paradise is only temporary.

When I flew from Singapore to Bangladesh last year, I had a layover in Guangzhou, China. When my Singaporean friends asked me where I was heading, I said my destination was Bangladesh. I didn't say, "I can't wait—I'm flying to Guangzhou!" Maybe that analogy helps. In short, 2 Corinthians 5:8 doesn't rule out a "layover" in paradise.

Weren't Enoch and Elijah taken to heaven? Does their example refute the intermediate view? Not according to second-century French church leader Irenaeus.

The elders who were disciples of the apostles tell us that those who were translated [Elijah and Enoch] were transferred to that place. For paradise has been prepared for righteous men, those who have the Spirit. Likewise, Paul the apostle, when he was translated, heard words in this place that were unspeakable…So it is there that those who have been translated will remain until the consummation of all things, as a prelude to immortality (Irenaeus, 1:531).

Irenaeus believed that Elijah, Enoch, and Paul were all taken to paradise and not to heaven proper (2 Kings 2:11; Genesis 5:24; 2 Corinthians 12:4). And there they remained (to this day, according to the early church fathers).

## Conclusion

What do the experts say? When you consult the literature produced by professionals in the field, there is a broad consensus that it is not heaven, but paradise—where our thief rendezvoused with Jesus—that receives the souls of the righteous. Popular reference works may be based on secondary and tertiary sources, so they are sometimes less helpful.[12] More and more Christian scholars are realizing that our final state or reward does not come until Christ returns.[13] Others, like Alcorn, get it half right with their *intermediate heaven*—a modern term that is confusing and is not strictly biblical.[14]

This is a contrast to mainstream Protestant thought. "We believe that the faithful, after bodily death, go directly to Christ" (Second Helvetic Confession, 1562). Written for the Swiss Reformed churches, this confession was adopted by Protestants throughout Europe. Robert Peterson insists that the wicked go immediately to hell.[15] There are a handful of churches, outside the Orthodox, who teach the intermediate state of the dead in Hades. They are swimming against the stream. In evangelicalism, and especially the variety molded by the American experience, people don't want to wait for heaven any more than they want to wait in a line at a bank.

The evidence is clear. There was an early Christian consensus. The patristic quotations have no intrinsic authority—for authority we rely only on the word of God—but they illustrate the Scriptures, with which they are in harmony. Unless we are taken to be with the Lord in the last generation alive (1 Thessalonians 4:13-18), we too will spend some time in paradise before we go to heaven. So is it wrong to say that we go to heaven when we die? A more accurate statement would be that we go to heaven *after* we die. As wonderful as paradise will be, it's only a layover. Heaven is our final destination.

Sometimes we are threatened by new views even when those advancing them do not intend to challenge us. There's a lot to think about here, especially if you are from a tradition that omitted the intermediate state. My own denomination does not have a set doctrine concerning the afterlife. Thankfully, one's position was never made an issue of fellowship. Don't we all think more clearly when we breathe freely?

## In Brief

- The underworld—Sheol (from the Hebrew), or Hades (from the Greek)—is the waiting place of the dead.

- The dead wait there until the second coming, resurrection, and last judgment.

- Paradise is part of Hades; it is not a synonym for heaven.

- We shall receive our final reward only in heaven. We will be glorified only when Jesus appears (1 Peter 5:4).

- Christians differ on some of these issues, and there is no need to be dogmatic. Let's learn to tolerate and listen to dissenting voices and to dialogue on such topics with respect and without acrimony.

# Resurrection

## *Up from the Grave*

*We will all be changed, in a moment, in the twinkling of an eye, at the last trumpet; for the trumpet will sound, and the dead will be raised imperishable, and we will be changed.*

1 CORINTHIANS 15:51-52 NASB

Our sojourn in the intermediate state terminates once the Lord returns. This is the day of resurrection (John 5:25,28-29).

## A Dispute

I hadn't enrolled in seminary only to learn theology. I had a more important reason: to enlighten my fellow students, to teach my professors, to show that I was right. And one Catholic seminarian, Bernie Ezaki, just wouldn't back down. He kept insisting that the general resurrection (when humans are raised from the dead) would entail a *physical* body. I knew this was a superstition, that what really counted was the spiritual world, not the physical. And so I wouldn't back down either.

"It's a *spiritual* body, not a physical one," I argued, citing 1 Corinthians 15:44.

Bernie reminded me that our resurrection was somehow like Jesus's resurrection.

"What?" I retorted. "Jesus was *Jesus*! We're just people."

"But we will be transformed, St. Paul tells us."

"Yes, but Paul was talking about a spiritual transformation. We won't have any need for our bodies," I countered.

"But that *is* a spiritual transformation. Besides, do you think we'll just be floating around like ghosts?"

"Don't be silly." We then opened the Bible to 1 Corinthians 15. Bernie made his case. But I didn't need to really listen to him because I already knew what the Bible said about the resurrection.

"Douglas, I have 2000 years of church tradition on my side."

"Tradition, tradition…"

That argument finished more than 30 years ago. I would like to think that I was the one in the right, and that Bernie was won over by my superior wisdom, finesse, and (of course) tact. Alas, that's not how it went. He never changed his mind—good for him!—and I didn't either.

That is, until 15 years later, when I came round. Of course we have bodies. That's what Paul teaches, and when our Lord was resurrected, he had a body. And I'd honestly thought I had nothing to learn from Bernie—even though he exhibited a more gracious spirit than I and had the Scriptures on his side.

**Three Views**

*1. The spiritual body view.* As I now realize, our having a nonphysical, "spiritual body"—the notion that our bodies will be discarded—is common among Protestants and independent Christians. Truth is, I had never heard about a *bodily* resurrection, only about the resurrection of the Lord. To me, Bernie's idea sounded unbiblical.

Here's why it was right. God's creation was good. The ancient Gnostics denied this, as did the followers of Plato. And in the second century, Platonic thought snuck into the church. Here are a few of the key Platonic concepts:

- The body is evil, a prison for the soul.
- The soul is immortal. It is the real part of a human being.
- The physical world is illusory, less real than the spiritual world of ideas.

Ironically, Plato's ideas seeped into the church through several Christian apologists, men who explained why Christianity was superior to paganism and secular philosophy. But here's where the Bible is at odds with Plato:

- The body is good. Everything God created is good (Genesis 1:4,10,12, etc).

- Only God is immortal. Immortality is his gift to the redeemed, received at the last day (1 Corinthians 15:53-54). Nowhere are the unsaved said to be immortal (1 Timothy 6:16).

- The Bible never says that the physical world is less substantial than the world of spirit.

Plato was wrong! Not only that, but the "spiritual body" I had interpreted to be nonphysical (1 Corinthians 15:44) was nothing of the kind. The same word is used in 1 Corinthians 2:15 of the spiritual person, who of course had a body! In ancient Greek, the word was not the antonym of *material*, but of *unspiritual*.

*2. The spiritual view.* This view is common among liberal Christians. Jesus's rising was more of a comeback of the *idea* of Christ, not an actual resurrection. His followers rallied and, recalling the motivational words of their Lord, started the Christian movement. This theory is psychologically improbable in the extreme, and there is substantial evidence for the physical resurrection of Jesus.[1] Actually, this isn't that different from the atheists' take on Christ's resurrection. Liberal Christians say Jesus's body didn't really rise, just his spirit. The atheists say Jesus's body never rose, and some hold that the first Christians (like Paul) never thought the tomb was empty.[2]

*3. Bodily resurrection.* In the third view, our bodies will be resurrected and glorified just as Jesus's was. So we have the spiritual body view, the spiritual view—notice how similar they are?—and bodily resurrection with glorification.

### Firstfruits

Why is this third view the one with the strongest biblical support? Because Jesus was the firstfruits of the resurrection (1 Corinthians

15:20). A number of persons were raised from the dead in both the Old and New Testaments (2 Kings 4:34-35; 13:21; John 11:44; and many other passages). Strictly speaking, these aren't resurrections because these men, women, and children got their same old bodies back. Some scholars call them resuscitations. Maybe that's not the right word, but the word *resurrection* is misleading—unless we're talking about Jesus. They weren't transformed.

In other words, only one man has ever been resurrected, and the rest of us must wait till the last day. Jesus's body exhibited natural and supernatural qualities (Luke 24:39; John 20:19). He walked through closed doors. Yet he still had his scars. His body shows us what ours will look like when we are resurrected.

### Restoration

When our bodies are resurrected, how will they be transformed? There will be continuity and discontinuity. We will still have our own bodies. This is not easy to grasp, so the apostle Paul gives us an analogy. Our body is like a seed.

> But someone will ask, "How are the dead raised? With what kind of body will they come?" How foolish! What you sow does not come to life unless it dies. When you sow, you do not plant the body that will be, but just a seed, perhaps of wheat or of something else. But God gives it a body as he has determined, and to each kind of seed he gives its own body...
> So will it be with the resurrection of the dead. The body that is sown is perishable, it is raised imperishable; it is sown in dishonor, it is raised in glory; it is sown in weakness, it is raised in power; it is sown a natural body, it is raised a spiritual body (1 Corinthians 15:35-38,42-44).

I doubt you could sketch an oak tree just by seeing an acorn if you'd never seen a tree, let alone an oak. Yet there is continuity—the seed (acorn) undergoes continuous transformation. One day it is a tall oak. Without the acorn, there is no oak. After our bodies are sown in the ground, a transformation will occur. The metamorphosis takes place "in a flash, in the twinkling of an eye, at the last trumpet" (1 Corinthians 15:52). The transformation will be one that makes us more like our

Lord, even as we strive to emulate him in this life (Romans 8:29; 1 John 3:2).

We should resist the temptation to speculate about the nature of the resurrection body, whether by presumption or by argument from silence. Several writers assume our resurrection body will be young (thirtysomething) or without wrinkles and gray hair.[3] Quite a few suggest there will be "selective purging of painful memories," which is reasonable if not explicit in Scripture. Some assume that because Scripture never mentions bedtime or mealtime, we will not sleep or eat. (And yet isn't a great banquet one of the images of the kingdom of God [Matthew 22:2; 25:10; Luke 14:16]?) One even hazards the guess, "No food will be needed in heaven, but incredible gourmet delights will nonetheless be enjoyed."[4] We just don't know. It is certainly presumptuous to claim that our perfect body in heaven will have no limitations.[5] What we do know is that our resurrection body will be like Christ's glorious body (Philippians 3:21).

As theologian and apologist William Lane Craig notes, resurrection entails physical healing (our bodies are fully resurrected), mental healing (no Alzheimers or mental impairments), and psychological healing (openness, wholeness).[6] A couple of years ago I was preaching an Easter message in Kharkov, the Ukraine. On the front row was a Christian sister with one arm. As I preached about the resurrection—Jesus's and ours—I looked right at her. She needed to hear the healing words of Scripture. This is a message the entire world desperately needs to hear.

Speaking of renewal, scholar N.T. Wright raises a valid question. "What's the point in having a resurrected body if there's no resurrected environment?"[7] He refers, of course, to Paul's words in Romans 8.

> I consider that our present sufferings are not worth comparing with the glory that will be revealed in us. For the creation waits in eager expectation for the children of God to be revealed. For the creation was subjected to frustration, not by its own choice, but by the will of the one who subjected it, in hope that the creation itself will be liberated from its bondage to decay and brought into the freedom and glory of the children of God.
>
> We know that the whole creation has been groaning as in the

pains of childbirth right up to the present time. Not only so, but we ourselves, who have the firstfruits of the Spirit, groan inwardly as we wait eagerly for our adoption to sonship, the redemption of our bodies. For in this hope we were saved (Romans 8:18-24).

We may confess ignorance as to exactly how Paul understands the creation to be subject to frustration, but he clearly speaks of its renewal.[8] This ties in nicely with the (literal) idea of the new heavens and earth (an intriguing possibility we discussed in chapter 6). On the other hand, Paul wrote in 2 Corinthians 5:17, "If anyone is in Christ, the new creation has come: The old has gone, the new is here!" This sounds as if the creation (like Christians, who are God's new creation in Christ) has already been renewed.[9] Has the renewal already commenced? Much to think about.

Because of the resurrection, we have hope. Christians do mourn when their brothers and sisters die (Acts 8:2; 1 Thessalonians 4:13), but when they die, there is hope.[10]

**Resurrection and Judgment**

The concept of the resurrection, developing out of the doctrine of Sheol (the shades in the underworld) and adumbrated in the Old Testament, comes into clear focus in the New Testament.[11] We also learn that only after the general resurrection has taken place does the last judgment occur.

When I was writing this chapter, I remembered that Easter sermon a few years back in the Ukraine. In it, I mentioned my argument with Bernie, and how slow I was to accept what the Bible said. Then it occurred to me, I never apologized to him. So I tracked Bernie down. As expected, he was gracious. Better late than never.

## In Brief

- The resurrection must take place before anyone goes to heaven or hell.
- The body is good, which is one reason God resurrects it.

- The bodies of the righteous will be transformed—glorified to be in some way like Christ's body.

- In his resurrection, Jesus went first, and we will follow.

## Questions for Self-Examination

- What things still need to change in my life in order for me to truly be holy? How much postmortem transformation would God have to work in me before I would be able to exist in his undiluted holiness?

- The intermediate state is seldom explored. Did I learn anything new about the intermediate state? Do I tend to believe everything Christian traditions, preachers, and books tell me about the afterlife, or do I think independently?

- Given the biblical doctrine of the resurrection, do I honor God with my body? Is such a conviction reflected in my eating? Do I control my body, or does it control me?

- Do I honor God's creation? Am I ecologically aware? Do I pollute, litter, or do anything else that shows disregard for God's earth?

Part 4

# One Way?

The path is narrow, and the world pushes back when truth is preached. As Christians we are called to be respond graciously. These chapters are designed to help us to respond soberly to God's judgment on a personal level, to think clearly about the issues, and to reinforce our faith in God's justice. When our hearts and minds are in tune with the Spirit of God, we will not back down when our faith is challenged. We will engage.

# Judgment Day

## *The Books Are Opened*

*When the author walks on the stage the play is over... it will
be too late then to choose your side. There is no use saying you
choose to lie down when it has become impossible to stand up.*

C.S. LEWIS

*A god who is never angered at sin and who lets evil go by
unpunished is not worthy of worship. The problem isn't that the
judgmentless god is too loving; it's that he is not loving enough.*

TREVIN WAX

As we have observed, much of the Christian world believes that those
who are right with God through Christ proceed immediately to
heaven when they die. This plays havoc with the New Testament Scriptures because the souls of the departed, after being in heaven, must
return to earth to rejoin their bodies so that they can be resurrected,
judged, and sent to heaven once again.[1] This may be possible, but play-
ing the Luke 1:37 (NASB) card ("nothing will be impossible with God")
doesn't make it any more likely.

The Bible speaks of an intermediate place—for the saved, a place
of waiting and reunion. Later Christ returns, and only then does judgment takes place. It is a day of reckoning, a settling of accounts. Most

liberal Christians and Jews deem the idea of a day of reckoning unworthy of civilized culture. Obviously, those with a high view of Scripture cannot so easily dismiss one of the fundamental doctrines of the faith (Hebrews 6:1-2).

Those who wear the name of Christian hold at least four positions on the relationship of the judgment day to heaven. First, there is the premillennialist position just critiqued, that judgment day is little more than a formality and takes place for millions of believers after they have already been welcomed into heaven. Then there is the classic Christian view, that no one is admitted to heaven or sent to hell until the day of resurrection

> Very truly I tell you, a time is coming and has now come when the dead will hear the voice of the Son of God and those who hear will live...
>
> Do not be amazed at this, for a time is coming when all who are in their graves will hear his voice and come out—those who have done what is good will rise to live, and those who have done what is evil will rise to be condemned (John 5:25,28-29).

A third view is that we die, and the next thing we know, it's the end of time. Luther taught soul sleep—the doctrine had its roots in the theological discussions of the early 1300s and is attractive in that it eliminates the messy business with the intermediate state of the dead (Hades).[2] But Paul's use of *asleep* in 1 Corinthians 11:30 and *sleep* in 15:51 is figurative. Sleep is a common metaphor for death. Luther's belief in soul sleep was discarded even within Lutheranism by the 1600s. Most parts of the church readopted the medieval view, led by Calvin, who asserted that rewards and punishments follow immediately after death.[3] But Jesus's promise to the thief on the cross, "Today you will be with me in paradise" (Luke 23:43), seems to militate against this view.[4]

A fourth understanding strives to combine the first two by some sort of time warp. "For God, time is not what it is with us. It may not make sense, but that's what happens." This is not very satisfying to most students of the Bible, though of course it's impossible to disprove.

What can we know for sure about the day of judgment?

## Who?

The entire world will be judged (Acts 17:31; Romans 3:6), as Ecclesiastes soberly concludes.

> Now all has been heard;
> here is the conclusion of the matter:
> Fear God and keep his commandments,
> for this is the duty of all mankind.
> For God will bring every deed into judgment,
> including every hidden thing,
> whether it is good or evil (Ecclesiastes 12:13-14).

Paul, writing to Christians, states, "We must all appear before the judgment seat of Christ, so that each of us may receive what is due us for the things done while in the body, whether good or bad" (2 Corinthians 5:10). When will we appear before the Judge? Once he has returned, at the last trumpet, at which time the physical resurrection and judgment of the dead will take place (John 5:24-27; 1 Corinthians 15:25-55). Paul also tells us that everyone will give an account of himself to God (Romans 14:12). The context of this passage has to do with the way we treat our brothers and sisters in Christ.

In short, the Scriptures hold that believers, not just outsiders, will be judged. Christ may have taken our place on the cross, but this does not undo the biblical truth that we are accountable to God for every word and action.

## What?

This judgment is declarative, not investigative. God won't be examining the records of our lives to determine, in something like a courtroom scene, whether we "made it"—something often dramatized with appeal to the "book of life" passages.

> Then I saw a great white throne and him who was seated on it. The earth and the heavens fled from his presence, and there was no place for them. And I saw the dead, great and small, standing before the throne, and books were opened. Another book was opened, which is the book of life. The dead were judged according to what they had done as

recorded in the books. The sea gave up the dead that were in it, and death and Hades gave up the dead that were in them, and each person was judged according to what they had done. Then death and Hades were thrown into the lake of fire. The lake of fire is the second death. Anyone whose name was not found written in the book of life was thrown into the lake of fire (Revelation 20:11-15).

We should be cautious as we read the last book of the Bible, but the picture of God judging the world clearly corresponds with many other biblical passages, especially in the prophets and the teaching of Jesus. It may be doubted whether there will be any investigation. The drama of the judgment scene above is to impress on us the seriousness of God's purposes, the inevitability of failure for his opponents, and the surety of victory for his followers. Above all, the "great white throne" judgment scene assures us that God's judgment is always just.

The book of life is an ancient theme. It is found in Psalm 69:28—a request that the enemies of God be blotted out of the book of life. We also recall Moses's words as he pleaded for his idolatrous compatriots: "'But now, please forgive their sin—but if not, then blot me out of the book you have written.' The LORD replied to Moses, 'Whoever has sinned against me I will blot out of my book'" (Exodus 32:32-33).

Christians' names are written in this book (Philippians 4:3; Revelation 21:27), in contrast to those who do not follow Christ (Revelation 13:8; 17:8). Many Christians hold that our names were written in the book before we were ever born, in accordance with God's sovereign plan. This does not fit well with Exodus 32, where the Lord speaks of removing sinners from the book. In my opinion (which I cannot prove), in principle everyone's name is written in the book of life when he or she is born. Only sin causes it be expunged. And this is a possibility even for Christians (Hebrews 6:4-6; 10:26-31; 2 Peter 2:20-22).

In the judgment, God will declare what we knew all along: our final destiny. At this point the righteous will be escorted into the glory of heaven, but the wicked will be cast into the lake of fire. Those who loved God will be saved forever, but those who rejected him will be destroyed.

We may know that we are saved before that great day (1 John 2:3-6; 5:13), but we must be diligent to live holy lives, realizing that the God we serve is a consuming fire (Deuteronomy 4:24; Isaiah 33:14; Hebrews 12:29). Some compare the judgment day for Christians to an awards banquet.[5] This fits well with a number of Scriptures we are inspecting in this book—indicating that God's just judgment leads to differing outcomes even for the saved—but it does not fit with Paul's admonition.

> Therefore, my dear friends, as you have always obeyed—not only in my presence, but now much more in my absence—continue to work out your salvation with fear and trembling, for it is God who works in you to will and to act in order to fulfill his good purpose (Philippians 2:12-13).

God's judgment is no investigation. It is a declaration of a future we presumably knew the moment we died and went to Hades.

### When?

When will the judgment take place? It will take place after death (clearly) but not immediately. There is more than one way to read Hebrews 9:26-28.

> [Christ] he has appeared once for all at the culmination of the ages to do away with sin by the sacrifice of himself. Just as people are destined to die once, and after that to face judgment, so Christ was sacrificed once to take away the sins of many; and he will appear a second time, not to bear sin, but to bring salvation to those who are waiting for him.

Judgment will not happen until after the resurrection of the dead. There is little to add apart from a reminder that no one knows the time of Christ's return. Therefore we must be ready at all times, living by faith (Luke 18:8).

### Where?

Judgment takes place before the judgment seat of God. Is this a literal seat? Does God wear robes, as in Isaiah's mind-numbing vision (Isaiah 6:1-8)? The answer is that it doesn't matter. The truth about what will happen does not change or go away just because some of the descriptions have metaphorical elements. These elements convey truth—in this case, moving us to reverence and awe (Malachi 2:5; Hebrews 12:28)—and confirm that the Lord is sovereign and righteous.

### Why?

Why couldn't God just forgive everyone, as some critics of biblical faith inquire? The answer is that God is just (Deuteronomy 32:4; Habakkuk 1:13; Revelation 16:7). He does not and cannot wink at sin (Acts 17:30). Justice demands his righteous judgment of our sin, the Bible explains it, and our consciences confirm it (Romans 2:5,14-15; see John 16:8).

I have walked in the killing fields of the genocidal Pol Pot in Cambodia, where 2 million people were killed. At Yad Vashem, during a recent visit to Israel, I was horrified and repulsed by the inhumanity of the Nazis, who killed 13 million people in the holocaust. At the slave fort at Cape Coast, Ghana, I was deeply moved by the degradation of the slave trade and was reminded of the Europeans' part in this dehumanizing four-century travesty, which left tens of millions dead. I recently entered the torture chambers of Idi Amin, who killed between 300,000 and 500,000 people in Uganda. If God does not punish evil, he is not good.

This side of the judgment, much of the vice in this world remains unrequited and virtue remains unrewarded (Psalm 73). Honest guys don't always finish first. Some pay for their honesty with their lives. If God does not recognize and take virtuous thoughts and deeds into account, he is not good. And if he is not good, he is not God.

### How?

Judgment is fair, and with something as complex as the judgment of a human life, we can trust only the righteous Judge (Genesis 18:25; Isaiah 11:4; Jeremiah 11:20; Ezekiel 33:20; 2 Timothy 4:8; 1 Peter 2:23). Judgment, according to Scripture, is based on several factors.

Does that sound complicated? That's why he's the Judge, not you or me. The bottom line is that God is fair (Psalm 98:9). He takes into account every aspect of our lives, including genetics, upbringing, social

| The Basis of God's Righteous Judgment | |
|---|---|
| Faith | Romans 3:26; Revelation 21:8 |
| Openness | John 3:19-21; 1 John 1:2–2:2 |
| Words | Matthew 12:37; James 1:26 |
| Lifestyle | 1 Timothy 4:16; 1 John 2:3-6 |
| Obedience | John 14:23-24; Acts 5:32; 2 John 6 |
| Following the word | John 8:31-32; James 2:14-26 |
| Love of truth | John 4:23; Romans 2:8; 2 Thessalonians 2:10 |
| Example to others | Matthew 18:6-7; Luke 17:1-3 |
| Responsibility | Luke 12:48; James 3:1 |
| Perseverance | Hebrews 3:14; 2 Peter 2:20-22 |
| Knowledge | Luke 12:47-48; John 9:41 |
| Sexual purity | Matthew 5:29; Hebrews 13:4 |
| Holiness | 1 Corinthians 10:1-13; Hebrews 12:14; 1 Peter 1:13-17 |
| Forgiveness | Matthew 6:14-15; James 2:13 |
| Care for needy | Matthew 25:31-46; James 1:27 |
| Effort | Matthew 25:14-29; Luke 13:24 |
| Honesty | James 5:12; Revelation 21:8 |
| Sincerity | Matthew 7:1-5; Romans 2:1-4 |
| Fruit | Luke 13:8-10; John 15:1-16 |
| Lordship of Christ | Matthew 7:21; Luke 6:46 |
| Motives | Romans 2:16; Corinthians 4:1-5 |
| Heart | Matthew 22:37; Romans 10:9; Philippians 3:19 |
| Standing for Christ | Matthew 10:32-33; Revelation 21:8 |

conditioning, brain chemistry, willpower, all our choices, and the true intentions behind every choice.

I realize that some bristle at such a list. "It smacks of salvation based on works." The danger of legalism is a serious one, and we need to always be on our guard. But we shouldn't overreact either, as Luther did when he removed James from the Bible on account of its teaching that we are justified by works.[6] The early church saw no contradiction between justification by faith and justification by works, for they are two sides of the same coin. We should strive for the same maturity, the same heart.

## Work Out Your Salvation

In view of all the Scriptures that speak of holiness, it is fair to say that the modern church has swung so far in the other direction from "works righteousness" that it has become spiritually anemic, pathetic, and inert. Paul told us to work out our salvation with fear and trembling (Philippians 2:12). He also told us that faith means doing the works the Lord has prepared for us (Ephesians 2:8-10). But is this the attitude toward discipleship we can expect when we read Christian authors? I am well aware that there are some—Francis Chan, David Platt, and Lee Camp come to mind immediately—who insist on radical discipleship. They speak the truth in love, even when it hurts (Mark 10:21; Ephesians 4:15,25). I don't mean to be ungracious, but in my opinion, many others tone down Christ's call to carry the cross.

One writer claims that even if Christians pay for their sins with their lives, they are still saved, based on Acts 5:1-11; 1 Corinthians 5:5; 11:29-32. It's a comforting thought that Ananias and Sapphira, who lied to the Holy Spirit and the apostle Peter, were saved after all. I don't think we can rule it out, but such conclusions reach far beyond the text. The same author suggests that uncommitted Christians will be saved but will not reign with Christ. He then claims that 1 Corinthians 3:11-15 refers to "the perpetually *carnal* and *backslidden* Christian," despite the fact that the context is church building and not our personal spiritual lives.[7] This reminds us of the errant doctrine of purgatory, which is also built on this text yet ignores the context.

Another bestselling writer claims she saw a vision of hell. People burn there while disobedient Christians hang around the entrance to the lake of fire. They are not admitted into the kingdom, though they don't go to hell either. Such believers, she says, are doomed to loiter near the lake of fire because they went to church only once a week, failed to tithe, and did not read their Bibles enough. She later claims that Jesus told her only 20 percent of Christians are obedient.[8] But does the term "disobedient Christian" sound odd? It should.

Both authors seem to be justifying the status quo, merely reflecting the commonly accepted view that one can be a true Christian without holiness. Nor is this a new view. One eminent nineteenth-century evangelist preached holiness and yet softened the demands of Jesus. He assured his audiences that a great many careless Christians will make it to heaven, as Lot was saved from Sodom. But these Christians are "waterlogged," or weighed down with earthly treasures.[9]

What a shock such a position would have been to the early Christians, some of whom gave their lives rather than compromise with the world. And there is an underlying contradiction, an oxymoron. In what sense is someone a Christian who is not following Christ?

## Perfect Judgment

Of course, Christians are not the only ones who balk at the judgment. Unbelievers too resist the teaching of Scripture. Non-Christians are quick to say, "Do not judge!" One suspects they learned this phrase from churchgoers who live double lives and don't want to be exposed. How we answer this protest is so crucial that the next chapter is devoted to this matter.

Others protest that hell cannot possibly be unfair. Punishment is infinite, regardless of the degree of sin. If you will pardon the severe analogy, allow me to illustrate. One man is in the oven set at 300 degrees, another at 1000 degrees. But the "level" of punishment is irrelevant if he's there forever because 300-degree infinity is the same as 1000-degree infinity. An innocuous granny and Genghis Khan get the same punishment. And if this analysis is on track, it *would* be unfair. Here is where those who hold to an annihilationist viewpoint—that hell ends in the destruction of the sinner, after the appropriate point— seem to have a better answer for the critics.

Similarly, if there are degrees of appreciation of heaven—I would say "levels," but that sounds as if we will be segregated by spiritual accomplishments—then, once again, justice can be served. Jesus's common phrase "treasure in heaven" makes perfect sense.[10]

God's justice has always been a major concern of those with a heart for God (Genesis 18:25; Jeremiah 12:1-2; Romans 3:3-4; see also the entire book of Habakkuk). He is the one we look to as the Judge of the world—not you, not me. And that's great news. Our judgments would be biased, misdirected, incomplete. His are thoroughly correct, accurate, and fair.

## Prepare

Preparing for the last day is too crucial to put off. Augustine is credited with saying, "God has promised forgiveness to your repentance, but He has not promised tomorrow to your procrastination." Someone else said, "Many who plan to seek the Lord at the eleventh hour die at ten thirty."

Couldn't God just let it all slide—dismiss our sin? No, not if he is holy. God longs to forgive us in Christ. But he has done his part. The ball is now in our court, not his.

## In Brief

- All mankind will be judged in their physical bodies after the return of Christ and the general resurrection.

- God's judgment is just and will take our entire lives into account.

- The judgment is an expression of God's moral character. If he did not reward good and punish evil, he would not be God.

# "Do Not Judge"

## *Is Judgment Ungracious?*

*Tolerance gets a lot of the credit that belongs to apathy.*

Our feel-good culture bristles at the notion of judgment. This makes it difficult to get others to consider seriously God's right to judge or to assign rewards or penalties. It may even feel undemocratic that some pass muster at the last day and others don't. So let's take a moment to unpack the common view, even among believers, that judgment is somehow ungracious.

I recently attended a talk by apologist Josh McDowell, who loves to research and follow trends. A dismaying fact he shared was that John 3:16 ("God so loved the world...") may still be the most familiar Scripture, but is no longer the most quoted. Now it's Matthew 7:1 ("Do not judge"). And a lot of people doing the quoting are church attenders. This reminds me of the years we lived in Scandinavia.

When we lived in Sweden (1989–1992), I was taken aback at how liberal the society was. In our apartment building, only half of the couples were married. Of course, these days in the United States, this has lost its ability to shock. Decades of indoctrination in liberal values by way of television, public schools, the judiciary, and liberal theology have taken their toll. In response to the culture in which I was working in Stockholm, I put together a Bible study for the benefit of our church, although it can be used effectively as a small-group study, a spiritual training (discipling) handbook, or even a guided study for a seeker. Americans today are like the Scandinavians a few decades ago: mortified by the thought that we might be identified as extremist, unreasonable, intolerant, or (worst of all) religiously fanatic.

The study was called *Judge Not!* It should be useful for anyone who has heard that we should never judge. Certainly, a judgmental spirit is wrong and unbecoming of a believer, but this doesn't necessarily mean that all judging is wrong. Quite often, when someone pleads, "Do not judge," he is exhibiting a defensive spirit—as well as a lack of knowledge of God's word. The truth is, the Bible distinguishes a number of types of judging—some good, some bad.

Here are 12 kinds of judgments. As you proceed through the list, take the time to look up the Scriptures.

*1. Hypocritical judging* (Matthew 7:1-5; Romans 2:1). This is the kind of judging most people have in mind when they express the judgment that one should not judge. Jesus tells us to get the log out of our own eye so that we can see clearly enough to help our brother. Clearly he expects us to do a certain amount of judging, but not hypocritically.

*2. Discerning who is receptive to the gospel* (Matthew 7:6; 10:11-13). Judging who is open to the gospel message and who is not is not unkind. In fact, it is fairest to all—both to the person at hand as well as to others who may be seeking the Lord.

*3. Superficial judging* (John 7:24). Get the facts and know the Scriptures. That is the only way to judge correctly. The person who fails to make a right judgment will make poor decisions and may even be duped by others who are shrewder. The entire book of Proverbs exhorts us to this sort of practical wisdom.

*4. Making an assessment* (Acts 4:19). The act of judgment itself is neutral. The usual Greek verb for *judge* or *discern* is *krinein*. It is not an inherently negative word. It means moving from premises to conclusions, assessing a situation, discerning, and the like. As we will urge in the next chapter, we ought to think clearly about the claims of the various world religions. This is not in itself ungracious. In fact, Paul insists that the spiritual man makes all sorts of judgments (1 Corinthians 2:15). That is good.

*5. Passing judgment on matters of opinion* (Romans 14:1). We must all take a stand on crucial issues, but it is wrong to judge others on the basis of nonessential or disputable issues. Of course, the apostles expect us to accept the weaker brother, not necessarily to leave him in a state of ignorance or weak faith. Yet the Lord will hold all of us accountable for how we use our freedom of thought and expression. Many passages in the Bible remind us of this truth.

*6. Final judgment* (Romans 14:10-12; Acts 10:42). This is the prerogative of God alone. Sentencing people to heaven or hell is "final judgment." Obviously, no human has the authority to send any other human being anywhere after death. Further, do not confuse warning with sentencing. They are different kinds of judging.

*7. Judging hearts and motives* (1 Corinthians 4:3-5). This is highly problematic. Yes, out of the mouth comes the overflow of the heart, so there may be some clues to what is going on in someone's heart or mind, and yet Proverbs says that only a person of understanding can draw out the innermost intent (20:5). Paul adds that he does not even judge himself. Let's not get tied in knots trying to analyze everybody—including ourselves![1]

*8. Disciplinary judging* (1 Corinthians 5:12-13). Church discipline requires that action be taken when serious sin is affecting the congregation. This may include expelling the unrepentant.

*9. Judging disputes* (1 Corinthians 6:2). This requires judgment (discernment). The apostle assumes that Christians have the collective wisdom to settle their own disputes without going public.

*10. Critical judging* (James 4:11-12). Grumbling—for example, rich Christians complaining against poor Christians or vice versa—is wrong. We are not to judge others in a critical, destructive manner (Ephesians 4:29). Before I correct someone else, I need to examine my heart (as far as that is possible). Am I trying to guide, help, or educate (all in love), or is my intent to defeat, tear down, and humiliate (in pride and arrogance)?

*11. Interpreting the Scriptures* (1 Corinthians 10:15; 11:13). We are all encouraged to correctly study and interpret God's word. This entails exercising judgment.

*12. Doctrinal nitpicking* (Colossians 2:16). Some people refer to inconsequential or outmoded doctrines to determine whether others are saved. The central teachings of Scripture indicate the core doctrines. Not all biblical teachings are equally important, nor are they all essential for salvation. This is not to say that we should refuse to draw the line when it comes to such key doctrines as the one body, Spirit, hope, Lord, faith, baptism, and God mentioned in Ephesians 4:3-6. The Bible is too long, the lost are too many, and life is too short for us to get bogged down in nonissues.

## Conclusion

John 3:16 is too short a snippet to lead most people to repentance, but at least it says something. Matthew 7:1, in the hands of most who wield it nowadays, says nothing at all. Apathy masquerades as tolerance. Or, as someone put it, "The fellow who boasts about his open mind may only have a vacant one."

What should we do when people (often nonbelievers) correct us and tell us not to judge? Here are some suggestions. Ask, "Do you know what Jesus was teaching by saying that?" They may not know. Explain, "Jesus didn't want us to be hypocrites. He wanted us to look at our own lives and clean them up in order to be able to help others compassionately." Then ask, "Are you aware that Jesus used that very statement to teach us how to render a clear judgment and to help others make good changes in their lives?" They will most likely not be aware of this, and this should take the discussion to a more productive level.

In our modern era, taking a conclusive stand for anything is often considered ungracious! Yet we have seen that the common plea "Do not judge" is a gross oversimplification. We all must make many judgments every day. Let's be sure we are doing it in the right spirit. Judge not![2]

## In Brief

- Forbidden forms of judgment include hypocritical judging, superficial judging, condemning others' opinions, final judgment, judging motives, critical judging, and doctrinal nitpicking.

- Acceptable forms of judgment include discerning who is receptive to the gospel, making a "right" judgment, making a general assessment, disciplinary judgment, judging disputes, and interpreting the Scriptures correctly.

- "Do not judge" is thus often a simplistic and evasive move to exonerate oneself. We Christians are called to judge wisely, beginning with ourselves (2 Corinthians 13:5).

# 14

# Alternative Views

## *Moonlight*

*I am the way and the truth and the life. No one
comes to the Father except through me.*

JESUS CHRIST

We have studied what the Bible says about heaven and hell. One
third of the planet self-identifies as Christian. What do the other
two thirds say? And what about the dissenting voices even within
Christianity (broadly defined)?

Fewer and fewer church members appreciate the difference between
their faith and the other world religions. Why? Three reasons come to
mind. First, many nominal Christians rarely read the Bible and are
unfamiliar with most of the fundamentals. Second, they have not sur-
veyed the other religions. It's simpler, after all, to parrot the common
notion that all religions are the same despite their wide diversity and
disagreement.[1] Third, and probably most important, they do not want
to misstep. There is tremendous pressure to appear tolerant and politically correct.

The *World Christian Encyclopedia* lists 19 major world religions.
These in turn may be subdivided into 270 major groups and numerous smaller ones. At least 34,000 separate Christian groups have been
identified. (The majority are independent churches, not tied in with

the major denominations.)[2] Needless to say, there is a wide spectrum of opinions about heaven, hell, and the afterlife. In this chapter we will briefly survey the views of the afterlife promoted by several of the major religions and Christian sects.

## Atheists and Agnostics

Atheists and agnostics comprise 15 to 20 percent of the world's population.[3] Many believe in some kind of spiritual energy, and most are intrigued by the supernatural, but they do not hold any serious belief in heaven and hell. Some are hopeful that if they are wrong about God, they will still find a place in heaven. If one in six persons on the planet is an unbeliever, we who know Christ have work to do.

## The Most Influential World Religions

### Muslims

More than 20 percent of the world follow the way of Muhammad. Many of the tenets of Islam, which became a religion only in the seventh century AD, were derived from Judaism and Christianity. Heaven is conceived as a garden or a luxurious oasis in the desert. Heaven and hell are both vividly described in the Qur'an. I asked a highly respected imam to speak about the Muslim belief.

> Muslims generally believe that good souls will go to heaven and bad souls to hell. The Quran (7:46) also mentions a third place: the heights. Various scholarly opinions have been offered as to who will inhabit the heights. Usually, these opinions hover around the central idea that some people are not good enough to merit heaven and not bad enough to be consigned to hell. Moreover, from the Quranic description it is clear that the dwellers of the heights would eventually be admitted to heaven. Heaven is believed to be the abode of eternal bliss in the presence of God. Believers will enjoy seeing God, and they will bask in the knowledge that God is pleased with them. Hell, on the other extreme, holds in store some of the most gruesome tortures imaginable. Most Muslims believe that heaven and hell are everlasting. Some significant Muslim scholars, however, have held the view that hell will have a limited duration.[4]

There are different Islamic views, such as that of the heretical Ahmadiyya Muslims (numbering in the tens of millions), who believe in progressive enlightenment in heaven.[5] But the mainstream view is represented above and resembles to some extent the Roman Catholic heaven, purgatory, and hell.

### Hindus

About 20 percent of all humans are Hindu. Hinduism combined belief in heavens and hells with incarnation. The fire of cremation brings the soul to heaven. After some time in a heaven, one is reborn, and the cycle continues.[6]

Neither heavens nor hells are ultimate. At the end of it all, our soul returns to the world soul like a drop returning to the sea of consciousness. We will have no personal individual existence.

### Buddhists

Buddhism, which developed out of Hinduism, identifies numerous heavens (inhabited by numerous gods) and multiple hells. But there is an important difference from Hinduism. The Buddha (sixth century BC) taught that there is no individual self. This applies to the gods as well, which makes classical Buddhism atheistic, not theistic. Heaven is constructed from one's consciousness, and even then the consciousness is an epiphenomenon of a nonexistent self. In fact, all distinctions are invalid and relationships are illusory because there is no other, just as there is no self. Whereas in Hinduism all become one, in Buddhism it would be fair to say all become (or discover that all along they were) nothing.

How interesting that even when God is removed from the equation, heaven and hell reappear. The natural human tendency to believe in morality and accountability led to theistic Buddhism, at least at the popular level.

### Jews

Orthodox Jews believe in an eternal hell. But many Jews, including those I grew up with in New Jersey, are secular. Most Jews in the world, whether residing in Tel Aviv or Brooklyn, are atheists or agnostics. In the words of secular Jew Lisa Miller, an author and journalist who contributes to the *Washington Post,* "When you are facing the sheer cliff of your own mortality, the modern Jewish emphasis on this life rather than the next can feel brutally insufficient."[7]

Such a perspective is unfortunate, considering that heaven, hell, and the afterlife are intimated in the Hebrew Scriptures.[8] In addition, the Old Testament speaks frequently of Sheol (the Hebrew equivalent of the Greek Hades), the waiting place of the dead. Many Jews even believe in a purgatory.[9] When Jews return to their scriptural roots, they find that their Bible dovetails perfectly with the Christian New Testament, in which the truth about the afterlife is more fully developed.

## Major Christian Divisions

### Protestants

Most of the world's 800 million Protestants believe that one goes to heaven or hell at the moment of death—no purgatory. As we have seen, this is a fairly recent development, born of reaction to the theology of the Middle Ages.

### Catholics

The planet's 1.2 billion Roman Catholics believe that the dead proceed at once to heaven, hell, or purgatory. Purgatory is for those who "die in God's grace and friendship, but are still imperfectly purified."[10] The original concept of Hades (the intermediate state of the dead) was gradually transformed into purgatory during the third and fourth centuries. By the fifth, belief in purgatory was widespread. The most detailed descriptions of heaven, purgatory, and hell are found in Dante's *Divine Comedy.* Here the lowest part of hell, reserved for Satan, is ice cold.[11] There is no doubt that Dante's writing crystallized medieval Christian thought, also framing popular understandings for future generations.

### Orthodox

The Orthodox (300 million in all) believe in a temporary judgment. All proceed to the underworld—the wicked to the dark part of Hades, the righteous to paradise (Abraham's bosom). In Hades they experience a foretaste of what is to come. There is no purgatory, though it is believed that the dead can be affected by prayers of the living. At the end of the world, humans will end up in heaven or hell.

## Sects Born in a Christian Milieu

Many groups have arisen in the United States that are far from the Christian center. This is not surprising, given the spirit of individualism and religious freedom as well as the absence of a state church. Among their ranks are such groups as the Mormons (Latter-day Saints), Seventh-day Adventists, Jehovah's Witnesses, Christian Scientists (all these groups were founded in the nineteenth century), and Scientologists (founded in the twentieth). We will consider three of these groups and the ever-fashionable New Age Movement.

### Mormons

Founded by Joseph Smith (1805–1844), the Latter-day Saints posit three heavenly kingdoms (celestial, telestial, and terrestrial). The ultimate hope of every Mormon male is to become god of his own planet. Heaven and "the heavens" (astronomical) are confounded. Nearly everyone will end up in one of these three heavens, and few will remain in hell eternally.[12]

### Christian Science

Mary Baker Eddy (1821–1910), founder of Christian Science, denied the reality of evil as well as the historical crucifixion and resurrection of Christ. God is universal wisdom. There is no eternal hell. Instead hell and heaven are states of mind. "Heaven is not a locality, but a divine state of Mind in which all the manifestations of Mind are harmonious and immortal." It is "harmony; the reign of Spirit; government by divine principle; spirituality; bliss; the atmosphere of Soul."[13]

### Jehovah's Witnesses

The Witnesses, founded by Charles Russell (1852–1916), also deny hell, equating it with the grave. Taking Revelation 7 and 14 literally (though not that literally, otherwise only Jewish men would be there), they limit heaven to 144,000 persons, who will rule over the "great flock" on earth (even though in Revelation 7:9 and 19:1, this multitude is depicted as being in heaven). Most of the saved will live on a renewed earth.[14]

### New Age Movement

This movement is a fusion of Eastern religion (Buddhism, Taoism, Hinduism) and Western philosophical ideas. Its salient features include astrology, channeling, crystals, witchcraft, nature worship, sin and evil as illusory, and all paths leading to God. The central New Age teaching is that we are God. If we realize this core truth, things will go our way, the world will orient itself around our wishes, and we will be fulfilled. Naturally, there is no hell. Universalism, the belief that none will be lost and that the afterlife will be pleasant for all—is the norm.

Each person must find his or her own path. The afterlife may be a higher plane of consciousness, reincarnation, or even nonexistence. New Age writers and speakers include James Redfield (*The Celestine Prophecy*), Rhonda Byrne (*The Secret*), Paulo Coelho (*The Alchemist*), Carlos Castaneda (*The Teachings of Don Juan*), and Eckhart Tolle (*A New Earth*). To these could be added the even better-known Edgar Cayce, Madame Blavatsky, Jeane Dixon, Shirley MacLaine, Deepak Chopra, and probably Dan Brown (of *Da Vinci Code* fame).

### Summary

On our planet are manifold views of the afterlife, from nebulous states of mind to the highly specific Islamic paradise. Yet the Christian concept of heaven is significantly different. It is not a psychological state, but a true place. It is not explicitly described—what we imagine about heaven and hell must be garnered from symbolic or allusive passages. The heaven of the Bible is also highly relational and social.

To these characteristics might be added another. "While other religions may think of heaven (now) as a place of felicity, light, untainted glory—the New Testament tradition never entertains such thinking. It is a place of conflict, and will ultimately be renewed."[15] If the biblical phrase *new heaven and earth* means that both heaven and earth must be cleansed and created afresh (an increasingly accepted view among Christian theologians and writers), then there is merit to this suggestion.[16]

Few human religious movements are completely benighted. It isn't hard to find some truth even if it is blended with error. Yet the difference between the doctrines of the Bible and all others is like the difference between moonlight and sunlight. One is only reflected and is weaker. The other has its own incandescence and is blindingly powerful.

If the difference between biblical religion and others is so great, was it really necessary to take time to listen to these dissenting voices? Yes, because people are confused about truth—not only people outside the fold but also those inside.

A survey of 35,000 American adults conducted in 2007 shows that 70 percent believe there are many paths to God—all equally valid. 68 percent said that there was more than one true way to interpret the teachings of their own religion. Michael Lindsay of Rice University said that "the survey shows religion in America is, indeed, 3000 miles wide and only 3 inches deep."[17]

The problem is that people do not know why they believe what they believe, and certainly do not understand the uniqueness of the Christian system. Universalism and pluralism have become the politically correct positions, and because people do not know their Bibles they can subscribe to such beliefs, dismissing Jesus's statement, "I am the way and the truth and the life. No one comes to the Father except through by me" (John 14:6).

Once we realize how great the differences are among the religions of the world, it will be more natural for us to accept Jesus's doctrine of the narrow road, which we will look at in the next chapter.

## In Brief

- Concepts of heaven and hell among the world's religions, including Christian sects, range from wild guesses to glimpses of genuine insight.

- No others come close to the biblical view, for they lack the profound understanding of *relationship* in the biblical teaching about heaven.

- Most regard heaven and hell as ultimate solutions to
  the problems of a moral universe even when their faith
  includes no original belief in God or a judgment day. This
  suggests mankind has God's law "written on their hearts,
  their consciences also bearing witness, and their thoughts
  sometimes accusing them and at other times even defending them" (Romans 2:15).

# The Narrow Road

## *Is God Just?*

*These are the days when the Christian is expected
to praise every creed except his own.*

G.K. Chesterton

This is our third consecutive chapter on judgment. This topic may be inconvenient and distressing for some, but judgment day is on the way. We had better think clearly about it. As we've seen, it is woefully simplistic to condemn judging (which itself would be an instance of judging). We must specify which kind of judging we are referring to. It is prudent to ponder God's justice in judgment in light of the narrow road.

People of faith ought to be deeply concerned with God's justice. We should be bothered to think that most of the world may not make it at the last day. It should bother us even more to think that God may have got it wrong—that some folks got a raw deal and that a cosmic miscarriage of justice is in the wings. Ever since Abraham (Genesis 18:25) and Lot (2 Peter 2:7), men and women of faith have wrestled with this issue.

## The Narrow Gate and the Narrow Door

The passage on the narrow gate, Matthew 7:13-14, is probably more familiar than a similar passage in the third Gospel, but the essence is the same.

> Someone asked him, "Lord, are only a few people going to be saved?"
>
> He said to them, "Make every effort to enter through the narrow door, because many, I tell you, will try to enter and will not be able to" (Luke 13:23-24).

We presume that the Lord knows who will be saved, and the percentages are not our concern. Notice how Jesus answered the man. He does not give a yes or a no. The answer is not a piece of information, but an imperative to the heart. He says, "Make every effort..." How many people are doing that—truly putting God first? Am I doing that?

## Two Paths

There are two doors (or gates) because there are two paths. We might prefer a third (more comfortable, more balanced) route, but this is not offered. In fact, the theme of two paths runs through every book of the Bible. You find it in Psalm 1 and the many other psalms that contrast the way of the righteous and the way of the wicked. It's in Acts (the Christians were called "The Way"). It's all over the Proverbs. I once preached a sermon proving the point. We moved through every book of the Bible. It took an hour, but we all left with deeper conviction. That's the purpose of this chapter.

One of my favorite passages touching on the narrow road is Isaiah 35:8 (NASB).

> A highway will be there, a roadway,
> And it will be called the Highway of Holiness.
> The unclean will not travel on it,
> But it will be for him who walks that way,
> And fools will not wander on it.

The Lord calls us to holy living. To be spiritual, not worldly (James 4:4; 1 John 2:15-17). To resist temptation in all its forms—egocentrism, materialism, sexual sin, laziness, drunkenness, bitterness...The New Testament includes some 30 lists of sins, so I am always stunned when people say the Bible isn't all that specific or that sin is whatever you think is wrong for you (but not necessarily for them).

And yet holiness is more than just resisting sin. Christ calls us to follow him—something active, not passive. We are called to be passionate, to catch fire for him (Romans 12:11; Revelation 3:14-20). If you commit yourself to the highway of holiness, there will be pushback. If Jesus got it, we will get it (Luke 6:22-23,26; John 15:18; 2 Timothy 3:12). "Blessed are you when people insult you, persecute you and falsely say all kinds of evil against you because of me" (Matthew 5:11). You will be misunderstood, labeled, and libeled. What sort of labels are slapped on true disciples of Christ, and how should we respond?

Of course we should always respond kindly and respectfully. This tends to disarm our critics. We can also respond intelligently.

- *Christians are narrow-minded.* Some are. Don't deny it. But true followers of Christ are truth seekers. The Greek word *mathetes,* "disciple," is used of Jesus's followers many times in the Gospels and dozens of times in Acts. It means "student."

- *Christians are exclusivists.* Truth is naturally exclusive. The correct answer rules out the incorrect ones. But rather than giving such a philosophical answer, turn the accusation on its head. Christianity is actually *inclusive*—far more so than the other world religions. Everyone is welcome! You don't have to belong to a certain culture or speak a certain language. It is open to men, women, minorities—everybody! There is a grand, inclusive vision in the Apocalypse: "After this I looked, and there before me was a great multitude that no one could count, from every nation, tribe, people and language, standing before the throne and before the Lamb" (Revelation 7:9).

- *Christians are unloving.* Sadly, there is some truth in this charge, at least historically. But there is nothing unloving about sharing the truth with the lost. Might the message be initially unpleasant? Definitely (Acts 24:24-25). But love speaks the truth (Mark 10:21). Actually, we're being unloving if we don't speak up.[1]

- *Christians are intolerant.* They are bigots. Chesterton addressed this concern: "It is not bigotry to be certain we are right; but it is bigotry to be unable to imagine how we might possibly have gone wrong."[2]

But what's going on here? In the not-so-distant past, Christianity was respected in Western culture. Yes, I realize that it was a dilute form of the original apostolic faith. But it is more so in our day, and still it is opposed even more vehemently. You would think the world wouldn't care, and yet religion—mainly Christian religion—is increasingly banished from the public square. Why is this?

## Tolerance False and True

Modern man has redefined *tolerance*. The word has undergone a subtle transition from tolerance of persons (with whom we disagree) to tolerance of ideas (as though they all have equal merit). Intolerance is unpopular, so we are willing to grant that all religious ideas are viable—provided, of course, that they are not too extreme. But to say that we tolerate another fellow's religion scarcely means we agree with him. On the contrary, it implies that we *disagree*. Of course, others are entitled to their own religious beliefs, but it is nonsense to say all ideas are equally true. (How can all ideas be equally true when they contradict each other?)

Modern man is confused about faith. He thinks that faith creates truth. That is, if you believe it, it is true (at least for you). If you believe in heaven and hell, fine. It may be real for you but not for me because I don't look at things that way. However, faith does not create truth. Faith can be completely mistaken about what is true, and we can place our faith in the wrong thing. It would certainly be better to have a weak faith in a strong bridge than a strong faith in a weak bridge. Christians could be wrong about the strength of their bridge, but they do not pretend that the bridge exists only for those who believe it is there.

If religious ideas cannot stand the test of criticism, they ought to be given up. After all, they are either well grounded or ill founded, true or false. If faith is so fragile that it is toppled by investigation, it isn't true in the first place, nor is it worth your believing it.

## What About Those Who Haven't Heard?

At this point in the discussion you can expect this question—what about those who haven't heard? The question seems to assume that if Christ hadn't come, we wouldn't have this problem, and people wouldn't be lost. Wouldn't they be saved by common decency? (Which, if you haven't noticed, is in short supply these days.) After all, most people grow up in a culture where they are not very likely to hear the gospel message. There are over a billion Hindus in our world and even more Muslims. Another billion plus live under governments that are atheistic, secular, and intolerant of religion. Even in the so-called Christian lands, the gospel has been so diluted and distorted, and so-called Christians are so far from the spirit of their supposed Lord, that potential seekers are often turned off.

So is God fair to hold these people accountable? No, not if this means they were put in an impossible situation. But yes it is if they are responsible for wrongdoing.[3] After all, people in the so-called Christian lands aren't the only ones who envy, lie, cheat, fornicate, hate, and so on. But we were *not* put in an impossible situation. *We put ourselves into it.* Sin was our own choice. We all chose it, just as Eve and Adam did (Genesis 3:6; Romans 3:23).

If someone had never sinned, he would not need Christ for forgiveness. But can we even imagine someone so virtuous that he or she sinned only three times a day? I know of no one so virtuous! That's more than 1000 sins a year, tens of thousands of sins in a normal lifetime. This doesn't sound so good anymore, does it? The New Testament tells us that if righteousness could be attained through the law, Christ died for nothing (Galatians 2:21).

Ecclesiastes 7:20, Romans 3:23, and many other biblical passages underscore the ubiquity of sin. It is everywhere! But this is hardly like a physical contagion, for which someone may quickly be excused should he or she become sick. There is a moral dimension. The contagion of sin is contracted by our multiple freewill choices. That is why John 3:18 says those who do not believe in Christ are *already* condemned. They remain in darkness until they respond positively to the light.

My practical experience in counseling and sharing the gospel around the world has convinced me that no one is without sin. And I bet if you have been active in sharing your faith or have been a student of human nature, you no longer hold a naive view that people don't need God, that we are anything but the lost sheep the Bible says we are. The whole world is in darkness. Matthew 7:13-14, Galatians 3:22, 1 John 5:19, and many other Bible passages paint a picture of a world in bondage to sin.

Sometimes I'm more worried about those who *have* heard. What will happen to them? So many don't live as though the judgment day is real. The principle of Luke 12:47-48 applies to everyone—punishment is proportional, and those who haven't heard will receive a lighter sentence. But what about the principle of John 12:47-48? Those who have heard have no excuse. And nearly all of us reading this book have been exposed to the gospel message.

## Saved by Sentimentality?

Romans 1 says the whole world is without excuse. Certain things may be known about God from nature. When people want to excuse the ignorant, they are making an odd proposal in terms of logic and in light of Jesus's teaching in John 12. Imagine that the lost could have been saved without the gospel, just by being decent persons (salvation by works). If that were true, and if Christians shared the truth with them and they rejected it, they would be lost! For Jesus said, "Whoever rejects you rejects me" (Luke 10:16). That is, exposure to the gospel would have damned them. Bad news indeed! Better to let the sleeping world lie in sin and ignorance. That way billions would have a shot at salvation on their own.

But it gets even more interesting. Insincere objections are often posed—what about the pygmies? The ones we care about are those we know, love, or respect. We don't worry about the countless billions about whom we know nothing. When the Muslim hears the gospel, he seldom agonizes over the implications for the Buddhists. He is concerned for his own friends, family members, and perhaps the imam at the mosque. The woman brought up in lukewarm churchianity does not worry excessively about the fate of the Hindus. She is concerned about her parents or grandparents. Or maybe about where her pastor really stands in terms of his relationship with God, given that he kept her on the church roll for years despite her lack of Christian discipleship. The college student who has been exposed to liberal ideas about enlightenment and salvation hardly sweats over the ultimate destiny of the Jews, Shintos, Taoists, or native Americans. He cares a lot more about what his friend thinks. Or what his girlfriend thinks!

If our feelings allow the whole world to be lost *except* for those we most care about, a double inconsistency emerges. First, the lost become saved by sentimentality. It is our *feeling* about them that makes them right with God, rather than their personal response to the gospel! Salvation by faith is replaced by salvation through third-party sentimentality. Second, rather than truly respecting others' decisions about God, we assure ourselves that somehow they are in fact believers in Christ, or at least that they would jump at the opportunity given a second chance. Many of these non-Christians would feel deeply insulted if they knew how little we respected their judgment. We can't have it both ways—free will for ourselves but not for them. Either a person's own response to the gospel is determinative or it is not.

But of course all of this is both nonsensical and unbiblical. Ignorance is not bliss. Otherwise, why did Jesus give us the Great Commission?

This can only mean that the lost are actually lost. Jesus is the only way (John 14:6; Romans 10:13-15). And since faith comes by hearing the word, someone needs to tell them. Who would that be, if not Christ's followers?

If God alone has the right of final judgment, we must allow him to say who is saved and who is lost. Of course he could consider the trajectory of someone's life—the direction and momentum. ("The way he was beginning to seek, within five years he would have been open to the gospel...") But we do not know this for a certainty. That is, we ought not to pronounce lost those who have turned to God in faith and repentance, nor ought we to pronounce saved those who have not.

### God Forgives

God is the Judge (James 4:12). Final judgment is his call, not ours. It is *his* prerogative to forgive sins. "Who can forgive sins but God alone?" (Mark 2:7) Let's say you owe the IRS a huge sum. I may wish you well and hope you won't have to pay, but that's wholly different from having the authority to cancel your debt. God may let some who have never heard into the kingdom, but unless he tells us so, we have no right to speak for him or to dispense exceptions.

Luke 23 is in the Bible for a reason. The story of the thief on the cross (Luke 23:39-43) is not intended to show us that a quickie confession can take the place of true faith, repentance, and baptism, but it does tell us something about the nature of God. Even at the last moment there may be hope. God is good. We may have biblical hope that those who turn to Christ in their final moments may find salvation.

The early Christians believed in a "baptism of blood." Those who did not make it to the water before their martyrdom were considered saved. Moreover, there were *a few* persons in biblical times who were right with God even though they were not part of God's people, such as Melchizedek (Genesis 14:18-20) and Jethro (Exodus 3:1; 18:1). Further, just as Abraham was saved by looking to God—though without a complete understanding of Christ—so others *might* turn in faith and repentance to their Creator even without someone preaching the gospel to them. Yet the Bible does not affirm this. To go any further than this—and perhaps even this far—is speculation.

We need not stake our hope on divine exceptions to the clearly articulated gospel message, for in fact the lost *do* respond to the gospel! Hundreds, thousands, millions embrace it with a sincere heart. Hindus hope in Christ. Muslims make Jesus their Lord. Buddhists are baptized. Hardened atheists soften. And those brought up around the Bible *but not in it* rethink their spiritual experiences and give their lives to the Lord in faith and repentance. I have seen all these responses with my own eyes. I want to be part of this process. I believe you do too.

### He Has the Whole World in His Hands

God knows how to deal with the billions in nations where the gospel has not penetrated.

> [The Lord] comes to judge the earth.
> He will judge the world in righteousness
>   and the peoples with equity (Psalm 98:9).

He is the just Judge (James 4:12; 1 Peter 2:23). The road is narrow, but not in order to keep club membership from expanding. It is narrow because of the freewill choices men and women have made.

Christians know what the world needs to hear—the solution to its true problems. May we share this message with courage and confidence and without delay. For, in the words of Carl F.H. Henry, "The gospel is only good news if it gets there in time."

## In Brief

- The path to eternal life is narrow. We must exert effort to find it and stay on it.

- There are only two paths, as the entire Bible attests.

- Tolerance of persons is biblical. Tolerance of ideas, a modern development born of relativism, is nothing more than political correctness. True tolerance requires disagreement if the term is not to be meaningless.

- God will judge fairly those who haven't heard. Though sin is a universal problem and Christ is God's only solution, the Bible assures us that the Lord will judge all nations with equity.

## Questions for Self-Examination

- If Christ returned tomorrow, would I be ready? When it comes to the narrow road, am I living on "the highway of holiness"?

- Is there anything that makes me doubt God's justice—something in life or in Scripture that feels unfair? Am I serious about finding practical answers?

- Have I rationalized the metaphor of the narrow road, or have I internalized it? Have I ignored it, or have I made it a central conviction in my life? How is my conviction lived out in outreach as I share Christ with others?

Part 5

# Questions

We have covered a lot of ground, and we ought to have a renewed appreciation for heaven and hell. Getting clarity on core Christian doctrine is most helpful, but it's also nice to get answers to more peripheral questions.

We will now explore a number of sometimes confusing topics. For most questions, the answers are near at hand.

# Out of Their Bodies
# or Out of Their Minds?

## Near-Death and Out-of-Body Experiences

*I know a man in Christ who…was caught up to*
*the third heaven. Whether it was in the body or*
*out of the body I do not know—God knows.*

THE APOSTLE PAUL

My Swedish tutor was a rational woman, fluent in Russian, German, French, Swedish, and English. Birgitta was sensible, modest, and intelligent—just like her husband. During our three years in Stockholm, we learned a lot about one other. I knew about her battles with cancer and her political and philosophical views. She was not a believer. So when she told me she'd been declared clinically dead in hospital but came back, I had no reason to suspect deceit, psychosis, or error. *Something* happened. She was not out of her mind, just out of her body. And she's hardly alone. Like most who have out-of-body or near-death experiences, she proceeded through a dark tunnel toward a light but was sent back, not permitted to stay in the blissful place. The sequence is universally familiar.

Tens of thousands of the living have had experiences of a world beyond this one. Quite a few are well documented. Some clung to life, others were given up for dead—and not a few were brain-dead. In a 2001 study of 350 patients published in the *Lancet,* the world's oldest medical journal and certainly one of the most respected, physician Pim van Lommel discovered a number of near-death experiences (NDEs) even after brain function had ceased.[1] Some experienced what they understood to be heaven, others the opposite, while some experiences were devoid of religion altogether. In some cases, the blind see.[2] Subjects meet dead relatives.[3] On occasion they behold angels, demons, and God himself.

NDEs and other phenomena transporting the subject to the world beyond are the focus of this chapter. They are an accepted part of popular culture, and biblically informed folks will be asked what they think about NDEs. We will take a look at five highly publicized cases. Four of the journeys were heavenly, one hellish. As James Garlow and Keith Wall conclude, not all NDEs are peaceful events.[4] A friend and fellow author has met several persons who experienced burning flames in their NDEs.[5] There are many recent works on out-of-body and near-death experiences, but I hope that a quick peek at five cases, each resulting in a bestselling book, will provide the opportunity to apply a balanced biblical perspective to the common range of NDEs in contemporary Western culture.[6]

### Don Piper, *90 Minutes in Heaven*

Don Piper (no relation to the theologian John Piper, whom we mentioned in passing in chapter 7), died in a grisly car crash and spent an hour and a half in heaven. Piper recognized many of the (deceased) persons he saw in heaven. Interestingly, all the people Piper encountered during his NDE were the same age as when he last saw them. In many NDEs people tend to appear younger than they were at the time of death.[7] Piper notices several details that match the traditional picture of heaven, including pearlescent gates and streets of gold.

His account has the ring of truth, though as he admits, he didn't reveal all the details until nearly two years after the accident. But if he told no one about his experience for many months, how can he be sure he didn't "experience" it later, especially during the times he was so heavily medicated? I am not doubting that he had a significant experience, only calling into question whether the details were remembered or synthesized.

### Choo Thomas, *Heaven Is So Real!*

Thomas considers herself to be an end-times prophetess. God began speaking directly to her in 1995, and she was specially selected by Jesus to accompany him on weekly visits to heaven, which typically follow a period of bodily convulsion. There she beheld streets of gold and literal mansions—showing she has misunderstood the archaic sense of the King James word *mansions*. She sees beach houses, but if we literalize Revelation, there is no more sea (21:1). She also visited her own personal mansion with her name engraved on a golden plaque, a silver bathtub, and velvet chairs.

Thomas goes into tedious detail about what she has seen (Colossians 2:18-19). Her Jesus endorses December 25 as his birthday even though the date has almost certainly come into Christianity from paganism. Her visions also support other features of her personal theology: strict tithing, a premillennial rapture, speaking in tongues, and laughing in the Spirit. She learns that a war will begin in 1998. She is told we are to eat fish. God speaks King James English. He purposes to make her rich so that she can bless others. Jesus assures her that she is a beautiful woman.

As Thomas admits throughout the book, she rejects all suggestions that she is anything less than a prophetess or that the heavenly dances Jesus taught her to perform should not be performed in the churches she visits. It is difficult not to conclude that she is narcissistic.

When an NDE clearly contradicts Scripture or orthodox biblical scholarship, warning bells should begin to ring. We know that the Bible is true. We don't know that a particular report of an NDE is true, so the Bible must always take precedence over an NDE story regardless of how much we may want to believe it.

If her story is so lacking in biblical credibility, why mention it here? Because it is endorsed by David Yonggi Cho, senior pastor of Yoido Full Gospel Church, the largest church in the world with a membership of 1 million. Cho was "deeply impressed and inspired by it." He agrees that "Sister Choo Thomas...traveled to heaven with Jesus several times, and He took her sightseeing in heaven…I have received a lot of insight about heaven and have been blessed…Among religious books, it has become the number one bestseller in Korea."[8]

## Colton Burpo, *Heaven Is for Real*

Our third story is somewhat more credible. Todd Burpo (Colton's father) is a Christian pastor. He is highly personable, sharing a lot from his own life. He repeatedly emphasizes how he and his wife tried not to lead their little boy on or to put words in his mouth. Todd writes the story of three-year-old Colton, who underwent emergency appendix surgery under anesthesia. He did not die. Colton's recollections of his heavenly visit are divulged over the period of several years.

At first he rose above his body—a common experience during surgeries and near-death experiences. He knew that his parents were praying for him, that his mother was on the telephone, and that they were in separate rooms. According to the little boy, his visit to heaven lasted three minutes—into which it sounds like a full day's activities were crammed. The boy recognized the Father (who was "really big"), the Holy Spirit, and of course Jesus, who loves the little children. Jesus had a rainbow horse and wore white clothes and a purple sash. There were red marks on his feet and palms. The boy later points out Jesus in a sketch by Akiane Kramarik, *Prince of Peace*. Jesus has light eyes and streaks in his hair, which appears to be permed. He looks little like a Middle Easterner—more like a white American. The sketch is included in *Heaven Is for Real*.

Other humans were in heaven, especially children, many of whom Colton later named. They sported wings and halos, which sounds like something out of the children's book *The Littlest Angel*.[9] The imagery of Revelation is literalized, with thrones, Jesus on the right side of God, and the archangel Gabriel on the left. Heaven is the new Jerusalem of Revelation (it is not on earth). Angels carry swords in heaven, and the battle of Armageddon is apparently to be fought with swords and bows and arrows. There are dogs in heaven. And so are two family members that Colton (who was three years, ten months old) had never met.

He talks to his dead sister (a fetus of two months at the time of the miscarriage). This tugs on the heartstrings of the reader (and of Colton's mother). He also sees his deceased grandfather, though as a younger man. Colton later recognized his grandfather in a picture taken of him when he was in his thirties; he did not recognize him in later pictures. Colton's mother was shocked because she hadn't thought her father would be in heaven. She later learned that he had accepted Christ 28 years before his death, yet for the next three decades did not manage to tell his family members about his conversion.

Part of me wanted to believe that the boy wasn't making it all up—that his mother hadn't prompted him—but this last detail made it impossible for me to accept. Jesus taught that if we are ashamed of him, he will be ashamed of us (Mark 8:38). If we disown him, he will disown us (2 Timothy 2:12). If his grandfather became a true disciple of Christ, how could his own family members not know? The boy's experience had become a tool for his parental sentimentality.

The theology of *Heaven Is for Real* reads as though it has been taken out of a children's Sunday school workbook. A nearly four-year-old would have heard a great deal of talk about God and the Bible. It's not so easy to account for the details of the miscarried sister and grandfather, assuming they weren't added by his parents. We weigh the work as a whole; we are not required to accept everything just because one or two details cannot be explained.

The account repeatedly contradicts the testimony of the Old and New Testament and the early Christian writers. By placing people in heaven in the first place, it demonstrates little familiarity with biblical teaching on the afterlife but a lot of familiarity with mainstream American evangelical teaching. In addition to immediate transit to heaven, there is a literal battle of Armageddon, the new Jerusalem (heaven), and conversion through the sinner's prayer—which is not likely to appeal so strongly to other Protestants, Catholics, Orthodox, or non-denominational Christians.

The author admits a history of mental illness in the family (his father). Perhaps this is relevant. Although it's certainly a fascinating story, in so many places it feels hokey—though not as flagrant as the bizarre account of Choo Thomas. Despite the often expressed opinions of the pastor-father, I am afraid the account does not impress me as celestial. Whatever little Colton experienced, it was not a visit to heaven.[10]

### Bill Wiese, *23 Minutes in Hell*

Bill Wiese visits hell in a startlingly intense dream and in follow-up visits in waking dreams. He is in a subterranean chamber at the center of the earth ("I sensed it to be approximately thirty-seven hundred miles deep"), tormented by demons. The fire is literal. The details all come from the King James Version, and Wiese has clearly misunderstood the Elizabethan English. (In the KJV, *Sheol* is mistakenly rendered *hell*.)

Wiese repeatedly mistakes Sheol for hell, and so he conceived of hell as a pit, a literal prison, with snakes and maggots and fires that torture the lost forever and where the demons use the foulest profanity.[11] His book promotes the idea that when the lost die, they proceed immediately to hell—its most serious error. The misunderstandings of the KJV and even basic hermeneutics have led Wiese to make dozens of minor errors as well. The story is truly shocking but only marginally scriptural.

*23 Minutes in Hell* shares publishers with Choo Thomas's book. All four we have listed so far are *New York Times* bestsellers.

### Eben Alexander, *Proof of Heaven*

Eben Alexander's case is unusual in that he himself is a neurosurgeon and has often spoken with patients emerging from comas. He was well versed in the NDE scenario but only from the physician's side. Then, after being stricken with acute bacterial meningitis and spending a week in a coma in 2008, his entire perspective was radically altered.

> My coma taught me many things. First and foremost, near-death experiences, and related mystical states of awareness, reveal crucial truths about the nature of existence. And the reductive materialist (physicalist) model, on which conventional science is based, is fundamentally flawed. At its core, it intentionally ignores what I believe is the fundament of all existence—the nature of consciousness...
>
> That we can know things beyond the ken of the "normal" channels is incontrovertible. An excellent resource for any scientist who still seeks proof of that reality is the rigorous 800-page analysis and review of all manner of extended consciousness, *Irreducible Mind: Toward a Psychology for the 21st Century.*[12] This magnum opus from the Division of

Perceptual Studies at the University of Virginia catalogues a wide variety of empirical phenomena that appear difficult or impossible to accommodate within the standard physicalist way of looking at things. Phenomena covered include, in particular, NDEs occurring under conditions such as deep general anesthesia and cardiac arrest that—like my coma—should prevent occurrence of any experience whatsoever, let alone the profound sorts of experiences that frequently do occur. Also noteworthy, the American Institute of Physics sponsored meetings in 2006 and 2011 covering the physical science of such extraordinary channels of knowledge.[13]

The neurosurgical community is in perfect position to recognize and collect the crucial reports of patients who survive journeys deep in coma from a variety of conditions. These reports will prove invaluable in further comprehending the nature of existence. But remember that patients tend not to report these unusual experiences unless specifically asked what they might remember. So ask them![14]

Alexander insists that NDEs are not on the same level as visions or hallucinations, and the evidence is strong that he is correct in his assessment. His testimony as a former skeptic is especially valuable.

## Further Perspectives

Alexander's case, and probably Piper's, cannot be easily dismissed, and they force us to weigh each case on its own merits. In total, the first four books we discussed have sold about nine million copies, and the fifth is positioned to become another bestseller. The public appetite for the transcendent is enormous, but people need truth, not speculation. In all five cases, *something* happened. I was not especially interested in explaining away these stories, but often the details don't support biblical teaching.

Moving on from these specific cases, what are we to make of NDEs and out-of-body experiences in general?

It is well known that electrical stimulation of the brain's temporal lobe can generate a haunting experience, a sense of some alien presence. Severe accidents can trigger an NDE, especially when head trauma and heart stoppage occur. The NDE makes sense in terms of physiology.

Common elements of the NDE are a sense of well-being, disembodiment, visions (of persons, events, and objects), a tunnel leading to light, interactions with other beings (human or divine), a sober and often positive evaluation of one's life, and return to consciousness. Most of this can be explained by the drop in oxygen levels, buildup of carbon dioxide, reduction in neural firing, shutdown of the visual cortex, and euphoria triggered by dopamine and endorphins in the brain.

Michael Shermer, president of the Skeptics Society and a man I have debated three times, underwent temporal lobe stimulation. Shermer, who is an agnostic, got himself hooked up—all the wires attached to his head—and had an NDE. Any direct connection with the afterlife seems unlikely.[15] Science does not explain every detail in an NDE, including knowledge of events the subject could not have been directly aware of, but it should make us hesitate to assign a supernatural explanation.

For Christian writer and former White House policy analyst Dinesh D'Souza (whose own daughter had an NDE), the evidence is inconclusive.[16] D'Souza admits that NDEs do not prove life after death. Survival does not prove immortality, but it is clear that in some persons consciousness lingers for a while after death.[17]

I circled back to check with two men whose opinions I highly respect. I approached Gary Habermas (apologist, historian, and philosopher of religion) for his take. He hesitated to confirm the veracity of the Burpo story but kept his options open. "I don't say we know exactly where NDErs may go, heaven or otherwise. But there is an incredible amount of evidence that something objective is happening."[18] Habermas and coauthor J.P. Moreland note, "It makes sense that the identification of the figure will come from the patient's own background...For instance, no American claimed to have seen Shiva, Rama, or Krishna... So there are important reasons that certain factors of interpretation comment more on a person's beliefs, society, and culture than they do on the facts themselves."[19] Neither author rejects NDEs or the supernatural. They are both Bible believers. They approach NDEs with great care not to draw unwarranted conclusions.

Finally, I contacted David Bercot, an expert on early Christianity and a personal friend. After commenting on the possibility of hallucination or fraud, Bercot concluded that such NDE experiences generally contradict the evidence of the early church.[20] In short, in the New Testament and first three centuries of Christianity, there was a strong consensus that all the dead went to Hades, not heaven (as we demonstrated in chapter 10).

## In Brief

- NDEs are universal, happening to members of every culture and religion.

- Experiences tend to reflect the faith background of those undergoing them.

- Many, but not all, can be rationalized in terms of physiology or psychology.

- NDEs strongly imply the existence of a spiritual world. They also suggest the existence of an afterlife, though they do not prove it.

# Angels, Ghosts, and Other Things You've Wondered About

## Seven Further Questions

*He who asks a question is a fool for five minutes; he
who does not ask a question remains a fool forever.*

CHINESE PROVERB

Like the issues we considered in our last chapter, most of the seven questions we'll now address concern what happens to the dead—where they are and how they exist.

## Do We Become Angels When We Die?

The Greek and Hebrew words translated *angel* literally mean "messenger." The words sometimes refer to human messengers but usually denote heavenly beings.[1] The latter appear to be genderless or male. Two are named: Gabriel and Michael. Angels can be good or evil (Jude 6).

As a churchgoing youngster, I came to believe that we become angels when we die, at which time we receive a halo and begin harp lessons. This was not altogether worrying to me because the thought of being in the clouds was quite appealing. (I still remember being amazed by the cottony clouds the first time I was in an airplane.) It was not so much the church, but the children's book *The Littlest Angel* that shaped these early ideas. This is not the teaching of the Bible. Jesus never said we will become angels when we die, though in respect to marriage we will be *like* the angels (Matthew 22:30).

The Scriptures present angels as anonymous servants (Hebrews 1:14). We are forbidden to worship them (Colossians 2:18; Revelation 19:10), and one day we will even judge them (1 Corinthians 6:3). Why, then, do some Christians like to swap angel-sighting stories? We ought to be awed by Christ, not by lesser beings (Hebrews 1:4). Dubious angelic anecdotes and the sensationalism of the popular media should be suspect. Moreover, not all angelic visitors were immediately recognized as such; it would be easy to be mistaken (Hebrew 13:2).

### Do We Come Back as Ghosts?

The skeptic would suggest most ghost stories, or perhaps all, result from some combination of unfounded superstition, altered states of consciousness, and optical illusion. But doesn't the Bible affirm their existence?

No, it doesn't. In Matthew 14:26 (and the parallel account in Mark 6:49), the disciples mistake Jesus as a ghost when he walks on water. They may have been similarly tempted as they beheld his resurrection body (Luke 24:37-39). He never bothers to disabuse them of their superstitious beliefs, but we should not take this as tacit confirmation. The Lord was often stretched to give the Twelve an account of their natural obtuseness. But if the Lord left it open, couldn't there be ghosts wandering the earth, especially if their deaths have not been avenged?

Given the biblical teaching that the dead are in Sheol (Hades), it is highly unlikely that any of these subterranean spirits are in our world. I have heard stories I cannot so easily explain away, but the Scriptures are surely more solid than the claims of the paranormal. In 1 Samuel 28 Saul engaged in necromancy. Through a medium he contacted Samuel, who was at peace in Sheol. When I teach people in Latin America or Africa about ghosts, they often point to this passage. "Look—Samuel was a ghost." In some sense the witch "brought him up" (1 Samuel 28:11-14), but this was a temporary event, and it is not even clear that Samuel actually left the underworld. It has little in common with the ghost stories most of us are familiar with. Nor does Job 4:15 support the popular notion that ghosts are the spirits of dead humans. The spirit in this passage was perhaps angelic, or Eliphaz (the speaker) may have been relating a vision.

The Bible does affirm the existence of spirit beings, some benevolent and some malevolent. Some ghostly sightings could possibly be the work of spirits. This is not to say they are demons—in the Bible demons seek bodies in which to dwell (Matthew 17:14-18; Mark 1:21-26; Luke 11:24-26).[2] In short, whatever ghosts are, they aren't human. The spirits of the dead do not come back.

As for communication with the dead, the Bible forbids necromancy (Deuteronomy 18:11). Regardless of whether this is even possible (I suspect it is), such activity has a destructive effect on our lives and is inherently sinful. If you are more of a skeptic than I am, you will appreciate the detached and wry perspective offered by Dinesh D'Souza: "There are parapsychologists, even today, who credit such accounts, but I cannot take them seriously. If the dead could communicate with us, one would expect that they would do so more regularly. How likely is it that, given the millions upon millions who have died, a mere handful would return, through the kind facilitation of some somber intermediary, not to give us any important information but rather to speak mostly gibberish?"[3]

### What About the Great Cloud of Witnesses?

If, as the evidence suggests, the dead aren't in heaven yet, then they aren't *up* there looking *down* on us. (This was always a disconcerting idea anyway. Are dead people watching me work, eat, bathe, and so on?) Then what about Hebrews 12?

> Since we are surrounded by such a great cloud of witnesses,
> let us throw off everything that hinders and the sin that so
> easily entangles. And let us run with perseverance the race
> marked out for us, fixing our eyes on Jesus (Hebrews 12:1-2).

The Old Testament saints who are celebrated in Hebrews 11 have finished the race, keeping the faith till the end. Jesus himself has gone before us, and now we follow him, also running in the stadium. This is not a cloud of literal spectators, nor did Jesus literally run a race. Both are metaphors, but a good few Christian writers take them literally. Some hold that the angels observe and rejoice in our progress (Luke 15:10).[4] This is certainly a beautiful thought, but it is stretch. One wonders whether the dead are aware of anything the living are doing.[5]

### Are Unbaptized Babies in Limbo?

In medieval Catholic theology, unbaptized babies were consigned to hell, though with milder punishment than the other damned souls.[6] Later the view softened. Babies would not go to heaven, nor were they responsible enough to be condemned to hell. They therefore went to limbo.[7] Most Protestants agree that infants should not face eternal torment.[8] The Roman church has now officially dropped limbo, and in 2007 Pope Benedict XVI encouraged Catholic educators to phase it out. Yet it is not clear what real change has taken place because the church can only hope children will not be damned, entrusting them to the mercy of God.[9]

The Bible does not explicitly say what happens to babies, or to those with severe mental challenges, or to any others who could not possibly come to a saving faith. Matthew 18:1-5, Mark 10:14, and other Scriptures suggest these persons die in a state of grace.

### Is There Any Evidence for Reincarnation?

A few years ago I reconnected with a Jewish high school friend in Israel, where his family resides. His wife had been having recurring dreams. She saw bleak buildings, barbed wire, and a number tattooed on her arm. After several dreams—always the same view, always the same number—she decided to do some research. Looking up the number, she found out it belonged to a girl killed in a concentration camp, and then she saw pictures of the camp itself—the very camp about which she had been dreaming. Her conclusion: She was the reincarnation of this girl. My conclusion: I have no idea.

Most anecdotes are not nearly so detailed. But another font of anecdotes is equally difficult to analyze—the NDEs we considered in the last chapter. Many enthusiasts about NDEs also believe in reincarnation. On the other hand, N.T. Wright points out that seeing dead relatives would seem to argue against reincarnation.[10]

Belief in reincarnation has a long history. Hinduism has taught reincarnation for many thousands of years.[11] Status and the body you inhabit in the next life (such as canine, porcine, or "untouchable") depend on your conduct in the present life. Actions (karma) determine the level at which you are reborn. Eventually all souls graduate until their souls become one with the world soul. Individual existence and communal existence then disappear. Reincarnation ultimately negates the social dimension of humanity. It is a pagan belief, although it has become increasingly popular in the West thanks to Edgar Cayce, Jeane Dixon, Shirley MacLaine, John Denver, George Harrison, Deepak Chopra, and a host of others.

The Scriptures, however, do not leave room for a belief in reincarnation (Hebrews 9:27). Reincarnation does not take seriously the biblical view of humanity as spirit, soul, and body (1 Thessalonians 5:23). Besides, in Eastern thought, reincarnation is something to be escaped, not desired. In contrast, in the West, where it has become fashionable to espouse reincarnation, it is viewed as something positive—a chance to start over. Few Westerners are likely to have any idea about the real source of the concept or why no one who really comprehends it would desire its doleful cycles. Snob appeal may lead some to claim, "I'm Cleopatra," or "I was Napoleon."[12]

Proponents claim that John the Baptist was Elijah reincarnated. In Matthew 17:11-13, Jesus says John the Baptist was the Elijah to come, but in John 1:21 the Baptist denies it. Is this because Malachi only speaks of a prophet to come "in the spirit of Elijah," not Elijah himself? Was John's denial a way to steer his disciples away from the idea of an actual reincarnation? Yes, I think so. Many expected Elijah to return to the earth literally, and this notion persists in Jewish tradition even today, with the empty seat left for him at the Seder Supper. John does come in the spirit (and clothing) of Elijah, his ninth-century BC counterpart (Malachi 3–4; Matthew 11; 16; see also 1 Kings 17–19), though as he said, he wasn't literally Elijah.

Elijah appeared along with Moses at the Transfiguration (Matthew 17, Mark 9, Luke 9), so how could he have been reincarnated as John the Baptist? Worse for those advocating reincarnation, the classic belief requires the rebirth of a dead person, but Elijah never died (2 Kings

2:1-11). Furthermore, Luke 23:43 appears to refute reincarnation. How would Jesus meet the thief later that day if he were a different person? There is no biblical basis for importing the popular Eastern idea of reincarnation into Christianity, at least not based on the case of John the Baptist. Reincarnation is ultimately part of an impersonal worldview.

### Is Cremation Okay, or Should We Bury the Dead?

The Bible gives no verdict. I personally have no problem with cremation. In many cultures, corpses are routinely burned. In most, they are buried. In Zoroastrianism, they are intentionally exposed to the elements, allowing the birds to peck away the flesh until only a skeleton remains. Some people request that their ashes be scattered in special places. In other words, there is no consensus on how most respectfully to dispose of the bodies of the departed.

Many believers, however, are uncomfortable with cremation because they believe such a practice might interfere with our resurrection at the last day. The Bible does, after all, mention a bodily resurrection. Our new bodies will be spiritual according to Paul in 1 Corinthians 15, but they are bodies nonetheless. You can see why many believers are uncomfortable with cremation. Orthodox Christians oppose cremation (as do Muslims and Orthodox Jews).

If God is able to reconstitute the bodies of the dead—in whatever form they may be found in their new and altered state—surely he can accomplish this whether the body is drowned, buried in the sand, dismembered, eaten by animals or humans, or consumed by fire.[13] Our God, who created everything ex nihilo (from nothing), should clearly be able to (re)create our resurrected glorified bodies out of whatever he wants (Hebrews 11:3). Moreover, it is not intuitively obvious that we are honoring God more with our bodies in a moldering, decomposing state than in an incinerated one. This was also the position of the early church, although they encouraged burial (see, for example, Acts 8:2), both out of respect for the body as a holy temple and to distinguish themselves from the pagans, who normally cremated.

In the final analysis, given the silence of the Bible, the cremation issue will need to remain a matter of opinion.

## What Is the Third Heaven?

Paul had a mystical experience, although he was reticent, preferring not to give the details. "I know a man in Christ who…was caught up to the third heaven. Whether it was in the body or out of the body I do not know…I know that this man…was caught up to paradise and heard inexpressible things, things that no one is permitted to tell" (2 Corinthians 12:2-4).

Ancient Jews postulated three, seven, or even more heavens. The simplest understanding is that there are three. The lower heaven is the atmosphere, where the birds fly. The middle heaven is outer space, where the stars are located. Paul was caught up to the very presence of God, the third heaven. This seems to be the view of most commentators.[14] Emanuel Swedenborg (1688–1772) thought there were three degrees of closeness to God. The Mormons have their celestial, terrestrial, and telestial heavens. Both these opinions are unlikely in the extreme. Garlow and Wall reason that since *heavens* is plural, there must be more than one heaven.[15] While their conclusion is correct, their reasoning is not. The Hebrew and Greek words are plural, as is one of the common Hebrew words for the one God (*'Elohim*). It would be wrong to conclude there is more than one God.

The three heavens, then, are the sky, outer space, and the home of God.

## In Brief

- We do not become angels when we die. Biblically speaking, that would be a downgrade anyway.

- There are many notions about where the dead are and in what form they exist, yet the consistent testimony of Scripture is that they await the judgment day in Sheol (Hades). This casts considerable doubt on claims of reincarnation and human ghosts.

- The dead are not observing the living. The cloud of witnesses mentioned in Hebrews 12 is metaphorical.

- The Bible does not specify what happens to those who die in infancy, though most Christians presume that they are in the hands of a gracious God.

- Cremation appears to be a viable option for believers.

- The three heavens are the abodes of birds, stars, and God, respectively. The same Hebrew or Greek word is used in every case.

### Questions for Self-Examination

- Is my faith experience truly real to me? Do I think there would there be any major changes required in my life if I had an NDE?

- Am I more captivated by sensationalism (claims of seeing angels, ghosts, or other paranormal activity) or by the vast needs of the world around me? Do I major in the minors or in the Great Commandment and the Great Commission (Matthew 22:37-39; 28:18-20)?

- When people ask me a question, are all my answers equally emphatic, or am I able to use words like *probably* or *it seems*? Do I discern levels of clarity and certainty? In conversation am I careful to distinguish between Bible truths and speculation?

Part 6

# Finally

I hope you have been stimulated to think more deeply about eternity and to depend on the word of God as you navigate these choppy and sometimes murky waters. We read the Bible primarily to be transformed and not just to gather information, so after summarizing, our closing chapter will lead us through a different kind of study. If we desire heaven, putting Jesus's words into practice is the most important thing we could possibly do (Matthew 7:24-27; Luke 6:46).

# Treasure

## *The Paradox*

*It has been said that there will be three things that will surprise us when we get to heaven: one, to find many there whom we did not expect to find there; another, to find some not there whom we had expected; a third, and perhaps the greatest wonder, will be to find ourselves there.*

DWIGHT MOODY

I t is time to bring together our study, first with a brief review and then with a challenge.

### Think Again

In the first part of this book we reevaluated our presuppositions, hoping that our vision of eternity and God's eternal word would be less clouded by our own subjectivity. We saw that appreciating the nature of poetry, parable, and apocalypse goes a long way when we're trying to make sense of the metaphors in God's word. In short, we err in reading the whole Bible literally just as we do by reading it all metaphorically. Everyone contemplates the divine through certain lenses, and a careful method reduces glare, blur, and wrong thinking. Oliver Wendell Holmes Sr. (1809–1894) quipped, "The mind of a bigot is like the pupil of the eye; the more light you pour on it, the more it will contract."[1] As students of Scripture, our prayer must be that our eyes open, not close (Psalm 119:18; Ephesians 1:18).

## Destinations

In the next section we explored heaven, which is primarily relational, and hell, which is characterized by punishment, deprivation, and destruction. Some scholars believe hell is remedial, others assert that it comes to an end (annihilation), and most are convinced it is endless torment. A case can be made for all three positions, and the early church never made one's position on hell a matter of fellowship.

## Postmortem

When one assembles the various pieces from the relevant Scriptures, the sequence of afterlife events is simple. Death is followed by existence in an intermediate state, Hades (called Sheol in the Old Testament). This is sometimes called paradise for the saved, though it often remains unnamed in the case of the damned. On Jesus's return, the dead are raised while the living meet him directly, and then all face judgment, believers and nonbelievers alike. After the judgment, we proceed to our eternal destiny. The case for purgatory is based on logic alone because there is no direct scriptural support. Nevertheless, Protestants, Catholics, and Orthodox all agree that some degree of transformation must take place after death before we are ready to live eternally with God.

## One Way?

In our modern era, a black-and-white position (either you go to heaven or you go to hell) is offensive. This is no reason to reject it, though some believers could do better to present their position with gentleness and respect (1 Peter 3:15-16). We must reject the "do not judge" mentality of our age, not shirking our responsibility to think clearly about ultimate issues. Tolerance has been subtly redefined, altered from tolerance of persons to tolerance of ideas, and for the most part the Christian church has bought into this misguided thinking. But best wishes do not alter reality. Jesus proclaimed a narrow road, and we should not doubt God's justice in judging the world. God has the prerogative to save whom he will. No Scripture indicates that the unevangelized end up in heaven.

## Questions

In the fifth section we considered near-death experiences, concluding that the evidence is mixed. Some anecdotes are characterized by exaggeration or fabrication, but others have the ring of truth. Scientific and psychological analysis explains a lot but still leaves some questions unanswered. On the whole, we can agree that such experiences point to a world beyond our present experience. We also discussed a number of other topics related to the afterlife, including reincarnation, limbo, cremation, soul sleep, ghosts, angels, the cloud of witnesses, and the three heavens. In the end, there are two destinations, two destinies—heaven and hell.

## Can I Know Where I'm Headed?

The Bible assures us we can know we are on the right track. "I write these things to you who believe in the name of the Son of God so that you may know that you have eternal life" (1 John 5:13). How can we be sure which destiny is ours? As Peter confessed, "Lord, to whom shall we go? You have the words of eternal life" (John 6:68). Jesus leads in the right way (John 14:5-9). Consider, then, some of his life-giving teachings. We will focus on the Sermon on the Mount (Matthew 5–7) as we conduct this short study.

## Jesus's Plan for Reaching Heaven (or What Kingdom Life Looks Like)

- Strive for the heart and character of Christ (5:3-9).
- Love your enemies (5:43-48).
- Deal with lust (5:28).
- Be a man or woman of integrity (5:33-37).
- Give to the needy and serve others (6:1-4,19-24; see also 25:31-46).
- Pray and fast (6:5-13,16-19).

- Always forgive (6:14-15).
- Resist the temptations of materialism (6:19-21,24-25).
- Stay focused (6:22-24).
- Trust the Lord rather than becoming anxious about daily necessities (6:25-34).
- Seek first his kingdom (God's rule in our lives) and his righteousness (living a holy life) (6:33).

You are likely to live in a highly materialistic society. It is hard for a wealthy person to be saved, according to Jesus (Matthew 19:23). Wealth exerts a tremendous pull on our hearts.

> Do not store up for yourselves treasures on earth, where moths and vermin destroy, and where thieves break in and steal. But store up for yourselves treasures in heaven, where moths and vermin do not destroy, and where thieves do not break in and steal. For where your treasure is, there your heart will be also (Matthew 6:19-21).

If you are like me, you have occasionally fantasized about money. What would I do if I found an attaché case full of hundred-dollar bills (like in the movies). I have never played the lottery, though friends recently bought Mega Millions tickets for themselves and for each of our family members. It was fun letting ourselves go even if we knew the mathematics were against us.

When I was a little boy, I found a $20 bill by the exit from a grocery store. My mother suggested we turn it in. We were glad we did; the cashier who had accidentally dropped it was in tears. This was in the 1960s, when $20 was two days' wages. She was so happy we found it, and we felt good having done the right thing.

A few weeks ago I was in Georgia—not the Georgia where we reside, but the Republic of Georgia in the Caucasus, the part of Asia between the Black Sea and the Caspian Sea, just south of Russia. I was there on a preaching trip, speaking to a retreat for citizens of Armenia, Azerbaijan, and Georgia. As I exited the airport, I saw green on the ground—four banknotes. "Look!" I said to my friend. "There's another one," he noticed. Someone had dropped $500! We looked around, hoping to spy the hapless dropster. The money had clearly just been lost, or the numerous taxi drivers, standing just feet from the bills, would have snatched them up. We thought about talking to the police (not a wise idea). We went to the information desk. We waited in the parking lot for half an hour. No luck.

I know the "health and wealth gospel" people would have looked up and said "Hallelujah—thank you, Jesus!" However, this wasn't the gospel Jesus preached, at least not in Matthew 6. Or in any other part of Matthew. I'm not saying God didn't put the money in my path, but if he did, I think it was more of a test than a reward. I felt a twinge of temptation. ("I've been working hard. It would be no nice to just keep the money.")

Money is often like that.

We took a few days to think (and pray) through the best way to use this unexpected gift. We decided the best thing to do was to share it with the underprivileged (which meant that neither of us was eligible—alas!). What does this have to do with heaven? Everything. It's about our heart and what truly excites and motivates us. If we can't get motivated to spend time with the Lord, read his word, share in fellowship with other believers, and tell the message to those who do not know him, what makes us think we would want to be in heaven? It's all about Christ.

When our treasure is in heaven, we pray, "Our Father…your kingdom come, your will be done, on earth as it is in heaven." Our words will be sincere. Desiring a holy life, we are preparing ourselves for eternity.

You will be there if your heart is there. Where's your heart—above or below (Colossians 3:2)?

## Warnings

Sober subjects, such as heaven and hell, deserve sober treatment. Jesus did not come to the earth to bring us material prosperity. He did not come to make us feel better about ourselves. He came so that we might fulfill the purpose for our very existence—eternal relationship with God. The stakes are so high, it is no wonder he left us with many warnings.

- You have to be a true seeker, or you won't make it (Matthew 7:7). The fact that only a few find (7:14) makes sense if only a few are seeking (6:33).

- If you're "about as good as the next fellow" (making equally minimal efforts to please the Lord), you will not make it. It's a narrow road (7:13).

- If you don't display the fruit of a person living out the truth, your heart is not pure. Others will be able to tell (7:15-20).

- Regardless of how religious you are or how intense the religious experiences you've had, without obedience you won't make it (7:21-23).

- If your life isn't built on the foundation of God's word, this life will not end up well. Expect destruction (7:24-27).

It's not *calling* him Lord that counts, but *making* him Lord (7:21). Really, there's no reason for anyone reading this book not to make it. All we need to do is to pay attention to God's word, open our hearts, and fix our thoughts on Jesus, as he has already gone before us (Hebrews 2:1; 3:1; 4:12; 6:19-20; 10:19-20; 12:2-3). If Jesus is the author and perfecter of our faith (Hebrews 12:2), whose Spirit lives within us (Romans 8:9-11), then we should never grow weary in doing good (Galatians 6:9). Our treasure is in heaven.

## Beyond Imagination

Heaven is ineffable, beyond words, surpassing our loftiest dreams, hopes, and ideation. Our minds boggle in contemplation of the abode of God—and no surprise, because our minds are stretched to capacity just to take in what he has revealed of himself in nature and in his word.

> Oh, the depth of the riches of the wisdom and
>    knowledge of God!
>    How unsearchable his judgments,
>    and his paths beyond tracing out!
> "Who has known the mind of the Lord?
>    Or who has been his counselor?"
> "Who has ever given to God,

that God should repay them?"
For from him and through him and for him are all things.
To him be the glory forever! Amen (Romans 11:33-36).

Heaven is indescribable. To know what we cannot possibly know—
that's a paradox.

We cannot capture it in words, but the Bible assures us that heaven
is our destiny, for eternal life is knowing Him (John 17:3).

# Appendix A

# Imagery in Isaiah

This appendix is a supplement to the treatment of Isaiah's figurative language in chapter 3. The list is not comprehensive, nor does it deal with the messianic texts (the prophecies of the Christ). The aim is to illustrate Isaiah's artistry more than to systematize his theology. Note especially how much of the imagery is picked up in Revelation.

1. *Two cities* are depicted, one unrighteous and one holy (1:21–2:5). One day, Zion (Jerusalem) will be redeemed with justice (1:27; 26:1-2). The new Jerusalem will be adorned with jewels (54:11-17), its gates left open (60:11), enjoying both security and prosperous commerce. *Imagery in Revelation*: Rome is pictured as the great harlot, and Jerusalem as the Holy City (chapters 17 and 21).

2. *Gentile nations* are accountable to God. There are two outcomes. First, the Gentiles may be humbled in judgment. A raging fire will punish Assyria; Topheth (Gehenna, or hell, the place of burning) has been prepared for its king (30:33). Insentient corpses will be consumed by worms and fire (34:3; 66:24). The idea of the wicked being tortured by fire and worms does not make its appearance until the apocryphal book of Judith, six centuries later, and it is far from obvious that Jesus's references to Isaiah 66:24 are to be understood in this later sense.

A second outcome for the Gentiles is also envisioned. They may become humble, streaming to Zion to learn about its God (2:2; 11:10; 60:3; 61:11; 62:2; 66:12). This prophecy of their conversion was fulfilled at Pentecost (Acts 2:5) and the Gentile mission (Isaiah 42:6; 49:6; 51:4; Acts 13:47). *Imagery in Revelation*: God judges Rome and all those who were under her spell (chapters 17–19).

3. *Elements of ancient mythology* are recycled. Israel's deliverance

is portrayed through the image of the slaying of Leviathan (27:1; see also Genesis 3:15; Romans 16:20; Revelation 12:9) or Rahab (51:9; see also Job 9:13; 26:12; Psalm 89:10). Borrowing pagan motifs and turning them on their heads hardly validates them. Rather, the new twist "demythologizes" the idolaters' faith and shows who is the true god. *Imagery in Revelation*: The primordial dragon appears in chapters 12, 13, 16, and 20.

4. *God comes* in judgment and vindication of the saints. For example, in 19:1 the Lord comes on the clouds of heaven (also Psalm 68:33)— not to bring the world to an end, but to bring the *Egyptians'* world to an end. The Lord comes in the fire of judgment (66:15). Other typical verses on God's coming may be found in Deuteronomy 33:26 and Micah 1:3. At the end of the book, we are still in Israel. The closing scene of Isaiah does not, strictly speaking, prophesy the end of history. Those slaughtered were judged for not keeping kosher (65:4; 66:17). It would be hard to apply this directly to the last judgment (the end of the world). Would people really miss heaven for enjoying barbecue or shrimp (Mark 7:19; 1 Timothy 4:3)? The passage makes much better sense in the context of Israelite history. *Imagery in Revelation*: Jesus is coming soon in 1:7; 3:11; 22:7,12,20.

5. *Blessing and punishment* are relayed in cosmic terms. Isaiah 30:18-26 looks ahead to an era of grace. Notice especially 30:26: "The moon will shine like the sun, and the sunlight will be seven times brighter, like the light of seven full days, when the LORD binds up the bruises of his people and heals the wounds he inflicted." If this were literally true, it would be no blessing at all. If the sun were septupled in intensity, we would be cooked. The heavens are rent (64:1) and vanish like smoke (51:6), and the earth wears out like a garment; yet Israel is a light to the nations (51:4). Israel will possess the land or earth (it's the same word in Hebrew) *forever*. As we saw in chapter 2, "forever" language is sometimes temporary. Israel eventually lost her land (Matthew 21:43; 24:1-35). Those who interpret Isaiah 60:21 as promising that Israel will possess the land forever seem not to appreciate the Semitic sense of *'olam*. They are inconsistent when they interpret *forever* literally in Isaiah 34:17 but not in verse 10 (else Edom would still be on fire).[1] Be sure to read 60:19-20. If we were to take these verses as prose, we would have

a contradiction: The sun never sets (verse 20), but there is no more sun (verse 19). With literary sensitivity, however, we realize that these are just two ways of communicating the same thing: The Lord will shine on his people. *Imagery in Revelation*: Thunder, lightning, earthquakes, falling stars, and the like appear throughout.

6. *Rising smoke.* This is an image of judgment (9:18), harking back to the punishment of Sodom (Genesis 19:28). When Edom is called to account for her sins, her punishment is eternal; smoke forever rises from her burning ruins (34:10). This, of course, is figurative. As one who has visited this part of the world many times, I can assure you that Edom is no longer smoldering. *Imagery in Revelation*: Smoke represents judgment in 14:11; 18:18; 19:3.

7. *Return from exile.* Judah's exile lasted from 605 to 536 BC. Israel's return is depicted as a second exodus—a highway in the wilderness (10:20-21; 11:15-16; 35:8). Israel will return from exile in sight of nations (66:19-20), a reversal of fortune anticipating the fall of Rome and vindication of the church. *Imagery in Revelation*: God's people are to come out of "Babylon," or Rome (18:4; see 17:18).

8. *A new world.* A new state of affairs follows God's expected intervention in history. The world of God's enemies is dismantled, and the world of God's people is renovated. A rich banquet is provided on the day of the LORD, with no death, tears, or sorrow (25:6-8; 51:11; 65:16,19). Israel returns to her land, and her borders are enlarged. The widespread claim that Israel will return to her land (based on such verses as Psalm 89:4; Isaiah 9:7; 61:7) fails to let Scripture interpret Scripture.[2] Amos 9:11-12 is qualified in Acts 15:16. The early church saw the fulfillment of Isaiah's vision in the Messiah and in the new covenant. Never did they speak of a modern state of Israel returning to her land.[3] This new world (65:17-25) is a delightful city. Exaggerated longevities (verse 20) are signs of God's extreme blessing, yet there is still death, so like 30:26, these are figurative, not literal. The wolf lies down with the lamb (65:25)—an image of peace, not a bizarre prediction of herbivorous canines.[4] *Imagery in Revelation*: The new heaven and earth is introduced in 21:1.

9. *The image of resurrection.* This appears in 26:19. In Isaiah's imagery, the resurrection includes more than just people's bodies; the entire

world is resurrected. The return from exile is pictured in cosmic terms (27:12-13). "A whole new world" will be created through Cyrus, the Persian king who is God's anointed agent, or Messiah (44:22–45:13). The "new heavens and new earth" (65:17) are set squarely in the context of Judaism (66:22-23). This is therefore not referring to the end of the world. *Imagery in Revelation*: The two witnesses come to life in 11:11, and 20:5-6 pictures the general resurrection.

*10. Marriage.* Instead of desertion, Israel and her God enjoy matrimony (62:4). Paul teaches on the groom-bride relationship between Christ and the church (Ephesians 5:22-33). The faith of Israel is relational. God desires not rule-keeping, but our hearts. *Imagery in Revelation*: The marriage of the Lamb is described in 19:7,9.

There are of course many other highly colorful and symbolic metaphors. As I scanned Isaiah for this part of the book, I was struck by 10:18; 11:4; 48:18; 51:3; 58:10; 59:10; 62:12; 64:6-7 (regarding clean garments, compare Revelation 3:4-5,18; 4:4; 16:15; 19:8).

# Appendix B

# Analysis of Alcorn

When I read Alcorn's 2004 bestseller *Heaven*, I expected to learn. I already knew that we agreed on some key points—Christian tradition needs to be reevaluated, there is an intermediate place of the dead, and the resurrection is physical. And yet the book fell short of expectations. Alcorn makes several thought-provoking points in interesting and sometimes compelling ways, but his methodology is inconsistent.

The numbers in parentheses below refer to pages in Alcorn's book.

## Inconsistent Literalization

About Revelation 5:6, Alcorn writes (as we have noted previously) "When Jesus is described as a lamb with seven eyes, it contradicts known facts to take that literally. But would it contradict known facts to believe that on the New Earth there will be a great city with streets of gold and gates made of pearls (Revelation 21:21), and with trees and a river (22:1-2)?" (472). But this approach fails to correctly read the genre of apocalypse and encourages speculation. The streets *are* gold, and the Lamb *does* have seven eyes—just not literally. Common sense is simply not enough if we are going to correctly interpret apocalyptic literature, and it has a way of breeding uncontrolled conjecture. Alcorn seems to be saying, "Why *not* take all the descriptions of heaven and the new earth literally?" If we are going to do so, we must be consistent. We can't just ignore the Scriptures that militate against our view.

He takes the image of the souls of martyrs under the altar (6:9) literally, concluding there are already people in heaven. But what about the earthquake of 6:12-13, so forceful that it causes the stars to fall to earth? The imagery works very effectively with ancient cosmology, but no earthquake could ever knock a star out of its place.

Isaiah's new earth has a new temple (Isaiah 44:28; 56:5; 60:7; 64:11; 66:6,20), whereas Revelation's does not (21:22). These details don't match, but the author sweeps the problem aside (97).

He claims there will be nations in heaven (21:24). What about 22:15—the dogs? Like the nations, they are outside the holy city. It is clear from context that John the Revelator is referring to people. If one is to take Revelation at face value, then there are *unsaved* persons outside the Holy City on the new earth. This poses a serious threat to Alcorn's position and shows the impossibility of sustaining his literalistic approach.

The books of Revelation 20:12 are literal books (324). What about 20:10,14? Was the false prophet (which represents idolatrous emperor worship) literally thrown into the lake of fire? How does that work? And how about death and Hades? In what sense were they cast into hell, especially considering that Hades held the souls of the righteous (20:13)? Was Hades being punished?

### Misinterpretation of the Apocalyptic Genre

*Revelation 21:2.* Alcorn affirms the present heaven is "up there," but the new heaven will be "down here." He admits the new heaven will come down out of the present heaven. But how can it be heaven if it came *from* heaven?

*Revelation 21:24.* Alcorn states repeatedly that there will be nations in heaven. This is highly problematic. Which nations does he have in mind? Nations are constantly evolving, dividing, recombining, and the like, much like the biological world itself. What is the definition of a nation? At which time period? The whole idea that there are nations (Gentiles, or pagans) at all outside the Holy City after the judgment day is an amazing leap.

*Revelation 6:9-11.* This is the image of the martyrs crying out in heaven. To extract from this picture the doctrine that dead humans are already in heaven not only contradicts the Scriptures (John 3:13; Acts 2:34) but also violates the rules of interpretation of metaphorical—and especially apocalyptic—language: Expect everything to be figurative. If Revelation is meant to tell us about heaven, there is no satisfying explanation for the presence of Gentile nations or "dogs" in heaven (21:24; 22:15). If these need not be literal, then why must the souls under the altar?

*Revelation 2:7.* "The tree of life's presence in the new Jerusalem establishes that elements of Eden, as physical as the original, will again be part of the human experience…that Heaven too has physical properties and is capable of containing physical objects" (57). Our author has gone far beyond the clear meaning of the text. There is a sort of physicality to our resurrection bodies and to heaven itself, but this hardly follows from the metaphors of Revelation.

*Isaiah 60:7.* In connection with the nations, in his commentary on Isaiah 60, Alcorn admits there is a problem with verse 7—why do we see animal sacrifices in heaven? But he dodges the problem passage entirely, offering no explanation.

*Revelation 21:16.* His literalistic Holy City is a cube 1400 miles in each direction. Yet the vision is not intended to satisfy a surveyor. Rather, it reminds us of the cube-shaped Holy of Holies in the temple of the old covenant, revealing that once again God will dwell with man in a breathtaking and phenomenal way.

*Isaiah 25:6-7.* Alcorn believes this refers to the new earth, where we will be vegetarians because animals no longer die (13). He writes, "So how could there be meat without animal death? Many people—I'm not one of them—eat meat substitutes and prefer the taste to real meat. How hard would it be for God to create meat substitutes that do qualify as meat in every sense of taste and texture, without coming from dead animals?" (307). What distorted exegetical gymnastics, all to uphold a literalist approach to Scripture. Similarly, with regard to Ezekiel 47:9-10, Alcorn takes the prophecies about animals in the millennium or in the new earth literally, so he finds it difficult to believe that anyone would be permitted to eat fish. "Either this is catch-and-release, purely for sport, or it suggests fish will still be eaten" (307).

## Pseudoscience

Our author suggests that the second law of thermodynamics (the tendency of systems to increase in entropy) came as a result of the fall of man (128). And yet entropy is integral to the existence of the very systems that make life possible in the first place. This is a common creationist argument, recycled even though it has long been discredited. Realizing he's in trouble, he throws us a footnote: "Some people argue that walking, breathing, digestion, and solar heating of the earth all involve the law of entropy. When I speak of that law, however, I mean specifically the parts related to death, decay, and the deterioration of things, especially living beings, as a departure from their ideal created state" (129). But this is a false distinction. In short, in the biological world, death is part of life.

"Some current earthly phenomena may not occur on the New Earth, including earthquakes, floods, hurricanes, and volcanoes" (259). Does he not know that all of these phenomena are necessary for the existence of life on planet earth? He continues, "These may be aberrations due to the Curse. God's Kingdom is described as one 'that cannot be shaken' (Hebrews 12:28)." This passage teaches us there will be no earthquakes in the kingdom of God? The passage in Hebrews is not talking about earthquakes at all!

Referring to the original oceans, which Alcorn thinks must have been potable, he writes, "God's originally created seas surely wouldn't have poisoned people if they drank from them. It seems that the Curse resulted in the contamination of the oceans" (274). This is wrong not only scientifically but also biblically. Even before the curse there was at least one thing in the garden that could hurt man: the tree of knowledge. To assume that God would not create anything that could hurt us is unwarranted.

### Theological Confusion

Alcorn follows the original NIV translation of Luke 16:23 (corrected in the 2011 edition), mistakenly rendering Hades (the intermediate place of the dead) as hell.

The term "intermediate heaven" is misleading because as we have seen, the Bible nowhere has anyone in heaven yet (John 3:13; Acts 2:34).

Romans 5:12 is interpreted to refer to physical death. It seems more probable that Paul means spiritual death, especially because biological life, on the basis of all scientific evidence, has always depended on death (such as cell death, the death of the microbes living inside us, the food chain, and so on). That is, when we sin, we die (Ephesians 2:1-3), and in Christ we come to life. Otherwise, consistency would demand that Christians be immortal in this life—be exempt from death!

"Scripture teaches that we're conceived lost and remain lost until we become saved" (354). In which passage? The poetic Psalm 51:5? The doctrine of original sin was invented in the late fourth century.

"God determined the exact time and places you would live" (357). Alcorn has misread Acts 17:26, relying on the original NIV mistranslation (corrected in the 2011 edition), which is hyper-Calvinist. Had he consulted other versions or if he read Greek, he would know that this is not what the text says at all.

"Christians should be involved in the political process" (223). But if this is so, why did Jesus avoid politics? (See, for example, John 6:15.) The early church avoided politics altogether. Why is that? Were they disobeying God's word?

The fourth kingdom of Daniel 2 is taken to refer to the end of the world, not to the kingdom of God established during the days of the Roman Empire, as the text has it. And yet the antichrist is to arise from the Roman kingdom (229). Where in the Bible is this (explicitly) stated?

Our author also thinks that the term "all flesh" in Luke 3:6 (NASB) includes animals (398). However, the phrase *pasa sarx* in the New Testament refers to humans and is usually a technical term meaning "both Jews and Gentiles" (Matthew 24:22; Mark 13:20; Romans 3:20; 1 Corinthians 1:29; Galatians 2:16; 1 Peter 1:24). Maybe he is right and we will see our pets in heaven, but he has hardly proven the idea!

In speaking of unfulfilled promises (149), Alcorn seems not to appreciate that God has already fulfilled his promises to Abraham in Genesis 12:2-3. The land promise was fulfilled (Joshua 21:43), as was the nation promise (Exodus 19:6; Isaiah 1:4). The spiritual promise has also been fulfilled through Christ and the true seed of Abraham (Galatians 3:8-9).

"The Biblical ideal is for every man to own property—a place where he can have dominion and rule under God" (210). This is tied in to his idea that heaven includes real estate on earth. But if this is so, why did Adam and Eve originally serve only as stewards in the garden? And what about Leviticus 25:23? Perhaps the Lord will give us land or even worlds to govern, as Alcorn claims, but why can't we admit the Scriptures simply aren't definitive on the matter?

## Speculation

By literalizing details in Isaiah and Revelation—highly symbolic passages with specific historical contexts—Alcorn finds meat substitutes and catch-and-release fishing in the new earth. He thinks our eyes might function as telescopes and microscopes. He posits that on the new earth, Jesus Christ may appear in multiple bodies simultaneously in order to have simultaneous fellowship with many people in different parts of heaven. Extinct animals will probably return to life. *Jurassic Park*, move over! Certainly we will see our pets in heaven, and don't be surprised if there are talking animals too (307, 283, 189, 399-405).

## Disregard for Context

Alcorn ignores the religious (Jewish) and historical context of Isaiah, whose promises were fulfilled in the return from exile. For example, Isaiah 60:7 has animal sacrifices in heaven. Alcorn admits the problem but doesn't deal with it. The entire book of Revelation applies most directly to the persecuted church during the time of the Roman Empire. We may extrapolate some of its principles, but we cannot lift passages from their context and then reinterpret them according to our enlightened common sense.

## Sentimentality

Alcorn asserts that according to 1 Corinthians 3:12-15, *anything* our hands have ever made will be redeemed. But Paul is clearly speaking about church building. Then Psalm 90:17 suggests that whatever our hands have made will be recovered in heaven. Nothing good will ever be truly lost, whether our children's kindergarten finger paintings or the works of the great masters. Everything worthwhile will reappear! The idea has great sentimental appeal, and there are plenty of things I wish I could receive back (including documents, toys, and pets), but nothing in Scripture supports it.

## Conclusion

Although he is right to emphasize that at the resurrection we will have transformed bodies (as 1 Corinthians 15 clearly states), much of what he has written about heaven in this book—its location, activities, and its nature—is unpersuasive. The handling of biblical texts is inconsistent.

I'm sure *Heaven* has encouraged many people all over the world, and not only the many Christian celebrities who have endorsed it. Yet Alcorn's interpretive method is cause for concern. As Paul wrote, "Examine everything carefully" (1 Thessalonians 5:21 NASB).

# Notes

## Chapter 1: A Fresh Look

1. If you are not sure that the Bible is God's message for us, you might appreciate my book *Compelling Evidence for God and the Bible: Finding Truth in an Age of Doubt* (Eugene: Harvest House, 2010). This work lays out the reasons for faith. And if you're one of the persons intrigued by vampire fever, visit www.jacobypremium.com and listen in.

## Chapter 2: The Lens of Eternity

1. William G.T. Shedd, *The Doctrine of Endless Punishment: Its Historical, Biblical and Rational Defense* (New York: Charles Scribner's Sons, 1886), 87.

2. William Crockett et al., *Four Views on Hell* (Grand Rapids: Zondervan, 1996), 26.

3. Bruce Milne, *The Message of Heaven and Hell: Grace and Destiny* (Downers Grove: InterVarsity, 2002), 151. Thoughtful theologians like Peter Kreeft and Ronald Tacelli agree that eternity doesn't mean endless time. See their *Handbook of Christian Apologetics: Hundreds of Answers to Crucial Questions* (Downers Grove: InterVarsity Press, 1994), 300, 307.

4. William F. Arndt and F. Wilbur Gingrich, *A Greek-English Lexicon of the New Testament and Other Early Christian Literature* (Chicago: University of Chicago Press, 1979), 27-28. This understanding is also supported in the more popular-level *Vine's Complete Expository Dictionary of Old and New Testament Words* (Nashville: Thomas Nelson, 1984), 72-73.

5. The Old Testament was written in Hebrew (99 percent) and Aramaic (1 percent), yet these Semitic languages were spoken by fewer and fewer Jews as the first millennium BC drew to a close. Therefore the Jewish scholars of Alexandria translated the Scriptures into Greek. The result, called the Septuagint, became the Bible for most Jews and the early church. The *'olam/ aion* equivalence is well known, and my work may be easily verified. (The Latin word *septuaginta* means "70," so the Septuagint is therefore often noted as LXX. According to tradition, 70 translators were involved.)

6. F. LaGard Smith, *After Life: A Glimpse of Eternity Beyond Death's Door* (Nashville: Cotswold Publishing, 2003), 15. Emphasis original. Smith adds, "To be eternal is to have a lasting nature. To have the kind of qualities which endure despite the passing of time (if, in fact, there is any time at all) (162).

7. Dallas Willard, *Knowing Christ Today: Why We Can Trust Spiritual Knowledge* (New York: HarperOne, 2009), 139.

8. Among the 60 or so volumes I read as I researched this book, Ron Rhodes' *The Wonder of Heaven: A Biblical Tour of Our Eternal Home* (Eugene: Harvest House, 2009, p. 169) is typical. Many Christian thinkers are questioning the immortality of the soul, though a sizable number still retain the belief.

9. The figure was near 80 percent in 2003 (www.barna.org/barna-update/article/5-barna -update/128-americans-describe-their-views-about-life-after-death). A 2001 *Newsweek* poll puts the new figure around 70 percent (www.prabhupadanugas.eu/?p=18640). Americans tend to believe not only that they will always be around but also that they are heaven-bound. Are we a nation of optimists?

10. See Bryan W. Ball, "The immortality of the soul: Could Christianity survive without it? (Part 2 of 2)," *Ministry*, May 2011. www.ministrymagazine.org/archive/2011/05/the-immortality-of-the-soul.

11. For example, Luke 18:18-30; Romans 2:7; 6:23; Titus 1:2.

12. Tertullian, *On the Resurrection of the Flesh*, 3.

13. According to first-century Jewish historian Josephus, the Essenes (second century BC–first century AD) believed in the immortality of the soul (Josephus, Wars of the Jews 2:154-55). So here was one Jewish sect more or less contemporary with early Christianity that may have anticipated the church's acceptance of the Platonic idea by a century.

    As journalist and author Lisa Miller notes, in 1824, Reform Judaism altered Maimonides' thirteenth principle from physical resurrection to the immortality of the soul (*Heaven: Our Enduring Fascination with the Afterlife* [New York: Harper Perennial, 2010], 138-39).

14. Stanley J. Grenz, *Theology for the Community of God* (Grand Rapids: Eerdmans, 1994), 585.

15. In 1513 Pope Leo X issued a papal bull (*Apostolici regimis*) stating, "We do condemn and reprobate all who assert that the intelligent soul is mortal...all who adhere to the like erroneous assertions shall be shunned and punished as heretics." In 1520 Martin Luther published a defense of 41 of his propositions, in which he described the pope's insistence on the immortality of the soul as one of many "monstrosities in the Roman dunghill of decretals" (twenty-seventh proposition).

16. Grenz, *Theology for the Community of God*, 638.

17. The development has antecedents around 500 BC. Some Greeks began to hope in the survival of the individual soul apart from the body. This took the Greeks in a different direction from Hebrew thought, where the body was considered to be good (not merely a prison house for the soul) and in fact essential to the resurrection of the dead.

18. Scholars of the 1900s who reject the immortality of the soul are numerous, including persons of such stature as Oscar Cullmann (1902–1999). Oscar Cullmann, *Immortality of the Soul or Resurrection from the Dead?* (London: Epworth, 1958). Reformed scholars Ridderbos and Hoekema also disagree with Calvin on the immortality of soul. Widely read reference works such as *The IVP Bible Background Commentary* emphasize that only God is immortal (1 Timothy 6:16). John H. Walton, Victor H. Matthews, and Mark W. Chavalas in the camp, such as Helmut Thielicke, Simon Tugwell, and Murray Harris (*The IVP Bible Background Commentary: Old Testament* [Downers Grove: InterVarsity, 2000], 148). New Testament evangelical giant N.T. Wright is one of the most prominent living scholars to challenge the Greek concept (*Surprised by Hope* [New York: HarperOne, 2008], 28, 160-61). Others include Philip Edgcumbe Hughes, *The True Image* (Grand Rapids: Eerdmans, 1989), 402-7; Stephen Travis, *I Believe in the Second Coming of Jesus* (Grand Rapids: Eerdmans, 1982), 199; John Wenham, *The Goodness of God* (Downers Grove: InterVarsity, 1974), 34-31; John Stott and David L. Edwards, *Evangelical Essentials: A Liberal-Evangelical Dialogue* (Downers Grove: InterVarsity, 1988), 314-20; Crockett et al., *Four Views on Hell*, 135-66. Kenneth D. Boa and Robert M. Bowman Jr., *Sense and Nonsense about Heaven and Hell* ([Grand Rapids: Zondervan, 2007], 44-54) is representative of the newer thinking among popular authors, who agree that the soul is not immortal.

19. Rodney J. Scott and Raymond E. Phinney Jr., "Relating Body and Soul: Insights from Development and Neurobiology," in *Perspectives on Science and Christian Faith* (The Journal of the American Scientific Affiliation) 62, no. 2 (June 2012): 90-107.

20. Malcolm Jeeves, "Neuroscience, Evolutionary Psychology, and the Image of God," *Perspectives on Science and Christian Faith* 57, no. 3 (2005): 170-86.

21. Smith, *After Life*, 163.

## Chapter 3: Lenses of Interpretation, Part 1

1. Here are several books that will help you to become a better interpreter:

   - Mortimer J. Adler & Charles Van Doren, *How to Read a Book: The Classic Guide to Intelligent Reading* (New York: Touchstone, 1972). This volume will prove far more helpful than we would ever guess.

   - Gordon Fee & Douglas Stuart, *How to Read the Bible for All Its Worth*, 3rd ed. (Grand Rapids: Zondervan, 2003).

   - Gordon Fee & Douglas Stuart, *How to Read the Bible Book by Book: A Guided Tour* (Grand Rapids: Zondervan, 2002).

   - J.I. Packer, *God Has Spoken* (London, 1979). Rightly emphasizes the authority of God's word. Golden! The standard volume on Bible interpretation.

   - David Winter, *But This I Can Believe* (London: Hodder & Stoughton, 1980). Helps us approach the Bible realistically and logically, thereby bringing our expectations into line with the nature of the biblical text.

2. I. Howard Marshall, *Biblical Inspiration* (London: Hodder & Stoughton, 1982), 84.

3. For the big picture of the Bible, perhaps you will benefit from my *A Quick Overview of the Bible: Understanding How All the Pieces Fit Together* (Eugene: Harvest House, 2012).

4. The three most quoted Old Testament books, in order, are Psalms, Isaiah, and Deuteronomy.

5. Edom's fall is announced in many prophetic works, including the short book of Obadiah.

6. Prophecies alternate from blessing to woe and may take sudden leaps into the future, often without warning.

## Chapter 4: Lenses of Interpretation, Part 2

1. Gerhard Kittel and Gerhard Friedrich, *Theological Dictionary of the New Testament*, vol. 5 (Grand Rapids: Eerdmans, 1967), 769, note 37.

2. Karel Hanhart, "The Intermediate State in the New Testament" (doctoral dissertation, University of Amsterdam, 1966), 192-93.

3. Joachim Jeremias, *The Parables of Jesus*, trans. S.H. Hook (London: SCM, 1963), 186.

4. N.T. Wright, *Christian Origins and the Question of God*, vol. 2, *Jesus and the Victory of God* (London: SPCK, 1996), 255.

5. Stanley J. Grenz, *Theology for the Community of God* (Grand Rapids: Eerdmans, 1994), 593.

6. N.T. Wright, *Surprised by Hope* (New York: HarperOne, 2008), 48.

7. His name is Dives in the older versions—Latin for "rich."

8. Allegorical interpretation is also well illustrated in the medieval period.

9. See 4 Maccabees 13:17. In Apocalypse of Zephaniah 11:1-2 (first century BC–first century AD), Abraham acted as intercessor for those in the fiery part of Hades. Hades was typically thought of as having two sections: an upper, light, blessed part, and a lower, dark, dolorous part.

10. David W. Bercot, ed., *A Dictionary of Early Christian Beliefs* (Peabody: Hendrickson, 1998), 191-97.

11. Regarding Hades in Luke 16 interpreted as hell, see Timothy Keller, *The Reason for God: Belief in an Age of Skepticism* (New York: Riverhead Books, 2008), 80; William G. T. Shedd, *The Doctrine of Endless Punishment: Its Historical, Biblical and Rational Defense* (New York: Charles

Scribner's Sons, 1886), iv, 24, 29; Michael E. Wittmer, *Christ Alone: An Evangelical Response to Rob Bell's Love Wins* (Grand Rapids: Edenridge Press, 2011), 25, 27-29; James L. Garlow and Keith Wall, *Heaven and the Afterlife* (Minneapolis: Bethany House, 2009), 139; Timothy J. Demy and Thomas Ice, *Answers to Common Questions About Heaven & Eternity* (Grand Rapids: Kregel, 2011), 53; Bill Wiese, *23 Minutes in Hell* (Lake Mary: Charisma House, 2006), 2, 96, 115; Randy Alcorn, *Heaven* (Carol Stream: Tyndale House, 2004), 63; Sharon L. Baker, *Razing Hell: Rethinking Everything You've Been Taught About God's Wrath and Judgment* (Louisville: Westminster John Knox Press, 2010), 130; Max Lucado, *When Christ Comes* (Nashville: Thomas Nelson, 1999), 119-20. Regarding the angelic escort, see Paul Enns, *Heaven Revealed* (Chicago: Moody Press, 2011), 40.

12. As in his interaction with the Sadducees in Matthew 22:23-32.

13. Robert A. Morey, *Death and Afterlife* (Minneapolis: Bethany, 1984), 30-31, 84-85.

14. Alan F. Johnson and Robert E. Webber, *What Christians Believe: A Biblical and Historical Summary* (Grand Rapids: Zondervan, 1989), 66.

15. Part of the following section has been adapted from chapter 22 of my book *A Quick Overview of the Bible: Understanding How All the Pieces Fit Together* (Eugene: Harvest House, 2012).

16. *Apocalypse* derives from the Greek *apokalypsis*, just as *Revelation* comes from the Latin *revelatio*.

17. Jim McGuiggan, *The Book of Revelation* (Dallas: Star Bible Publications, 1976), 14.

18. Here is a more complete list. Jewish apocalypse: 1 Enoch, Testaments of the 12 Patriarchs, Psalms of Solomon, Assumption of Moses, Apocalypse of Baruch, 4 Ezra, Apocalypse of Abraham, Prayer of Joseph, Book of Eldad and Modad, Apocalypse of Elijah, 2 Enoch, Oracles of Hystapses, Testament of Job, Testament of the Three Patriarchs, and Sibylline Oracles. Christian apocalypse: Apocalypse of Peter, Testament of Hezekiah, Testament of Abraham, Vision of Isaiah, Shepherd of Hermas, 5 Ezra, 6 Ezra, Apocalypse of Paul, Apocalypse of John, Apocalypse of the Virgin, Apocalypse of Sedrach, Apocalypse of Daniel, and Revelation of Bartholomew.

19. Many steady Bible readers understand Eden to be a literal place and take many of the details in the account of Adam and Eve as literally as possible. Yet when it comes to paradise at the other end of the Bible (Revelation 21–22), most take the details as symbolic. Why not the other way around? Why not take Revelation as literal and (early) Genesis as symbolic, as Ezekiel 28:13 does? Notice that in Ezekiel 28:13, which directly addresses the King of Tyre, the primordial Eden is described as a mountain. The apostle John fuses Genesis 2 with the imagery of Ezekiel 47 in the final chapters of the Apocalypse. In short, advocates of literalism tend to gloss over its difficulties.

20. Some images serve only as flourishes for dramatic effect (Revelation 6:12-14; 9:7-11).

21. Hans Lilje, *The Last Book of the Bible*, trans. Olive Wyon (Philadelphia: Muhlenberg, 1957), 246, 256.

22. Eugene H. Peterson, *The Contemplative Pastor* (Grand Rapids: Eerdmans, 1993), 41.

23. Bruce Metzger, *Breaking the Code: Understanding the Book of Revelation* (Nashville: Abingdon, 1993), 11.

24. Robert H. Mounce, *The Book of Revelation*, in *The New International Commentary on the New Testament* (Grand Rapids: Eerdmans, 1977), 12.

25. Craig S. Keener, *The IVP Bible Background Commentary: New Testament* (Downers Grove: InterVarsity Press, 1993), 813.

26. Wright, *Surprised by Hope*, 299.

27. Richard Bauckham, *The Climax of Prophecy* (Edinburgh: T&R Clark, 1999), 229.

28. Wayne Martindale, *C.S. Lewis on Heaven and Hell: Beyond the Shadowlands* (Wheaton: Crossway, 2005), 43.

29. Kenneth D. Boa and Robert M. Bowman Jr., *Sense and Nonsense about Heaven and Hell* (Grand Rapids: Zondervan, 2007), 155.

30. Ibid., 170.

31. F. LaGard Smith, *After Life: A Glimpse of Eternity Beyond Death's Door* (Nashville: Cotswold Publishing, 2003), 248.

32. Smith, *After Life*, 180.

33. McGuiggan, *The Book of Revelation*, 300.

34. Enns (*Heaven Revealed*, 84) is one of many. In the twentieth century, the grandfather of end-times literalists was Hal Lindsey. Hal Lindsey and Carole C. Carlson, *The Late Great Planet Earth* (Grand Rapids: Zondervan, 1970).

35. Keener, *The IVP Bible Background Commentary*, 759.

36. Enns, *Heaven Revealed*, 104.

37. Ron Rhodes, *The Wonder of Heaven: A Biblical Tour of Our Eternal Home* (Eugene: Harvest House, 2009), 13, 121; Enns, *Heaven Revealed*, 25; Alcorn, *Heaven*, 242.

38. Garlow and Wall, *Heaven and the Afterlife*, 186; see also Randy Alcorn, *Heaven*, 472.

**Chapter 5: The Good Place**

1. Jean-Paul Sartre, *No Exit*. Those are Garcin's final words.

2. If we take the description of hell in Lewis's *The Great Divorce* as reality, then hell is the place where a relationship with God and believers will not be possible—and the relationships in hell on earth will continue: distrust and envy of everyone, always searching for ways to use other people to get personal pleasure, gossiping and criticizing, stealing from the defenseless, being angry all the time, having the closest relationships with your addiction of choice, and always thinking of yourself first in every situation. In fact, those who love these attitudes and relationships will find hell very appealing.

3. Kenneth D. Boa and Robert M. Bowman Jr., *Sense and Nonsense about Heaven and Hell* (Grand Rapids: Zondervan, 2007), 168-69.

4. D.L. Moody, *Heaven Awaits* (New Kensington: Whitaker House, 1982), 21. Originally published 1894.

5. A similar line of thinking is found in Edwin A. Abbot, *Flatland* (Oxford: Blackwell, 1875).

6. C.S. Lewis, *Miracles* (London: Fontana, 1960), 111, 115. Jim McGuiggan develops Lewis's idea further at www.jimmcguiggan.com/reflections3.asp?status=John&id=1317.

7. For a great read on Lewis's thinking about the afterlife, see Wayne Martindale, *C.S. Lewis on Heaven and Hell: Beyond the Shadowlands* (Wheaton: Crossway, 2005).

8. Consider the following portion of the Qur'an: "The true servants of Allah will be well provided for, feasting on fruit, and honored in gardens of delight. Reclining face to face upon soft couches, they shall be served with a goblet filled at a gushing fountain…delightful to those who drink it… They shall sit with bashful, dark-eyed virgins, as chaste as the sheltered eggs of ostriches" (Surah 37). Similarly, Surah 78:29 offers "high-bosomed maidens, whom neither man nor jinnee will have touched before." This is nothing more than a natural, fleshly way of envisioning heaven, especially attractive if you are a man. The Qur'an calls paradise a "band of brothers" (Surah 15:47). "Eat and drink till your heart's content," Surah 69 says of the oasis of paradise.

9. Alice K. Turner, *The History of Hell* (New York: Harcourt & Brace, 1993), 106.

10. See, for example, Deuteronomy 9:3; Isaiah 47:14; Ezekiel 38:22.

11. Stanley J. Grenz, *Theology for the Community of God* (Grand Rapids: Eerdmans, 1994), 578.

12. The number of authors who subscribe to this view is too large to enumerate. See E.M. Bounds, *A Place Called Heaven* (New Kensington: Whitaker House, 2003), 12.

13. One of the most popular has been Hal Lindsey and Carole C. Carlson, *The Late Great Planet Earth* (Grand Rapids: Zondervan, 1970).

14. For some helpful material on the historical context of Revelation, from slightly different perspectives, see Gordon Ferguson, *Mine Eyes Have Seen the Glory* (Billerica: Discipleship Publications International, 1996); and Jim McGuiggan, *The Book of Revelation* (Lubbock: Star Publishing, 1978). For a totally different perspective—the judgments of the Apocalypse are all fulfilled in the destruction of Jerusalem in AD 70—see Max R. King, *The Spirit of Prophecy* (Warren: King, 1971).

15. Martindale, *C.S. Lewis on Heaven and Hell*, 27.

16. Nathan Bierma, *Bringing Heaven Down to Earth* (Phillipsburg: Presbyterian & Reformed, 2005), n.p.

17. Cited in Joe Beam and Lee Wilson, *The True Heaven: Not What You Thought, Better Than You Expected* (Abilene: Leafwood, 2010) 12.

18. C.S. Lewis, *Mere Christianity* (Glasgow: Collins, 1981), 119.

19. Cited by Lisa Miller, *Heaven: Our Enduring Fascination with the Afterlife* (New York: Harper Perennial, 2010).

20. Moody, *Heaven Awaits*, 39-40, 70, 138, 15; John F. MacArthur, *The Glory of Heaven* (Wheaton: Crossway 1996), 76-77, 129; Bounds, *A Place Called Heaven*, 32, 36, 58, 129; Max Lucado, *When Christ Comes* (Nashville: Thomas Nelson, 1999), 33 (However, Lucado agrees that one comes to heaven via an intermediate state [42]. "And for a season, your soul will be in heaven while your body is in the grave" [51]); J. Oswald Sanders, *Heaven: Better by Far* (Grand Rapids: Discovery House, 1993), 44; Enns, *Heaven Revealed*, 5, 13, 23, 133 (Enns, like several other evangelical writers, speaks of an "intermediate heaven," quoting approvingly Erwin W. Lutzer, *One Minute After You Die* [Chicago: Moody, 1997], 83: "All you will need to do is decide where you would like to be, and you will be there!"); Ron Rhodes, *The Wonder of Heaven: A Biblical Tour of Our Eternal Home* (Eugene: Harvest House, 2009), 11, 25, 114; Mark Cahill, *One Heartbeat Away: Your Journey into Eternity* (Rockwall: BDM, 2005), 250; James L. Garlow and Keith Wall, *Heaven and the Afterlife* (Minneapolis: Bethany House, 2009), 165; Bill Wiese, *23 Minutes in Hell* (Lake Mary: Charisma House, 2006), xiv, 50; Randy Alcorn, *Heaven* (Carol Stream: Tyndale House, 2004), xix. (By the way, Alcorn exaggerates the death rate by about 60 percent.)

21. Is this proleptic? The text is ambiguous. Philippians 3:20 has us registered in heaven when we become Christians, so it is not death that makes us part of the heavenly Jerusalem.

22. This was Tyndale's dying request: "O Lord, open the eyes of the King of England." Just two years later King Henry VIII authorized the Great Bible for the Church of England. It was largely Tyndale's own work. The KJV of 1611 drew heavily on Tyndale's work.

23. Henry Kriete, *Worship the King* (Woburn: DPI, 2000), 192.

### Chapter 6: Heaven on Earth

1. In the first-century Jewish document Testament of Levi, paradise is envisioned as existing on the earth. "He himself [the priestly Messiah] will open the gates of Paradise, take away the sword

which threatened Adam, and give the saints to eat of the tree of life" (Testament of Levi 18:10-11; see also 4 Ezra 8:52).

2. Jim McGuiggan, personal email, June 11, 2012.

3. At www.jimmcguiggan.com, McGuiggan argues that John 14:2-3,23,28-29 cannot refer to heaven. See also Don K. Preston, *We Shall Meet Him in the Air: The Wedding of the King of Kings* (Ardmore: JaDon Management Inc., 2010), n.p.

4. Craig G. Bartholomew and Michael W. Goheen, *The Drama of Scripture* (Grand Rapids: Baker Academic, 2004), 211.

5. Stanley J. Grenz, *Theology for the Community of God* (Grand Rapids: Eerdmans, 1994), 586.

6. N.T. Wright, *Surprised by Hope* (New York: HarperOne, 2008), 128-37.

7. My view is that the popular tribulation view is a modern innovation and a significant departure from apostolic doctrine. Nearly every time tribulation is mentioned in the New Testament, it refers to the trials believers must go through, not exquisite punishments for unbelievers. For more on this, please see my book *Your Bible Questions Answered* (Eugene: Harvest House, 2011), 239-40.

8. Wayne Grudem, *Systematic Theology* (Grand Rapids: Zondervan, 1994), 1160.

9. Of course, "elements" does not refer to hydrogen, helium, lithium, and the other entries in the periodic table. The ancient world had only four elements: earth, air, fire, and water.

10. William F. Arndt and F. Wilbur Gingrich, *A Greek-English Lexicon of the New Testament and Other Early Christian Literature* (Chicago: University of Chicago Press, 1979), 768-69.

11. Anthony Hoekema, *The Bible and the Future* (Grand Rapids: Eerdmans, 1979), 281.

12. Ben Witherington III, *Revelation*, in *The New Cambridge Bible Commentary* (New York: Cambridge University Press, 2003), 254.

13. Bartholomew and Goheen, *The Drama of Scripture*, 211.

14. Tim LaHaye, *Revelation Unveiled* (Grand Rapids: Zondervan, 1996), 154; James L. Garlow and Keith Wall, *Heaven and the Afterlife* (Minneapolis: Bethany House, 2009), 163-64; Kenneth D. Boa and Robert M. Bowman Jr., *Sense and Nonsense about Heaven and Hell* (Grand Rapids: Zondervan, 2007), 26 (tentatively); Tom A. Jones and Steve D. Brown, *The Kingdom of God*, vol. 1 (Nashville: Discipleship Publications International, 2010), 130-39; Paul Enns, *Heaven Revealed* (Chicago: Moody Press, 2011), 107.

15. In Isaiah, the kingdoms to be destroyed include Assyria, Egypt, Babylon, and Edom. In Revelation, the defeated kingdom is the Roman Empire.

16. The thesis is endorsed by Dallas Willard, Rob Bell, Richard J. Foster, Walter Brueggemann, Will Willimon, and many other well-known writers. Ben Witherington III, *The Paul Quest: The Renewed Search for the Jew of Tarsus* (Downers Grove: InterVarsity Press, 1998), 150-51; N.T. Wright, *Surprised by Hope*, 149.

17. Philo—On the Life of Moses 2.65; compare 1 Clement 9:4. Josephus—Antiquities 11.3.9. In ancient Greek the term can refer to restoring the stars in their orbits (so Arndt and Gingrich)—a kind of "reset." It is possible that the regeneration or renewal of Matthew 19:28 refers to a future time, though given the apostles' leadership in the foundational period of the church and their role in connecting Gentile Christianity with the Jewish Christian center, a first-century fulfillment is also defensible.

18. Geoffrey W. Bromiley, gen. ed., *The International Standard Bible Encyclopedia* (Grand Rapids: Eerdmans, 1982), 655.

19. F. LaGard Smith adopts such a position in his writings.

20. See, for example, Bruce Barron, *Heaven on Earth? The Social & Political Agendas of Dominion Theology* (Grand Rapids: Zondervan, 1992).

21. Premillennialism is a fairly modern view, blossoming in the latter part of the nineteenth century. Most of the 1800s were marked by millennialism, which asserted that the kingdom of God would be brought to earth through the evangelization and civilization of the world.

22. C.S. Lewis, *Miracles* (London: Fontana, 1960) 111, 115.

23. Randy Alcorn, *Heaven* (Carol Stream: Tyndale House, 2004).

24. Ibid., 472.

25. Ibid., 97.

26. Ibid., 324.

27. It is interesting to note that *Glorious Appearing*, the final book in the Left Behind series by LaHaye and Jenkins, offers a similar view of Jesus appearing to millions at the same time, giving each one personal instructions as to which group to stand with, the sheep or the goats. *Glorious Appearing* and *Heaven* were both released in 2004.

28. Alcorn, *Heaven*, 189, 283, 307, 399-405.

29. F. LaGard Smith, "LaGard's Review of 'Heaven,' by Randy Alcorn," unpublished critique, June 20, 2012.

30. Dinesh D'Souza, *Life After Death: The Evidence* (Washington DC: Regnery, 2009), 232.

31. Rick Warren, *Heaven*, inside cover. Interestingly, Warren also writes, "Life on earth is just a dress rehearsal before the real production…Earth is the staging area, the preschool, the tryout for your life in eternity" (*The Purpose-Driven Life* [Grand Rapids: Zondervan, 2002], 36). This seems to contradict his support for Alcorn.

32. Boa and Bowman, *Sense and Nonsense about Heaven and Hell*, 167.

33. Unfortunately, not all writers appreciate the "already but not yet" nature of the kingdom. Peter holds the keys to the kingdom at Pentecost, as scholars recognize. Yet Paul Enns claims that the kingdom (heaven) will be inaugurated at Jesus's second coming (*Heaven Revealed*, 27). But *heaven* is not a synonym for the kingdom. Moreover, the kingdom is here; it is Christ's rule on earth. Choo Thomas allegedly made multiple trips to heaven and learned that the kingdom is heaven (Choo Thomas, *Heaven Is So Real!* [Lake Mary: Charisma House, 2006], 46).

34. This is also the position of Jim McGuiggan (private conversation, June 9, 2012).

35. What he heard (not saw, interestingly) may have been ineffable, or he may have been forbidden to relate it. The word in 2 Corinthians 12:4 is ambiguous.

**Chapter 7: The Other Place**

1. John Piper, "The Echo and Insufficiency of Hell, Part 1: Behold the Kindness and the Severity of God (Romans 11:17-22)," sermon preached June 14, 1992, at Bethlehem Baptist Church. www.soundofgrace.com/piper92/06-14-92.htm.

2. Christopher W. Morgan, ed., *Hell Under Fire: Modern Scholarship Reinvents Eternal Punishment* (Grand Rapids: Zondervan, 2007), 71.

3. Matthew 5:22,29-30; 10:28; 18:8-9; 23:15,33 (and implicitly in 25:41). *Hell* also appears in the parallel passages in Mark and Luke.

4. John the Baptist mentions hell three times in Matthew 3:10-12.

5. Charles H. Spurgeon, "Paul's First Prayer," in *The New York Street Pulpit* (London: Passmore and Alabaster, 1856), 124.

6. Acts 10:42; 17:31; 24:25.

7. In a comprehensive study of preaching themes through the centuries, David L. Larsen has shown that hell was emphasized from the third to the twentieth centuries with a brief gap around the beginning of the Enlightenment. David L. Larsen, "Heaven and Hell in the Preaching of the Gospel: A Historical Survey," *Trinity Journal* 22 (2001): 237-59.

8. Max Lucado, *When Christ Comes* (Nashville: Thomas Nelson, 1999), 123; James L. Garlow and Keith Wall, *Heaven and the Afterlife* (Minneapolis: Bethany House, 2009), 191; N.T. Wright, *Surprised by Hope* (New York: HarperOne, 2008), 163.

9. C.S. Lewis, *The Great Divorce* (New York: HarperOne, 2001), 66-67.

10. John H. Walton, Victor H. Matthews, and Mark W. Chavalas, *The IVP Bible Background Commentary: Old Testament* (Downers Grove: InterVarsity, 2000), 603.

11. The English word *paradise* comes from the Greek *paradeisos*, which in turn derives from the Persian *pairidaeza*, meaning "enclosure." The Hebrew *pardes* is a cognate. The basic sense is that of an enclosed garden. The Septuagint regularly uses *paradeisos* not only in Genesis 2–3 but also in other books, with the meaning of either "paradise" or "garden": Numbers 24:6; Ecclesiastes 2:5; Song of Songs 4:13; Isaiah 1:30; 51:3; Ezekiel 28:13; 31:8-9; Joel 2:3.

   In some ancient Jewish literature, paradise is set in heaven: Enoch 39:3; 70:3; Josephus Bell 3:374; 4 Esr 7:36 and following; 2 Enoch 8. Kittel and Friedrich (*Theological Dictionary of the New Testament*, vol. 5, page 536) show that *pairi-daēza*, in the ancient Persian priestly Avestan, was at first an enclosure and then a park surrounded by a wall.

12. See, for example, Apocalypse of Zephaniah 11:1-2.

13. Job 40:20; 41:24; Proverbs 30:16 LXX; Sibylline Oracles 4:186; 1 Enoch 20:2; On the Life of Moses 2.433; On Rewards and Punishments 152.

14. Geoffrey W. Bromiley, gen. ed., *The International Standard Bible Encyclopedia* (Grand Rapids: Eerdmans, 1982), 654-56.

15. Ibid., 677-79.

16. Joshua 15:8; 18:16; 2 Kings 23:10; 2 Chronicles 28:3; 33:6; Jeremiah 7:31-32; 19:6-7. It is equated with hell and the last judgment in Ethiopic Enoch 90:26; 27:1-3; 54:1-6; 56:3-4 (Kittel and Friedrich, *Theological Dictionary of the New Testament*, vol. 1, 657-58).

17. In the pseudepigraphal 2 Enoch, the third heaven contains both paradise and hell (2 Enoch 8:1–10:3).

18. Franklin Graham, *The Name* (Nashville: Thomas Nelson, 2002), 20; Charles Stanley, *Charles Stanley's Handbook for Christian Living* (Nashville: Thomas Nelson, 1996), 245-48; Chuck Smith, *What the World Is Coming To* (Costa Mesa: Word for Today, 1993), 91.

19. Kenneth D. Boa and Robert M. Bowman Jr., *Sense and Nonsense about Heaven and Hell* (Grand Rapids: Zondervan, 2007), 115.

20. William G.T. Shedd, *The Doctrine of Endless Punishment: Its Historical, Biblical and Rational Defense* (New York: Charles Scribner's Sons, 1886), 151.

21. Interpreting hellfire metaphorically has a long pedigree. Luther and Calvin serve as two examples. Luther certainly accepted hell and is well known for his own despair and terror of hell. Calvin emphasized alienation from God and the wrath due the sinner. Yet both backed away from the purely literal view of the Middle Ages.

22. Matthew 8:12; 13:42,50; 22:13; 24:51; 25:30; Mark 9:18; Luke 13:28.

23. Peter Kreeft and Ronald K. Tacelli, *Handbook of Christian Apologetics: Hundreds of Answers to Crucial Questions* (Downers Grove: InterVarsity Press, 1994), 308.

24. Martin Luther, *The House Postils*, Twentieth Sunday after Trinity, Second Sermon (1533), section 17.

25. Brian Jones, *Hell Is Real (But I Hate to Admit It!)* (Colorado Springs: David C. Cook, 2011), 132. Jones offers minimal proof for the traditional position. His book is very motivational for evangelism, but despite the title, it contains virtually no evidence presented as to why hell is real.

26. Peter Lombard, *The Sentences*, book 4, *On the Doctrine of Signs*, distinction 50.

27. There is a similar theme in ancient Jewish literature, where the blessedness of the righteous is heightened by beholding torture of the wicked. See Assumption of Moses 10:10; 4 Esdras 7:93.

28. John Gerstner, *Repent or Perish* (Ligonier: Soli Deo Gratia, 1990), 64.

29. Peter Kreeft and Ronald Tacelli do better: "Hell is due more to love than to justice. Love created free persons who could choose hell. Love continues to beat upon the damned like sunlight on an albino slug, and constitutes their torture…The fires of hell are made of the love of God" (Kreeft and Tacelli, *Handbook of Christian Apologetics*, 306). They may be right, but the point and the analogy will be lost on most. Interestingly (in light of Matthew 7:14), Kreeft and Tacelli suppose that most of the world's population will not go to hell.

30. And 74 percent believe in heaven. Pew Forum on Religion & Public Life, *U.S. Religious Landscape Survey, Religious Beliefs and Practices: Diverse and Politically Relevant*. The questions were worded like this: "Do you believe in life after death?" "Do you think there is a heaven, where people who have led good lives are eternally rewarded? Do you think there is a hell, where people who have led bad lives and die without being sorry are eternally punished?"

**Chapter 8: No Exit**

1. The scholars were Jerry Walls (representing the traditional view of infinite torment), Thomas Talbott (espousing universalism), and Edward Fudge (conditionalism). June 12, 2012, Lipscomb University, Nashville.

2. New Testament scholar Craig Keener is ambivalent: Mark 9:48 may well be interpreted as destruction (annihilation), but Judith 16:17 (second century BC) had already taken it in the sense of eternal torment, so there is some cause for thinking Jesus may have believed in infinite punishment. Craig S. Keener, *The IVP Bible Background Commentary: New Testament* (Downers Grove: InterVarsity Press, 1993), 160.

3. Augustine, *The Enchiridion*, section 111.

4. See John Gerstner, *Repent or Perish* (Ligonier: Soli Deo Gloria, 1990), 53, for an example of a modern teacher who still believes that Satan will forever rule in hell.

5. Thomas Talbott, in *The Inescapable Love of God* (Boca Raton: Universal, 1999), starts with "God is love" and assumes that God's actions must be loving. Talbott makes a further, intriguing point (especially for those in the Calvinist camp). "And if it is not heretical for Calvinists to believe that all passive recipients of God's electing love will all be saved in the end, why should it be heretical for universalists to believe this as well?" Those who believe in predestination make assumptions similar to the universalists'. Even if we don't want to be saved, says the Calvinist, God's grace will be irresistible. If it is his will, we will be saved. Talbott's reasoning is sound, although it will not carry much weight with Arminians. See "Universalism, Calvinism, and Arminianism: Some Preliminary Reflections," section 5, at www.willamette.edu/~ttalbott/prolegomenon.shtml.

6. Robin A. Parry and Christopher H. Partridge, eds. *Universal Salvation? The Current Debate* (Grand Rapids: Eerdmans, 2003), xxiv.

7. There are varieties of universalism. Secular universalism holds that everyone will make it in the end. Christian universalism holds to the gospel truth that all who are saved are justified through Christ. This further divides into two types. In the first type of Christian universalism, everyone will eventually be saved by saying yes to the gospel. In the second type of Christian universalism, people can be saved by implicitly responding to the gospel. That is, they may be saved through Jesus Christ even though they are unaware of the fact, such as a devout Hindu or a pious Buddhist. Furthermore, some universalists construe hellfire as purifying. Being saved may be quite painful, but in the end, all mankind will make it.

8. Comment by Karl Rahner, cited in in M. Ludlow, *Universal Salvation: Eschatology in the Thought of Gregory of Nyssa and Karl Rahner* (Oxford: Oxford University Press, 2000), 15. Prominent evangelical universalists today include Sharon Baker, Jan Bonda, Robin Parry, and Thomas Talbott. These stand in sharp contrast to other universalist theologians, such as John Hick (*Death and Eternal Life* [Louisville: Westminster John Knox, 1994]; *Evil and the God of Love* [London: Fontana, 1974]). Hick does, however, support a theme that has been taken up by universalists like Talbott: human response to the wooing of divine love.

9. Edward William Fudge, *The Fire That Consumes: A Biblical and Historical Study of the Doctrine of Final Punishment*, 3rd ed. (Eugene: Cascade Books, 2011), 122.

10. Stanley J. Grenz, *Theology for the Community of God* (Grand Rapids: Eerdmans, 1994), 638; David W. Bercot, *The Early Christians and Three Views of Hell* (CD) (Amberson: Scroll Publishing, 2012).

11. James Charlesworth, "Pseudepigrapha, Early Judaism, and Christian Origins," lecture at King's College London, March 8, 1984. Charlesworth currently serves as director of the Dead Sea Scrolls Project at Princeton Theological Seminary.

12. Judith 16:17; 1 Enoch 27:2; 53:1-3; 91:9; 2 Enoch 40:12-13; 10:1-6; Sibylline Oracles 52:290-310; 2 Baruch 44:12-15,51-56; Testaments of the Twelve Patriarchs: Reuben 5:5, Gad 7:5, Benjamin 7:5; Jubilees 36:10; 4 Maccabees 12:12.

13. In Homer's *Odyssey*, Tantalus, Sisyphus, Tityus, and Ixion are doomed to endless punishment in Tartarus. Virgil's *Aeneid* also contains the idea.

14. Psalms of Solomon 3:11-12; Sibylline Oracles 4:175-185; 4 Ezra 7:61; Pseudo-Philo 16:3. Thus the Pseudepigrapha are divided. Technically Judith is not included in the list, but we list it because it belongs with the other references. (The term *Pseudepigrapha* refers to Jewish works of pseudonymous authorship. They were normally attributed to great figures of faith. None of these documents were accepted as canonical, with the lone exception of 1 Enoch, which is part of the Old Testament canon of the Ethiopic Orthodox Church.)

15. Regarding the usual sense of worms as agents of decomposition, "For when a man is dead, he shall inherit creeping things, beasts, and worms. Moths and worms shall have him to heritage, and a bold man shall be taken away" (Ecclesiasticus 10:11; 19:3).

16. Babylonian Talmud, Shabbat 33b.

17. Alberdina Houtman and Magda Misset-van De Weg, "The Fate of the Wicked: Second Death in Early Jewish and Christian Texts," in *Empsychoi Logoi—Religious Innovations in Antiquity: Studies in Honour of Pieter Willem van der Horst*, ed. Aberdina Houtman, Albert De Jong, and Magda Misset-van De Weg (Leiden: Brill, 2008), 405-24. The authors conclude also that the "second death" in Revelation was possibly inspired by Matthew 10:28 and Luke 12:4-5, and that annihilation was presupposed (page 410).

18. Targums Onqelos and Jonathan, on Deuteronomy 33:6; Isaiah 22:14; 65:6,15; Jeremiah 51:39,57.

19. Keener, *The IVP Bible Background Commentary*, 58.

20. Francis Chan and Preston Sprinkle, *Erasing Hell: What God Said About Eternity, and the Things We Made Up* (Colorado Springs: David C. Cook, 2011), 56.

21. A typical passage is Tertullian, On the Resurrection of the Flesh, chapter 35.

22. Clement of Alexandria—Paedogogus 1:8; Protrepticus 9; Stromata 6:6. Origen—De Principiis 1.6.2-4; Contra Celsum 5.15; 6:25.

23. Origen—Homilies on Ezekiel 1–2; Gregory of Nyssa—Oratio Catechetica Magna, chapter 26.

24. Here are the relevant references in the extrabiblical Christian literature of the first 150 years: Didache 1:1; 16:5; 1 Clement 9:1 (note, 2 Clement 17:6-7, which is normally not attributed to Clement, and dates from about AD 160, shows the infinite torment view); Ignatius Ephesians 11:1; 16:2; Smyrnaeans 6:1; Magnesians 5:1; Trallians 2:1; Polycarp Philippians 7:1; Martyrdom of Polycarp 2:3; 11:2; Barnabas 4:12; 20:1; 21:1; 21:3; Diognetus 10:7-8; Justin First Apology 12,17,45; 2 Apology 1,8,9.

25. Bercot, *The Early Christians and Three Views of Hell*.

26. William Crockett et al., *Four Views on Hell* (Grand Rapids: Zondervan, 1996), 14.

27. Through Augustine's influence, purgatory also became the standard accepted view, as did his doctrine of original sin, which served as an apologetic for infant baptism. In the fourth century the testimony is mixed; by the fifth, the medieval Catholic view of salvation and the afterlife develops rigid contours.

28. Traditionalist author Harry Buis admits that there was a certain state of fluidity before Augustine. *The Doctrine of Universal Punishment* (Philadelphia: Presbyterian & Reformed, 1957), 61.

29. Also at the Fourth Lateran Council (1215) and Vatican I (1870) as well as in the words of Pope Innocent IV (1224).

30. Traditionalists include Beale, Blanchard, Block, Braun, Cottrell, Davies, Dixon, Ferguson, Gerstner, Harmon, Helm, Hodge, Horton, Lucado, Mohler, Moo, Morey, Morgan, Packer, Peterson, Pettegrew, Ryrie, Spurgeon, Strong, Walvoord, and Yarbrough. This list includes professional academics (usually attached to universities) and popular authors. Representative of works supporting infinite torment is Crockett et al., *Four Views on Hell*. An older title has been resurrected and has sold very well in the (predominantly Calvinist) evangelical market—William G.T. Shedd, *The Doctrine of Endless Punishment: Its Historical, Biblical and Rational Defense* (New York: Charles Scribner's Sons, 1886).

31. Charles C. Ryrie, *Basic Theology* (Wheaton: Victor Books, 1986), 521. Walvoord claims, "If the slightest sin is infinite in its significance, then it also demands infinite punishment as a divine judgment" (Crockett et al., *Four Views on Hell*, 14). Cottrell states that on the cross Jesus "suffered the equivalent of eternity in hell for every sinner" (Jack Cottrell, *The Faith Once for All* [Joplin: College Press], 265).

32. Gerstner, *Repent or Perish*, 140. Emphasis in the original.

33. Robert Yarbrough refers to Isaiah 66:24 without explanation as though it were obvious that these corpses were conscious. Timothy Keller et al., *Is Hell for Real or Does Everyone Go to Heaven?* (Grand Rapids: Zondervan, 2004), 30.

34. Christopher W. Morgan, ed., *Hell Under Fire: Modern Scholarship Reinvents Eternal Punishment* (Grand Rapids: Zondervan, 2007), 39.

35. Brian Jones, *Hell Is Real (But I Hate to Admit It!)* (Colorado Springs: David C. Cook, 2011), 49.

36. For example, Shedd, *The Doctrine of Endless Punishment*.
37. Question 29. www.ccel.org/ccel/anonymous/westminster2.i.ii.html.
38. Friedrich Schleiermacher, *The Christian Faith* (Edinburgh: T&R Clark, 1989), 714-15. Søren Kierkegaard (1813–1855) also doubted the traditional concept on the basis of his profound faith in saving power of Christ. Jörgen Moltmann expected the ultimate restoration of all things. Jörgen Moltmann, *The Coming of God: Christian Eschatology* (London: SCM, 1996), 250. Hans Urs von Balthasar (1905–1988) argued that Christ descended into hell and made salvation possible for all. Hans Urs von Balthasar, *Dare We Hope That All Men Be Saved? with a Short Discourse on Hell* (San Francisco: Ignatius Press, 1988). See also Nigel M. de S. Cameron, *Universalism and the Doctrine of Hell: Papers Presented at the Fourth Edinburgh Conference on Christian Dogmatics* (Carlisle: Paternoster Press, 1992). Some evangelical theologians since the 1960s have endorsed or seriously contemplated postmortem evangelism (the dead might get a "second chance"). These include George Beasley-Murray, Charles Cranfield, Donald Bloesch, Clark Pinnock, Gabriel Fackre, Nigel Wright, George MacDonald, and Thomas Talbott.

    A great resource for this discussion is Robin A. Parry and Christopher H. Partridge, eds. *Universal Salvation? The Current Debate* (Grand Rapids: Eerdmans, 2003), which has valuable contributions from Thomas Talbott, I. Howard Marshall, Thomas Johnson, Jerry Walls, Eric Reitan, Daniel Strange, John Sanders, Morwenna Ludlow, David Hilborn, and Don Horrocks.
39. Emil Brunner, *Eternal Hope* (London: Lutterworth, 1954), 183; Geoffrey W. Bromiley, gen. ed., *The International Standard Bible Encyclopedia* (Grand Rapids: Eerdmans, 1982) , 677-79.
40. Nels Ferré, *The Christian Understanding of God* (London: SCM, 1951), 230.
41. Thomas Johnson, in Parry and Partridge, *Universal Salvation? The Current Debate*, 75-102.
42. Sharon L. Baker, *Razing Hell: Rethinking Everything You've Been Taught About God's Wrath and Judgment* (Louisville: Westminster John Knox Press, 2010), 115-117, 122, 141. For a similar case, see Jon Noe, *Hell Yes / Hell No* (Indianapolis: East2West Press, 2011), 125. Sharon Baker undergirds her position—that the fire of God's presence purifies—by an argument that slips past readers who have not been trained in Greek. She makes a connection between the word for sulfur, *theeion*, and the word for God, *theos* (page 143). But *theeion* comes from a different root than *theos* and the associated adjective, *theios/theion*.
43. Baker, *Razing Hell*, 93, 17. Baker claims that viewing God as violent feeds our own violence and reluctance to forgive and that in the traditional view the lost become scapegoats. She seems to ignore the biblical point of no return which one can reach even in this life (see, for example, Hebrews 6:4-6; 10:26-31). She admits that unquenchable fire would naturally annihilate body and soul (Matthew 3:12; 10:28), but she tries to find a way around this (pages 38, 47, 66, 143).
44. Rob Bell, *Love Wins: A Book About Heaven, Hell, and the Fate of Every Person Who Ever Lived* (New York: HarperOne, 2011), 50, 106-108.
45. Mark Galli, *God Wins: Heaven, Hell, and Why the Good News Is Better than "Love Wins"* (Carol Stream: Tyndale, 2011).
46. Chan and Sprinkle, *Erasing Hell*.
47. Brian McLaren, *The Last Word and the Word After That* (San Francisco: Jossey-Bass, 2005).
48. For the slimmer version, read Edward William Fudge, *Hell: A Final Word: The Surprising Truths I Found in the Bible* (Abilene: Leafwood, 2012). Also helpful is Edward William Fudge and Robert A. Peterson, *Two Views of Hell* (Eugene: Cascade Books, 2011). For a concise video approach to the topic, see www.rethinkinghell.com/2012/08/episode-3-the-goodness-of-god-with-john-stackhouse/#more-1450.

49. Fudge, *The Fire That Consumes*, ix, xi, xii. The book was first released in 1982. Editions followed in 1994 and 2011.

50. Fudge, *The Fire That Consumes*, 3, note 17.

51. Roger E. Olson, *On the Mosaic of Christian Belief: Twenty Centuries of Unity & Diversity* (Downers Grove: InterVarsity, 2002), 329.

52. Fudge, *Hell: A Final Word*, 128.

53. M. Eugene Boring, *Matthew*, vol. 8 in *The New Interpreter's Bible*, ed. Leander E. Keck (Nashville: Abingdon, 1994), 158. Similarly, Ulrich Luz, professor of New Testament studies at the University of Bern, writes, "The punishment for the wicked consists in their complete destruction, body and soul. Ulrich Luz, *Matthew 8-20*, in *Hermeneia: A Critical and Historical Commentary on the Bible*, trans. James E. Crouch (Minneapolis: Fortress, 2001), 101.

54. Paul's language on the destruction of the soul is identical to Plato's (Phaedo 115b-118a). The difference is that Plato believed the soul to be indestructible; Paul did not.

55. He continues, "But our emotions are a fluctuating, unreliable guide to truth and must not be exalted to the place of supreme authority in determining it. As a committed Evangelical, my question must be—and is—not what my heart tells me, but what does God's word say? And in order to answer this question, we need to survey the biblical material afresh and to open our minds (not just our hearts) to the possibility that Scripture points in the direction of annihilationism, and that 'eternal conscious torment' is a tradition which has to yield to the supreme authority of Scripture." John Stott and David L. Edwards, *Evangelical Essentials: A Liberal–Evangelical Dialogue* (Downers Grove: InterVarsity, 1988), 314-15.

56. F.F. Bruce, personal letter to John Stott. Quoted by Timothy Dudley-Smith, *John Stott: A Global Ministry* (Downers Grove: InterVarsity, 1999), 354.

57. See Richard Bauckham and Trevor Hart, *Hope Against Hope: Christian Eschatology at the Turn of the Millennium* (Grand Rapids: Eerdmans, 1999). Bauckham writes elsewhere, "The New Testament uses a variety of different pictures to describe hell: fire is one of them, destruction another, exclusion from the presence of God another. Burning in fire for eternity is the picture of God that got fixed in much traditional teaching about hell as though it were a literal description. The New Testament does not require us to think of hell in this way. Hell is not an eternal chamber of horrors across the way from heaven. Hell is the fate of those who reject God's love. God's love cannot compel them to find their fulfillment in God, but there is no other way they can find fulfillment. They exclude themselves from the Source of all being and life." "Hell," unpublished essay available online at richardbauckham.co.uk/index.php?page=short=essays.

58. N.T. Wright, *Surprised by Hope* (New York: HarperOne, 2008), 181-83.

59. Chan and Sprinkle, *Erasing Hell*, 104.

60. Morgan, *Hell Under Fire* 39; Gerstner, *Repent or Perish*, 122. John MacArthur similarly offers the reader eisegesis instead of proper exegesis in *The MacArthur Bible Commentary* (Nashville: Thomas Nelson, 2005), 843. Yarbrough (*Is Hell for Real or Does Everyone Go to Heaven?*, 30) simply refers to Isaiah 66:24 without any exegesis at all.

61. Jim McGuiggan, *The Book of Revelation* (Fort Worth: Star Bible Publications, 1976), 219.

62. Gerstner, *Repent or Perish*, 129-31, 153.

63. William Lane Craig, *On Guard: Defending Your Faith with Reason and Precision* (Colorado Springs: David C. Cook, 2010), 273. Shedd makes the same point in *The Doctrine of Endless Punishment*. Here's an interesting thought. If the wicked are able to heap up more punishment on the basis of postmortem choices to sin, then the lost continue to have some influence over

their fate. If this is so, and if sin affects their state (keeping them in hell), why is there no possibility of a change of heart?

64. Michael E. Wittmer, *Christ Alone: An Evangelical Response to Rob Bell's Love Wins* (Grand Rapids: Edenridge Press, 2011), 128-29.

65. F. LaGard Smith, *After Life: A Glimpse of Eternity Beyond Death's Door* (Nashville: Cotswold Publishing, 2003), 180.

66. Miroslav Volf, *Allah: A Christian Response* (New York: HarperOne, 2011), 297, note 29.

67. Keller et al., *Is Hell for Real or Does Everyone Go to Heaven?*, 36.

68. James Hastings, ed., *Dictionary of Christ and the Gospels*, vol. 2 (Edinburgh: T&T Clark, 1908), 785. For a more contemporary refutation of universalism, see Jerry L. Walls, "Why No Classical Theist, Let Alone Orthodox Christian, Should Ever Be a Compatibilist," *Philosophia Christi* 13, 1:105-24.

69. Kittel and Friedrich, *Theological Dictionary of the New Testament*, vol. 1, 387-93 *(apokathistemi, apokatastasis)*.

70. Peter Kreeft and Ronald K. Tacelli, *Handbook of Christian Apologetics: Hundreds of Answers to Crucial Questions* (Downers Grove: InterVarsity Press, 1994), 284. Philosopher Jerry Walls of Houston Baptist University makes an important point about free will. If free will and determinism are compatible as many theologians suppose, especially those in the predestinarian camp, then it is difficult to understand why God would not have set up the world such that eventually all would choose to embrace his will. Walls, "Why No Classical Theist, Let Alone Orthodox Christian, Should Ever Be a Compatibilist," 102.

71. Cited in Bill Muehlenberg, "Against Universalism," *Culture Watch*. www.billmuehlenberg. com/2011/03/12/against-universalism/.

72. Moreover, as we have seen, "day or night" need not be a literal phrase. See Isaiah 34:10; 1 Thessalonians 2:9; 3:10; Revelation 4:8; 7:15; 12:10.

73. Homer, *Iliad* 16.123,194; 1.599. Eusebius, *History of the Church* 6:41.

74. Herman Witsius, *The Economy of the Covenants Between God and Man*, book 1, chapter 5, section 42. (Witsius was professor of divinity at the universities of Franeker, Utrecht, and Leiden.) federaltheology.org/The%20Economy%20of%20the%20Covenants%20-%20Book%20I.pdf.

75. J.I. Packer, "Introduction," in Herman Witsius, *The Economy of the Covenants Between God and Man* (Phillipsburg: Presbyterian and Reformed, 1990). Accessed online at gospelpedlar.com/articles/Bible/cov_theo.html.

76. Jonathan Edwards, "Concerning the Endless Punishment of Those Who Die Impenitent," in *The Works of Jonathan Edwards*, ed. Edward Hickman, vol. 2 (Carlisle: Banner of Truth Trust, n.d.), 524; *The Fathers of the Church: A New Translation* (1954), vol. 24, *City of God, Books 17–22*, 169-70.

77. Ben Witherington III, "And Now—the Case for Permanent Residence in Hell," *The Bible and Culture* (Blog), March 19, 2011. www.patheos.com/blogs/bibleandculture/2011/03/19/and-now-the-case-for-permanent-residence-in-hell.

78. John Wenham, *The Goodness of God* (Downers Grove: InterVarsity, 1974), 27.

79. J.I. Packer, "Evangelical Annihilation in Review," *Reformed Review* 6 (1997): 43,47-48.

80. C.S. Lewis, *The Problem of Pain* (London: Collins, 1957), 115.

81. David W. Bercot, *The Early Christians and Three Views of Hell*.

82. My first work on the conditionalist view was Douglas Jacoby, "Heaven and Hell: Terminal

Punishment" (Unpublished paper, Stockholm, 1991). Available online at www.douglasjacoby .com.

### Chapter 9: A Third Place?

1. *Catechism of the Catholic Church*, 2nd ed. (2010), §1030.

2. Cited in Wayne Martindale, *C.S. Lewis on Heaven and Hell: Beyond the Shadowlands* (Wheaton: Crossway, 2005), 28.

3. At roughly the same time, the rabbis were coming up with their own purgatory. See Tosefta (a Jewish commentary on the Mishna) in the tractate Sanhedrin (13:3). By 1200 the Hasidim were saying Kaddish (a prayer of mourning) to help souls ascend up to heaven.

4. N.T. Wright, *Surprised by Hope* (New York: HarperOne, 2008), 166-67.

5. *The Catholic Encyclopedia*, q.v. "Purgatory." Article available online at www.newadvent.org/cathen/12575a.htm.

6. Jaroslav Pelikan and Helmut T. Lehmann, eds., *Luther's Works*, vol. 32, *Defense and Explanation of All the Articles* (St. Louis: Concordia, and Philadelphia: Muhlenberg and Fortress, 1955-86), 95.

7. Lewis admits that his words are "solely an imaginative proposal; they are not even a guess or a speculation at what may actually await us." C.S. Lewis, *The Great Divorce* (New York: HarperOne, 2001), x.

8. Wright, *Surprised by Hope*, 164, 172-73.

9. Jerry Walls, *Purgatory: The Logic of Total Transformation* (Oxford: Oxford University Press, 2012). See also his parallel works, *Heaven: The Logic of Eternal Joy* (Oxford: Oxford University Press, 2002), and *Hell: The Logic of Damnation* (Notre Dame: University of Notre Dame Press, 1992).

10. Zachary Hayes explains that all of us have many layers of selfishness, even at death. William V. Crockett et al., *Four Views on Hell* (Grand Rapids: Zondervan, 1996), 118.

11. Terence Nichols, *Death and Afterlife: A Theological Introduction* (Grand Rapids: Brazos Press, 2010), 174.

12. Wright, *Surprised by Hope*, 170-71.

13. F. LaGard Smith, *After Life: A Glimpse of Eternity Beyond Death's Door* (Nashville: Cotswold Publishing, 2003), 226.

14. Paul Enns, *Heaven Revealed* (Chicago: Moody Press, 2011), 21.

15. Crockett et al., *Four Views on Hell*, 106.

16. *The New Catholic Encyclopedia*, vol. 11 (New York: McGraw Hill, 1967), 825.

### Chapter 10: The Intermediate State

1. For example, Ron Rhodes believes that paradise is heaven and that Jesus's soul was in heaven from Good Friday to Easter Sunday. Ron Rhodes, *The Wonder of Heaven: A Biblical Tour of Our Eternal Home* (Eugene: Harvest House, 2009), 37, 46.

2. Jon Davies, *Death, Burial and Rebirth in the Religions of Antiquity* (London: Routledge, 1999), 52; cited in Christopher M. Moreman, *Beyond the Threshold: Afterlife Beliefs and Experiences in World Religions* (Lanham: Rowman & Littlefield, 2008), 16-17.

3. John H. Walton, Victor H. Matthews, and Mark W. Chavalas, *The IVP Bible Background Commentary: Old Testament* (Downers Grove: InterVarsity, 2000), 751.

4. Stanley J. Grenz, *Theology for the Community of God* (Grand Rapids: Eerdmans, 1994), 592.

5. George Eldon Ladd, *The Last Things* (Grand Rapids: Eerdmans 1978), 32.

6. Terence Nichols, *Death and Afterlife: A Theological Introduction* (Grand Rapids: Brazos Press, 2010), 195, note 16.

7. Gerhard Kittel and Gerhard Friedrich, *Theological Dictionary of the New Testament*, vol. 5 (Grand Rapids: Eerdmans, 1967), 768.

8. Alexander Roberts, ed., *The Ante-Nicene Fathers* (Peabody: Hendrickson, 1994). For a helpful compendium of the patristic teachings, see David W. Bercot, ed., *A Dictionary of Early Christian Beliefs* (Peabody: Hendrickson, 1998).

9. The Jewish book 1 Enoch, written between 300 and 100 BC, has Sheol divided into four compartments for the righteous, sinners, sinners who have already suffered in this life, and martyrs (1 Enoch 22).

10. When Christians spoke of paradise, they nearly always referred to the intermediate state. This differs from Jewish usage. The Jews believed paradise is yet to come and is not located in Hades (Kittel and Friedrich, *Theological Dictionary of the New Testament*, 771, note 52).

11. David, Jacob, Job, and many others in Scripture look forward to Sheol, so there is no way this can be hell.

12. See Kittel and Friedrich, *Theological Dictionary of the New Testament*, 771. This resource contains excellent articles on Hades and Paradise by Joachim Jeremias. In popular reference works, this view is found in the *Easton Bible Dictionary*. *Naves Topical Dictionary*, however, provides minimal information. *Vine's Complete Expository Dictionary of Old and New Testament Words* gets it partly correct, with Hades as the region of the departed spirits of the lost. In *Vine's* no distinction is made between heaven and paradise.

13. N.T. Wright, *Surprised by Hope* (New York: HarperOne, 2008), 22, 242.

14. Timothy J. Demy and Thomas Ice, *Answers to Common Questions About Heaven and Eternity* (Grand Rapids: Kregel, 2011), 44; Paul Enns, *Heaven Revealed* (Chicago: Moody Press, 2011), 133; Randy Alcorn, *Heaven* (Carol Stream: Tyndale House, 2004), 59; Kenneth D. Boa and Robert M. Bowman Jr., *Sense and Nonsense about Heaven and Hell* (Grand Rapids: Zondervan, 2007), 159-60.

15. Robert A. Peterson, *Two Views of Hell: A Biblical & Theological Dialogue* (Downers Grove: InterVarsity Press, 2000), 171.

**Chapter 11: Resurrection**

1. The most thorough source and the one that is most highly commended by other New Testament scholars and apologists is Michael R. Licona, *The Resurrection of Jesus: A New Historiographical Approach* (Grand Rapids: InterVarsity, 2010).

2. Two men I have debated (in 2009 and 2012, respectively) hold to this understanding. New Testament professor Robert Price calls himself a Christian atheist, and historian Richard Carrier is an atheist. Robert M. Price and Jeffery Jay Lowder, eds., *The Empty Tomb: Jesus Beyond the Grave* (New York: Prometheus Books, 2005); Robert M. Price, *The Incredible Shrinking Son of Man: How Reliable Is the Gospel Tradition?* (New York: Prometheus Books, 2003).

3. Todd Burpo and Lynn Vincent, *Heaven Is for Real: A Little Boy's Astounding Story of His Trip to Heaven and Back* (Nashville: Thomas Nelson, 2010), 123. See also Ron Rhodes, *The Wonder of Heaven: A Biblical Tour of Our Eternal Home* (Eugene: Harvest House, 2009), 85. Rhodes postulates, like many other writers from the Middle Ages to the present, a resurrection body "perhaps in the thirties." Enns claims that our bodies will have "perfect physical features" (*Heaven*

*Revealed* [Chicago: Moody Press, 2011], 165). See also Choo Thomas, *Heaven Is So Real!* (Lake Mary: Charisma House, 2006), 69.

4. Rhodes, *The Wonder of Heaven*, 144-45; see also Enns, *Heaven Revealed*, 80. And yet this is later contradicted by Rhodes's speculation that on the new earth there will be bumper crops, based on Isaiah 32:20,23; Hosea 2:22; and Amos 9:13, which he has misinterpreted.

5. The lack of appreciation for hyperbole and figurative language in general leads Bible readers into many impossible positions. Rhodes, *The Wonder of Heaven*, 115; Enns, *Heaven Revealed*, 77.

6. 274 "William Lane Craig on the difference the resurrection means to him," vimeo.com/47849560.

7. N.T. Wright, *Surprised by Hope* (New York: HarperOne, 2008), 149.

8. Some commentators believe that in the pristine world there was no death of any kind. Yet without death it does not appear that there would be any life. Think of the millions of microscopic organisms that live and die in our own bodies; they are essential if we are to live. Entropy itself drives biological processes forward. We don't need to understand the science of it all to accept what God says. Somehow the creation will be transformed.

9. Wright also comments that God's new world was born at Easter, not in the Enlightenment; Easter was the beginning of the new creation. "N.T. Wright on the difference the resurrection means to him," vimeo.com/47849824.

10. A point effectively made by Habermas. "Gary Habermas on the difference the resurrection makes to him," vimeo.com/47849678.

11. Wright shows that the resurrection developed out of Sheol, not Zoroastrianism. N.T. Wright, *The Resurrection of the Son of God* (Minneapolis: Fortress Press, 2003), 14. We see glimmers of the resurrection in Job 19:25-27; Isaiah 26:19; Ezekiel 37 (which refers to a national resurrection); and Daniel 12:1-3.

### Chapter 12: Judgment Day

1. F. LaGard Smith (*After Life: A Glimpse of Eternity Beyond Death's Door* [Nashville: Cotswold Publishing, 2003], 276, note 44) calls this yo-yo eschatology and underscores the special difficulties for those in the premillennialist rapture and tribulation camp. By their thinking, Christians who died in the first century and have been in heaven for nearly two millennia must come back to earth to be resurrected in the rapture. Then after seven years in heaven, they return to earth for the literal millennium (1000 years), finally proceeding to heaven for a third time before the destruction of the world. The truth is not always simple, but the convolutions of this perspective are suspicious.

2. Stanley J. Grenz, *Theology for the Community of God* (Grand Rapids: Eerdmans, 1994), 590-91.

3. In his *Psychopannychia* (1534), John Calvin argued that the soul is always conscious. The term comes from the Greek words for soul and night. The soul is awake all night, not asleep. See N.T. Wright, *Surprised by Hope* (New York: HarperOne, 2008), 71, 73.

4. As noted by Paul Enns, *Heaven Revealed* (Chicago: Moody Press, 2011), 21.

5. James L. Garlow and Keith Wall, *Heaven and the Afterlife* (Minneapolis: Bethany House, 2009), 144. A more balanced perspective may be found in Max Lucado, *When Christ Comes* (Nashville: Thomas Nelson, 1999), 105, 107.

6. I first noticed this when I read his German New Testament (translated in 1522). Four books had been removed from the New Testament as unworthy. Luther translated them but put them at the end in a sort of appendix. They were James, which teaches justification by deeds; Hebrews, which teaches that it is possible for a true Christian to drift away and lose his salvation; Revelation,

which is difficult to understand; and Jude, presumably because it quotes from the Old Testament apocryphal work 1 Enoch. He also added the word *alone* in places like Romans 3:28—a legacy that has stuck with Protestantism even though modern versions omit his insertion. We cannot commend Luther for chopping up the New Testament, but we can certainly admire him for his honesty.

7. Ron Rhodes, *The Wonder of Heaven: A Biblical Tour of Our Eternal Home* (Eugene: Harvest House, 2009), 17, 155, 182.

8. Choo Thomas, *Heaven Is So Real!* (Lake Mary: Charisma House, 2006), 45-46, 177.

9. D.L. Moody, *Heaven Awaits* (New Kensington: Whitaker House, 1982), 34, 46, 100, 108-9.

10. Found twice each in Matthew, Mark, and Luke.

## Chapter 13: "Do Not Judge"

1. The words of Edward John Carnell, in his inaugural address as president of Fuller Theological Seminary (1955), are apropos:

> Whoever meditates on the mystery of his own life will quickly realize why only God, the searcher of the secrets of the heart, can pass final judgment. We cannot judge what we have no access to. The self is a swirling conflict of fears, impulses, sentiments, interests, allergies, and foibles. It is a metaphysical given for which there is no easy rational explanation. Now if we cannot unveil the mystery of our own motives and affections, how much less can we unveil the mystery in others? That is, as we look into ourselves, we encounter the mystery of our own, the depths of our own selfhood. As we sing things like "Just as I am, though tossed about with many a conflict, many a doubt, fightings within and fears without, O Lamb of God, I come." And having recognized the mysteries that dwell in the very depths of our own being, how can we treat other people as if they were empty or superficial beings, without the same kind of mystery?

2. For a podcast with notes titled "Judging, Tolerance, Exclusivism," please visit jacobypremium .com and enter the keyword *judging*.

## Chapter 14—Alternative Views

1. For an expansive study of afterlife beliefs across the spectrum, see Christopher J. Johnson and Marsha McGee, *How Different Religions View Death and Afterlife*, 2nd ed. (Philadelphia: Charles Press, 1998). The survey is incomplete, but it succeeds in alerting the reader to the diversity and divergence among the world religions.

2. David B. Barrett, George Thomas Kurian, and Todd M. Johnson, eds., *World Christian Encyclopedia: A Comparative Survey of Churches and Religions in the Modern World, AD 1900-2000* (Oxford: Oxford University Press, 2001).

3. As it relates to God, hard agnosticism holds if such a being exists, he is unknowable. Soft agnosticism simply says, "I dunno."

4. Imam Shabir Ally (Islamic Information Centre, Toronto), personal correspondence, August 2, 2012. Used with permission.

5. Mirza Ghulam Ahmad, *The Essence of Islam* (Tilford, UK: Islam International Publications, 2004), 284.

6. Christopher J. Johnson and Marsha McGee, *How Different Religions View Death and Afterlife*, 2nd ed. (Philadelphia: The Charles Press, 1998), 266-300. The Parsees (Zoroastrians from the

sixth century BC onward) also have a new creation following the destruction of the old by Ahriman, the evil one. The theme of the new heaven and new earth is extremely ancient.

7. Lisa Miller, *Heaven: Our Enduring Fascination with the Afterlife* (New York: Harper Perennial, 2010), 28.

8. The afterlife is intimated in such passages as Job 19:25-27; Psalms 16:9-11; 17:15; 49:15; Isaiah 26:19; and Daniel 12:1-3.

9. Tosefta (a Jewish commentary on the Mishna) in the tractate Sanhedrin (13:3).

10. Catechism of the Catholic Church, 2nd ed. (2010), §1030.

11. In the ninth circle of Dante's inferno, traitors are frozen in a lake of ice. Here is Satan—not in a lake of fire, but in a lake of ice.

12. For more, see Johnson and McGee, *How Different Religions View Death and Afterlife*, 90-108. See also Kenneth D. Boa and Robert M. Bowman Jr., *Sense and Nonsense About Heaven and Hell* (Grand Rapids: Zondervan, 2007), 150-53.

13. Mary Baker Eddy, *Science and Health with Key to the Scriptures* (Boston: Writings of Mary Baker Eddy, 1906), 291, 587.

14. Boa and Bowman Jr., *Sense and Nonsense About Heaven and Hell*, 153-57.

15. Geoffrey W. Bromiley, gen. ed., *The International Standard Bible Encyclopedia* (Grand Rapids: Eerdmans, 1982), 654-56. Gerhard Kittel and Gerhard Friedrich (*Theological Dictionary of the New Testament*, vol. 5 [Grand Rapids: Eerdmans, 1967], 497-543) note that the heavens too are affected by divine judgment (Isaiah 51:60; 65:17; 66:22). Heaven can be shaken because it is physical—its pieces can fall.

16. Moreover, such an understanding could be supported from such passages as Job 15:15-16. However, these are the words of Eliphaz, and the reader must keep in mind that God rejected the words of Job's "miserable comforters," rebuking them for their presumption and theological error (Job 42:7-9).

17. Eric Gorski, "'MANY PATHS TO GOD' Grows in Acceptance," *South Bend Tribune*, June 24, 2008, page A3.

### Chapter 15: The Narrow Road

1. "There are those who hate Christianity and call their hatred an all-embracing love for all religions." G.K. Chesterton, *Illustrated London News*, January 13, 1906.

2. G.K. Chesterton, *The Catholic Church and Conversion* (New York: Macmillan Press, 1926), 34.

3. Philosopher William Lane Craig opines, "God in His providence has so arranged the world that those who would respond to the gospel if they heard it, do hear it. The sovereign God has so ordered history…Hence no one is lost because of historical or geographical accident. Any who wants or even would want to be saved will be saved." Although we can't disprove this, it seems contrived. William Lane Craig, *On Guard: Defending Your Faith with Reason and Precision* (Colorado Springs: David C. Cook, 2010), 280-81.

### Chapter 16: Out of Their Bodies or Out of Their Minds?

1. Pim van Lommel, Ruud van Wees, Vincent Myers, and Ingrid Elfferich, "Near-Death Experience in Survivors of Cardiac Arrest," *Lancet* 358, issue 9298 (2001): 2039-45.

2. Dinesh D'Souza, *Life After Death: The Evidence* (Washington DC: Regnery Publishing, 2009), 64, 244, note 15.

3. As N.T. Wright points out, this militates against reincarnation. *Surprised by Hope* (New York: HarperOne, 2008), 112.

4. James L. Garlow and Keith Wall, *Heaven and the Afterlife* (Minneapolis: Bethany House, 2009), 42-53.

5. Mark Cahill, *One Heartbeat Away: Your Journey into Eternity* (Rockwall: BDP, 2005), 104. Also recommended: Mark Cahill, *One Thing You Can't Do in Heaven* (Rockwall: 2005).

6. Other recent *New York Times* bestsellers on heaven and hell include Richard Sigmund, *My Time in Heaven* (Whitaker House, 2009); Dennis and Nolene Prince, *Nine Days in Heaven* (Charisma House, 2011); Mark K. Baker, *A Divine Revelation of Hell* (Whitaker House, 1997); Kevin and Alex Malarkey, *The Boy Who Came Back from Heaven: A Remarkable Account of Miracles, Angels, and Life Beyond This World* (Thomas Nelson, 2011).

7. One wonders what happens when other people have their own NDE. Are the people who appeared to Piper available to appear to others to whom they may also be connected?

8. Choo Thomas, *Heaven Is So Real!* (Lake Mary: Charisma House, 2006), xxv.

9. Charles Tazewell's *The Littlest Angel* has been in circulation for more than 70 years.

10. For more about the case of Colton Burpo, listen to "Heaven Is for Real—or Is It?," a podcast with notes at www.jacobypremium.com.

11. Garlow and Wall also describe Hades as a terrible prison, which they see as a holding tank for the hell-bound. *Heaven and the Afterlife*, 178.

12. Edward F. Kelly, et al., *Irreducible Mind: Toward a Psychology for the 21st Century* (Lanham: Rowman & Littlefield, 2007).

13. Daniel P. Sheehan, ed., *Frontiers of Time: Retrocausation—Experiment and Theory*, AIP Conference Proceedings 863 (College Park: American Institute of Physics, 2006); Daniel P. Sheehan, ed., *Quantum Retrocausation—Theory and Experiment*, AIP Conference Proceedings 1408 (College Park: American Institute of Physics, 2011).

14. Eben Alexander, "My Experience in a Coma," *AANS Neurosurgeon* 21, no. 2 (2012). Available online at www.aansneurosurgeon.org/210212/6/1611. From his book *Proof of Heaven: A Neurosurgeon's Journey into the Afterlife* (New York: Simon & Schuster, 2012).

15. Michael A. Persinger, S.G. Tiller, and S.A. Koren, "Experimental Stimulation of a Haunt Experience and Elicitation of Paroxysmal Electroencephalographic Activity by Transcerebral Complex Magnetic Fields: Induction of a Synthetic 'Ghost'?" *Journal of Perception and Motor Skills* 90, vol. 2 (2000): 659-74.

16. D'Souza, *Life After Death*, 1-2.

17. Ibid., 72.

18. Gary Habermas, private correspondence, August 13, 2011.

19. Gary R. Habermas and J.P. Moreland, *Immortality: The Other Side of Death* (Nashville, Thomas Nelson, 1992), 91-93.

20. David Bercot, personal correspondence, August 11, 2011.

**Chapter 17: Angels, Ghosts, and Other Things You've Wondered About**

1. Humans are in view in 1 Kings 19:2; Haggai 1:13; Malachi 2:7; 3:1; Luke 7:24; and possibly Acts 12:15. In Revelation 2–3, the messengers of the seven churches may be human church leaders.

2. The suggestion of James Garlow and Keith Wall, that ghosts are demons, is not persuasive. James L. Garlow and Keith Wall, *Heaven and the Afterlife* (Minneapolis: Bethany House, 2009), 68.

3. Dinesh D'Souza, *Life After Death: The Evidence* (Washington DC: Regnery Publishing, 2009), 54.

4. Garlow and Wall, *Heaven and the Afterlife*, 164; Timothy J. Demy and Thomas Ice, *Answers to Common Questions About Heaven & Eternity* (Grand Rapids: Kregel, 2011), 44; Brian Jones, *Hell Is Real (But I Hate to Admit It!)* (Colorado Springs: David C. Cook, 2011), 55; Paul Enns, *Heaven Revealed* (Chicago: Moody Press, 2011), 69.

5. As Solomon wrote in Ecclesiastes 9:5,10. Yet these verses represent the skeptical view of a believer who has compromised his faith (many verses in Ecclesiastes reveal this, including 4:13; see also 1 Kings 11:1-11), and many are leery of going to Solomon for doctrine about the afterlife.

6. For example, the Council of Carthage affirmed this in AD 418.

7. Geoffrey W. Bromiley, gen. ed., *The International Standard Bible Encyclopedia* (Grand Rapids: Eerdmans, 1982), 678. Limbo had three compartments—the main one, one for babies, and one for the Old Testament saints (until "the harrowing of hell").

8. For example, Ron Rhodes, on the basis of his understanding of original sin, concedes that babies are born damned, but he affirms that God saves them through Christ. Ron Rhodes, *The Wonder of Heaven: A Biblical Tour of Our Eternal Home* (Eugene: Harvest House, 2009), 161. See also Demy and Ice, *Answers to Common Questions About Heaven & Eternity*, 58-59.

9. Catechism of the Catholic Church, 2nd ed. (2010), §1261.

10. N.T. Wright, *Surprised by Hope* (New York: HarperOne, 2008), 112.

11. The Chandogya Upanishad (5.10.8) reads, "Those who are of pleasant conduct here—the prospect is, indeed, that they will enter a pleasant womb, either the womb of a Brahman, or the womb of a Kshatriya, or the womb of a Vaisya. But those who are of a stinking conduct here—the prospect is, indeed, that they will enter a stinking womb of a dog, or the womb of a swine, or the womb of an outcast." Kaushitaki Upanishad 12 teaches, "Either as a worm, or as a moth, or as a fish, or as a bird, or as a lion, or as a wild boar, or as a snake, or as a tiger, or as a person, or as some other in this or that condition, he is born again here according to his deeds, according to his knowledge."

12. To be fair, "Contrary to the popular stereotype of past lives fostered by the tabloid press, the vast majority of past lives are not those of Egyptian princesses or wives of Henry VIII. Most of the lives that are reported are barely identifiable within the known framework of history. We encounter African tribesmen, nomadic hunters, nameless slaves, Middle Eastern traders, anonymous medieval peasants, and so on, from all times and places; often they can barely name their chieftain or lord, let alone place themselves upon some totally irrelevant time map of European or ancient history." Roger J. Woolger, *Other Lives, Other Selves: A Jungian Psychotherapist Discovers Past Lives* (New York: Doubleday, 1987), 37-38.

13. See Exodus 15:4; 2:12; Judges 20:6; 2 Kings 9:36-37; Lamentations 4:10; 1 Samuel 31:12, respectively.

14. Joe Beam and Lee Wilson, *The True Heaven: Not What You Thought, Better Than You Expected* (Abilene: Leafwood, 2010), 34-35; Boa and Bowman, *Sense and Nonsense about Heaven and Hell*, 28-30; Rhodes, *The Wonder of Heaven*, 91-92; Enns, *Heaven Revealed*, 18-19; D.L. Moody, *Heaven Awaits* (New Kensington: Whitaker House, 1982), 88.

15. Garlow and Wall, *Heaven and the Afterlife*, 138.

**Chapter 18: Treasure**

1. Oliver Wendell Holmes Sr., "The Autocrat of the Breakfast Table," *Atlantic Monthly*, 1857–1858.

**Appendix A: Imagery in Isaiah**

1. Paul Enns, *Heaven Revealed* (Chicago: Moody Press, 2011), 86, 98.

2. For example, Enns, *Heaven Revealed*, 90.

3. Not even in Romans 9–11 does Paul hint at such a notion.

4. Enns gets it wrong again (*Heaven Revealed*, 89). There is in fact nothing in the passage to suggest this refers to a millennium.

# About the Author

Douglas Jacoby came to faith in Christ while a freshman at Duke University in 1977. He also attended Oxford University, Harvard Divinity School, University of London, and Drew University, receiving a bachelor of arts degree in history, a master of theological studies degree in New Testament, and a doctor of ministry degree in ministry and education. A lifelong student, Douglas is a serious bibliophile with special interests in theology, history, languages, and science. He also loves crime dramas, Scrabble, Words with Friends, and spicy food.

In his early twenties, Douglas joined a team of Britons and Americans planting a church in London. There he met his future wife, Vicki, and they married in 1985. The Jacobys have three grown children, born in England, Sweden, and China.

On church staffs, the Jacobys lived in London, Sydney, Birmingham, Stockholm, Philadelphia, Indianapolis, and Washington, DC. After 20 years in full-time church planting and leadership, Douglas began work as an independent scholar and teacher in 2003. His passion is to help believers to think critically about faith. As he says with only a touch of overstatement, "The unexamined faith is hardly worth living."

Dr. Jacoby's work includes writing, consulting, adjunct professorship at Lincoln Christian University, weekly podcasts, annual tours to Bible lands, debates, preaching, and teaching at churches, colleges, and other groups around the globe. He currently delivers some 400 talks a year and has visited more than 100 nations.

Douglas is a member of the American Scientific Affiliation, Society of Biblical Literature, Strength in Weakness Ministries, Biblical Archaeology Society, American Association of Christian Counselors, and Evangelical Philosophical Society.

www.douglasjacoby.com

# More Great Harvest House Books by
# Douglas Jacoby

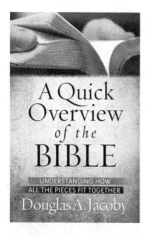

### A Quick Overview of the Bible

Douglas Jacoby bridges the gulf between the biblical world and the twenty-first century. He explains the big picture of the Bible, shows how the pieces fit together, provides the basic chronological outline of the Bible, and reveals the most important themes of the Old and New Testaments.

### Your Bible Questions Answered

Dr. Jacoby believes that pursuing answers about the Bible and God's truth is healthy for a thriving faith. With encouragement and clarity, he tackles your questions of greatest interest to help you grow in relationship with God and with others.

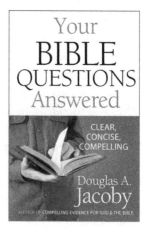

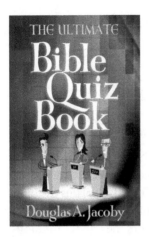

### The Ultimate Bible Quiz Book

Who led a rebellion against Moses and
Aaron?
Who was Jeremiah's secretary?
What was Peter's father's name?

These questions and countless more fill
these entertaining one-page quizzes, with
answers on the following page. Categories include important people in the Bible,
books of the Bible, and many others.

### Compelling Evidence for God and the Bible

In an age of doubt, it's rare to find
Christians who can speak clearly and
boldly about the reasons for their faith.
*Compelling Evidence for God and the Bible*
gives you solid reasons why the Christian
faith is not only true but also reasonable.
This easy-to-read apologetics work will
strengthen your faith, and it is the perfect
gift for nonbelievers and anyone new to
the faith.

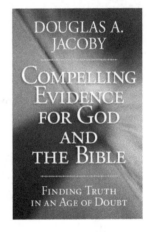

# More Books by Douglas Jacoby

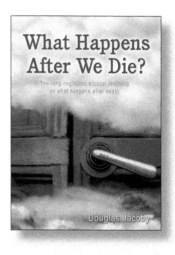

### What Happens After We Die?

In this book you'll find surprising insights into what the Bible teaches about the afterlife. You'll learn...

- commonly held beliefs about the afterlife
- what the early Christians believed about life after death
- why most Christians think heaven is now, even before Christ has returned
- who ends up in Hades
- what the Bible teaches about eternal punishment

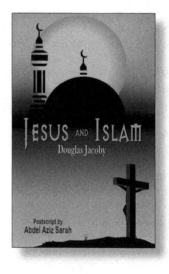

### Jesus and Islam

Readers may have a number of reasons for taking the time to study this book:

- Maybe you know nothing about Islam, and this is your first study of the religion.
- Perhaps you have taken a college-level class on Islam and seek to know more.
- Maybe you are a Westerner who is apprehensive about Islam and this fear has impelled you to increase your understanding.
- Or perhaps you are a Muslim and have an interest in the subject; you want to make sure that what the book says is fair.

Regardless of your background, we hope that *Jesus and Islam* will stimulate you to deeper study, and even some soul-searching.

Available from Illumination Publishers
## www.ipibooks.com

# More Books by Douglas Jacoby

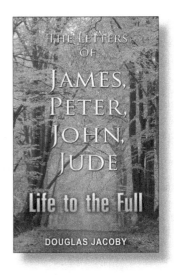

### Life to the Full

"Life to the Full"? Isn't that a line borrowed from the gospel of John? So why make it the subtitle of the book? Let me explain. Several words appear over and over again in the general letters, and "life" is one of them. These men did not write to impress the scholars. They wrote because they had found life, and wanted to pass it on. Of course it is not just mastering seven epistles that yields the abundant life. The entire word of God comes into play. Yet the life described and guaranteed in these timeless letters is the very life of Jesus. And because he lives forever, according to Hebrews 13:8, today we too can enjoy life to the full.

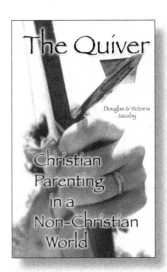

### The Quiver

The title of the book comes from Psalm 127, one of two psalms in the Bible penned by Solomon. In his analogy, the quiver holds the children; the quiver is the home. Quivers are nothing more than temporary housings for the projectiles they carry. To bring up children requires not only a "quiver," but also a "bow." How can the arrows be shot without the bow? The parents are the archers, who by skillful use of the bow launch the arrows. This requires a steady hand, a keen eye, and a calm spirit. The goal, of course, is to hit the target. Yes, the Lord has something specific in mind for us as parents. We dare not parent "at random."

Available from Illumination Publishers
# www.ipibooks.com

To learn more about Harvest House books and
to read sample chapters, log on to our website:

**www.harvesthousepublishers.com**

**HARVEST HOUSE PUBLISHERS**
EUGENE, OREGON

CPSIA information can be obtained
at www.ICGtesting.com
Printed in the USA
LVHW081903121122
733003LV00017B/690